GCSE

Maths

OK, so GCSE Maths is a serious business. The only way to get to grips with the skills you need is practice, practice, practice.

Luckily, this fantastic CGP Workbook is packed with practice questions covering every topic to help you feel totally confident in your exams.

You can thank us later. For now, it's time to get stuck in...

Workbook
Higher Level

Published by CGP

Illustrated by Ruso Bradley, Lex Ward and Ashley Tyson

From original material by Richard Parsons

Contributors:
Gill Allen,
Margaret Carr,
Barbara Coleman,
JE Dodds,
Mark Haslam,
John Lyons,
Gordon Rutter,
Dave Williams

Updated by: Martha Bozic, Sammy El-Bahrawy, Emily Garrett, Ruth Greenhalgh, Andy Park, David Ryan.

With thanks to Sarah George for the proofreading.

ISBN: 978 1 78294 380 8

Printed by Elanders Ltd, Newcastle upon Tyne.
Clipart from Corel®

Text, design, layout and original illustrations © Richard Parsons 2022
All rights reserved.

Photocopying this book is not permitted, even if you have a CLA licence.
Extra copies are available from CGP with next day delivery • 0800 1712 712 • www.cgpbooks.co.uk

Contents

How to Use this Book..2

✓ Use the tick boxes to check off the topics you've completed.

Section One — Number

Types of Number and BODMAS..3 ☐
Multiples, Factors and Prime Factors...4 ☐
LCM and HCF..6 ☐
Fractions..7 ☐
Fractions, Decimals and Percentages..9 ☐
Rounding Numbers..11 ☐
Estimating...12 ☐
Bounds...13 ☐
Standard Form..15 ☐
Mixed Questions..17 ☐

Section Two — Algebra

Algebra Basics..19 ☐
Powers and Roots..20 ☐
Multiplying Out Brackets..22 ☐
Factorising..23 ☐
Manipulating Surds...24 ☐
Solving Equations..25 ☐
Rearranging Formulas...27 ☐
Factorising Quadratics..29 ☐
The Quadratic Formula...30 ☐
Completing the Square...32 ☐
Algebraic Fractions..33 ☐
Sequences...35 ☐
Inequalities..37 ☐
Iterative Methods...40 ☐
Simultaneous Equations..41 ☐
Proof..42 ☐
Functions...44 ☐
Mixed Questions..45 ☐

Section Three — Graphs

Straight Lines and Gradients ... 47
$y = mx + c$ ... 48
Drawing Straight Line Graphs ... 49
Coordinates and Ratio ... 50
Parallel and Perpendicular Lines ... 51
Quadratic Graphs ... 52
Harder Graphs ... 53
Solving Equations Using Graphs ... 57
Graph Transformations ... 58
Real-Life Graphs ... 60
Distance-Time Graphs ... 61
Velocity-Time Graphs ... 62
Gradients of Real-Life Graphs ... 63
Mixed Questions ... 64

Section Four — Ratio, Proportion and Rates of Change

Ratios ... 66
Direct and Inverse Proportion ... 69
Percentages ... 71
Compound Growth and Decay ... 74
Unit Conversions ... 76
Speed, Density and Pressure ... 78
Mixed Questions ... 81

Section Five — Geometry and Measures

Geometry ... 83
Parallel Lines ... 84
Polygons ... 85
Triangles and Quadrilaterals ... 86
Circle Geometry ... 87
Congruent Shapes ... 89
Similar Shapes ... 90
The Four Transformations ... 91
Perimeter and Area ... 93
Area — Circles ... 95
3D Shapes — Surface Area ... 96
3D Shapes — Volume ... 97

More Enlargements..100
Projections...101
Loci and Construction..102
Bearings..104
Mixed Questions...105

Section Six — Pythagoras and Trigonometry

Pythagoras' Theorem..107
Trigonometry — Sin, Cos, Tan...110
The Sine and Cosine Rules..113
3D Pythagoras and Trigonometry..116
Vectors..117
Mixed Questions...119

Section Seven — Probability and Statistics

Probability Basics...121
Counting Outcomes..122
Probability Experiments..123
The AND / OR Rules..125
Tree Diagrams..126
Conditional Probability..127
Sets and Venn Diagrams...128
Sampling and Bias..130
Collecting Data...131
Mean, Median, Mode and Range..132
Frequency Tables — Finding Averages...134
Grouped Frequency Tables...136
Box Plots...137
Cumulative Frequency...139
Histograms and Frequency Density..141
Other Graphs and Charts..144
Scatter Graphs...146
Mixed Questions...147

How to Use this Book

- Hold the book upright, approximately 50 cm from your face, ensuring that the text looks like this, not sıɥʇ. Alternatively, place the book on a horizontal surface (e.g. a table or desk) and sit adjacent to the book, at a distance which doesn't make the text too small to read.
- In case of emergency, press the two halves of the book together firmly in order to close.
- Before attempting to use this book, familiarise yourself with the following safety information:

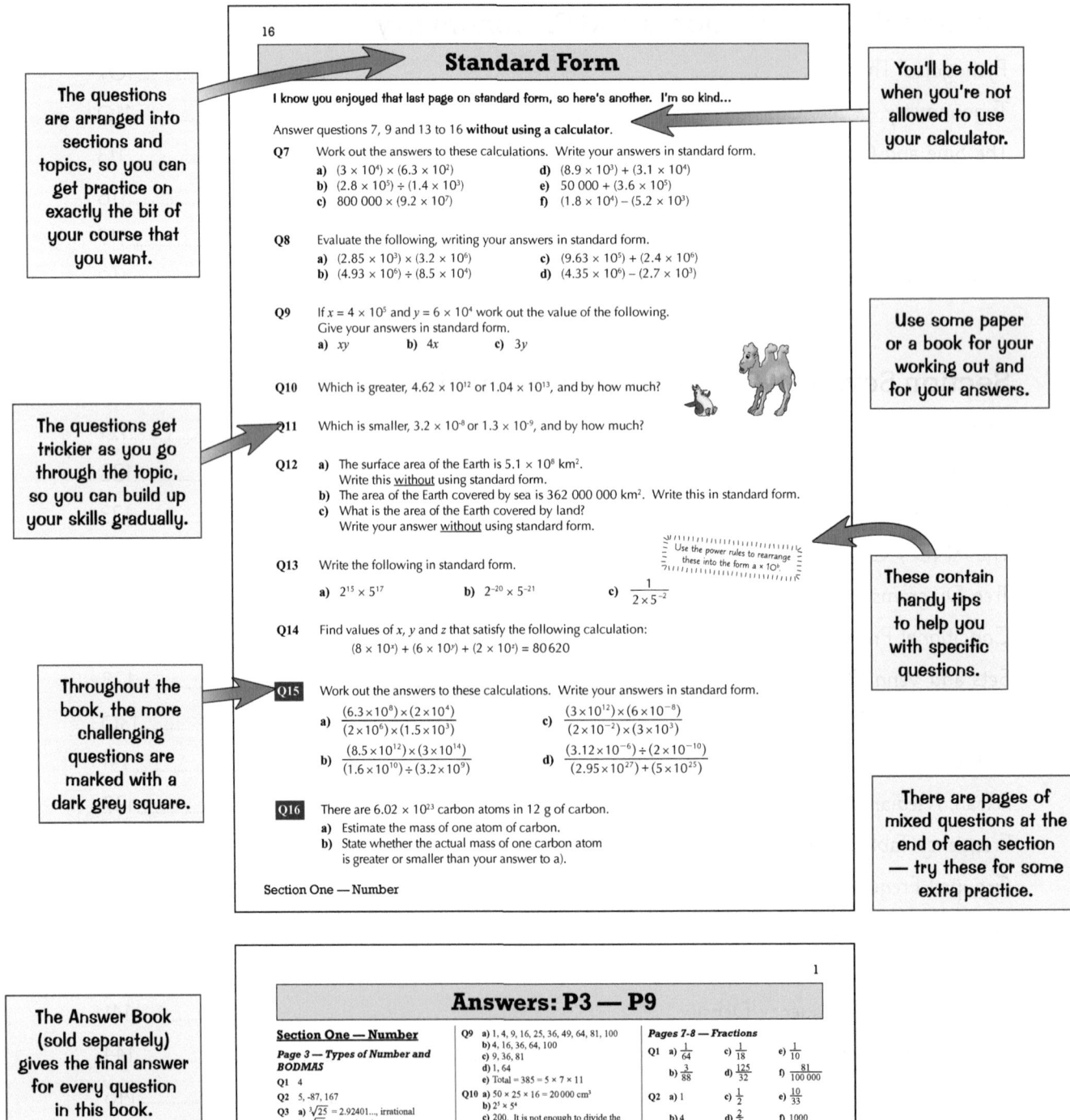

- You'll need a few extra things to answer some of the questions in this book — make sure you also have: a ruler, a pencil, a protractor, a pair of compasses, graph paper and, of course, a calculator.

Section One — Number

Types of Number and BODMAS

There are a few types of number that you really need to know — odd and even numbers, integers, prime numbers and rational and irrational numbers. Make sure you're happy with BODMAS too — that way you'll always do your calculations in the right order.

Q1 Sarah thinks of a positive number. She calculates that the square of the number is 256. What is the square root of the number?

Q2 Which of the following are integers?

$5 \quad 6\frac{3}{4} \quad 7.802 \quad -87 \quad -0.0003 \quad 7.\dot{4} \quad 167 \quad \pi$

Q3 Which of these are rational and which are irrational?

a) $\sqrt[3]{25}$ b) $\sqrt{16}$ c) $\sqrt{5}$ d) $\frac{3}{8}$ e) $8.4\dot{2}$ f) 0.2413

Q4 1 is the first odd number. It is also the first square number and the first cube number. Which is greatest:

a) the third odd number, the third square number or the third cube number?
b) the sixth odd number, the fourth square number or the second cube number?

Q5 Using any or all of the figures **1, 2, 5, 9** write down:

a) the smallest prime number
b) a prime number greater than 20
c) a prime number between 10 and 20
d) two prime numbers whose sum is 21
e) a number that is not prime

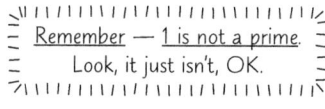

Remember — 1 is not a prime. Look, it just isn't, OK.

Q6 How many prime numbers are even?

Q7 What is the largest prime less than 120?

Q8 Without using a calculator, find the following:

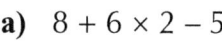

This is where you'll need to use BODMAS.

a) $8 + 6 \times 2 - 5$
b) $(8 + 2) \div 5 + 2$
c) $(3 + 4) \times 8 - 3^3$
d) $6 \div 3 + 8 \times 2$
e) $(5 \times 2 - 2) \div 2$
f) $\sqrt{(12 - 3)} + 4 \times 2^2$
g) $\sqrt{8 + 17} + 3 \times 4$
h) $(4 \times 8 - 10 \times 3)^2$

Q9 Without using a calculator, find the reciprocal of $\sqrt{(2+3) \times 8 - 4}$.

Q10 Without using a calculator, decide which of the following has the largest value.

$6^2, \quad 3^3, \quad$ the prime number between 35 and 40, $\quad 10 \times \sqrt{2 \times 5 + 6}$

Multiples, Factors and Prime Factors

Q1 From the numbers 1, 3, 6, 9 and 12, write down:
a) a multiple of 4
b) the prime number
c) two square numbers
d) three factors of 27
e) two numbers, P and Q, that satisfy both P = 2Q and P = $\sqrt{144}$

This is real basic stuff — you just have to know your times tables. And your primes, of course...

Q2 48 students went on a geography field trip. Their teachers split them into equal groups. Suggest five different ways that the teachers might have split up the students.

Q3 A school ran 3 evening classes: Conversational French, Cake Making and Woodturning. The Conversational French class had 29 students, Cake Making had 27 students, and the Woodturning class had 23. For which classes did the teacher have difficulty dividing the students into equal groups?

Q4
a) Write down the first five cube numbers.
b) Which of the numbers given in part **a)** are multiples of 2?
c) Which of the numbers given in part **a)** are multiples of 3?
d) Which of the numbers given in part **a)** are multiples of 4?
e) Which of the numbers given in part **a)** are multiples of 5?

Q5 Write down each number below as a product of its prime factors.
a) 18
b) 140
c) 44
d) 81
e) 550
f) 560
g) 288
h) 104

Remember — if a prime factor is repeated, you need to use powers. E.g. if 2 is a factor three times, you write 2^3.

Q6 Express the following numbers as products of their prime factors.
a) 1050
b) 1980
c) 546
d) 1260
e) 462
f) 3080

Q7
a) List the first five prime numbers.
b) If added together, what is their total?
c) Write down the answer to part **b)** as a product of its prime factors.

Multiples, Factors and Prime Factors

Q8 The prime factor decomposition of a certain number is $3^2 \times 5 \times 11$.
    a) Write down the number.
    b) Write down the prime factor decomposition of 165.

Q9   **a)** Write down the first ten square numbers.
    b) From your list, pick out all the multiples of 2.
    c) From your list, pick out all the multiples of 3.
    d) From your list, pick out any cube numbers.
    e) Add the numbers in your list together and write down the prime factor decomposition of the total.

Q10 Gordon is doing some woodwork and needs to calculate the volume of a wooden rectangular block (a cuboid). The length of the block is 50 cm, the height is 25 cm and the width is 16 cm.
    a) What is the volume (in cm³) of the wooden block?
    b) Express the number found in part **a)** as a product of its prime factors.
    c) Gordon needs to cut the block into smaller blocks with dimensions 4 cm × 5 cm × 5 cm. What is the maximum number of small blocks Gordon can make from the larger block? Make sure you show all your working.

Q11 The prime factor decomposition of a certain number is $2^3 \times 5 \times 17$.
    a) What is the number?
    b) What is the prime factor decomposition of half of this number?
    c) What is the prime factor decomposition of a quarter of the number?
    d) What is the prime factor decomposition of an eighth of the number?

Q12 Jovi and Marah were playing a guessing game. Marah thought of a number between 1 and 100, which Jovi had to guess. Jovi was allowed to ask five questions, which are listed with Marah's responses in the table below.

Jovi's Questions	Marah's Responses
Is it prime?	No
Is it odd?	No
Is it less than 50?	Yes
Is it a multiple of 3?	Yes
Is it a multiple of 7?	Yes

Use the questions to narrow down the possible numbers — keep going until you only have one left.

What is the number that Marah thought of?

LCM and HCF

 **Top tip** LCM is the Least Common Multiple and HCF is the Highest Common Factor. The basic method is to list the multiples or factors of each number and pick out the answer. But sometimes the question will ask you to use prime factors to calculate the LCM or HCF — so make sure you can use this method too.

Q1
a) List the first ten multiples of 6, starting at 6.
b) List the first ten multiples of 5, starting at 5.
c) What is the LCM of 5 and 6?

Q2
a) List all the factors of 30.
b) List all the factors of 48.
c) What is the HCF of 30 and 48?

Q3 For each set of numbers find the HCF.
a) 40, 60
b) 10, 40, 60
c) 10, 24, 40, 60
d) 15, 45
e) 15, 30, 45
f) 15, 20, 30, 45
g) 32, 64
h) 32, 48, 64
i) 16, 32, 48, 64

Q4 For each set of numbers find the LCM.
a) 40, 60
b) 10, 40, 60
c) 10, 24, 40, 60
d) 15, 45
e) 15, 30, 45
f) 15, 20, 30, 45
g) 32, 64
h) 32, 48, 64
i) 16, 32, 48, 64

Q5
a) Express 15 and 18 as the product of their prime factors.
b) Using your answer to part a), find the LCM of 15 and 18.

Q6
a) Express 90 and 120 as the product of their prime factors.
b) Using your answer to part a), find the HCF of 90 and 120.

Q7
a) Given that $48 = 2^4 \times 3$ and $72 = 2^3 \times 3^2$, find the LCM of 48 and 72.
b) Given that $60 = 2^2 \times 3 \times 5$ and $126 = 2 \times 3^2 \times 7$, find the LCM of 60 and 126.

Q8
a) Given that $120 = 2^3 \times 3 \times 5$ and $150 = 2 \times 3 \times 5^2$, find the HCF of 120 and 150.
b) Given that $140 = 2^2 \times 5 \times 7$ and $600 = 2^3 \times 3 \times 5^2$, find the HCF of 140 and 600.

Q9 Lars, Rita and Alan regularly go swimming. Lars goes every 2 days, Rita goes every 3 days and Alan goes every 5 days. They all went swimming together on Friday 1st June.
a) On what <u>date</u> will Lars and Rita next go swimming together?
b) On what <u>date</u> will Rita and Alan next go swimming together?
c) On what <u>day of the week</u> will all three next go swimming together?
d) Which of the three (if any) will go swimming on 15th June?

This is just a LCM question in disguise.

Q10 Ifeoma has a lot of toy birds — 36 parrots, 42 puffins and 84 penguins. She wants to give them all away to some friends so that they each receive exactly the same number of toys, but they each get only one type of bird. What is the least number of friends she can give the toys away to?

Fractions

 A page full of fractions, how exciting. I know you're itching to get started — just remember, you'll need to use common denominators when adding and subtracting.

Answer the following questions **without using a calculator**.

Q1 Carry out the following multiplications, giving your answers in their simplest form. Any answers larger than 1 should be given as an improper fraction.

Don't forget to see if you can cancel down before multiplying.

a) $\frac{1}{8} \times \frac{1}{8}$ c) $\frac{3}{18} \times \frac{1}{3}$ e) $\frac{6}{28} \times \frac{7}{15}$

b) $\frac{3}{32} \times \frac{4}{11}$ d) $1\frac{1}{4} \times 3\frac{1}{8}$ f) $\frac{9}{10} \times \frac{9}{100} \times \frac{1}{100}$

Q2 Carry out the following divisions, giving your answers in their lowest terms.

'Lowest terms' and 'simplest form' mean the same thing — just cancel down as far as you can.

a) $\frac{1}{8} \div \frac{1}{8}$ c) $\frac{3}{18} \div \frac{1}{3}$ e) $1\frac{1}{4} \div 4\frac{1}{8}$

b) $\frac{2}{3} \div \frac{1}{6}$ d) $1\frac{1}{4} \div 3\frac{1}{8}$ f) $\left(\frac{9}{10} \div \frac{9}{100}\right) \div \frac{1}{100}$

Q3 Evaluate the following, giving your answers in their simplest form. Give any answers that are larger than 1 as improper fractions.

a) $\frac{1}{8} + \frac{1}{8}$ c) $\frac{3}{4} + \frac{7}{15}$ e) $1\frac{3}{4} + 4\frac{4}{5}$

b) $\frac{1}{6} + \frac{2}{3}$ d) $1\frac{1}{4} + 3\frac{1}{8}$ f) $\frac{9}{10} + \frac{9}{20} + \frac{1}{30}$

Q4 Caley is making some punch for her birthday party. She mixes $\frac{1}{2}$ litre of cranberry juice, $1\frac{1}{2}$ litres of apple juice, $\frac{2}{3}$ litre of orange juice and $\frac{4}{5}$ litre of pineapple juice. She has a bowl that will hold $3\frac{1}{2}$ litres. Is this big enough to contain all of the punch?

Q5 Evaluate the following, giving your answers in their simplest form. Give any answers that are larger than 1 as improper fractions.

a) $\frac{7}{8} - \frac{2}{8}$ c) $\frac{3}{4} - \frac{1}{3}$ e) $1\frac{1}{8} - 4\frac{3}{5}$

b) $\frac{2}{3} - \frac{1}{6}$ d) $3\frac{1}{8} - 1\frac{1}{4}$ f) $\left(\frac{9}{10} - \frac{9}{100}\right) - \frac{1}{30}$

Q6 Evaluate the following, giving your answers in their lowest terms. Give any answers that are larger than 1 as mixed numbers.

a) $\frac{1}{2} + \frac{1}{4}$ e) $6 \times \frac{2}{3}$ i) $3 + \frac{8}{5}$

b) $\frac{2}{3} - \frac{1}{4}$ f) $\frac{4}{5} \div \frac{2}{3}$ j) $\frac{2}{3}\left(\frac{3}{4} + \frac{4}{5}\right)$

c) $\frac{1}{5} + \frac{2}{3} - \frac{2}{5}$ g) $\frac{5}{12} \times \frac{3}{2}$ k) $\left(\frac{1}{7} + \frac{3}{14}\right) \times \left(3 - \frac{1}{5}\right)$

d) $5 - \frac{1}{4}$ h) $\frac{5}{6} - \frac{7}{8}$ l) $\left(\frac{3}{4} - \frac{1}{5}\right) \div \left(\frac{7}{8} + \frac{1}{16}\right)$

Section One — Number

Fractions

The cunning bit with long wordy questions is picking out the important bits and then translating them into numbers. It's not that easy at first, but you'll get better.

Answer questions 7 – 9 **without using your calculator**.

Q7 Write each of these times as a fraction of 1 hour. Give each fraction in its simplest form.
    a) 5 minutes   **b)** 15 minutes   **c)** 40 minutes

Q8 The Sandwich Club of Great Britain are going on their annual picnic.
    a) The boxes they use to transport their sandwiches are 10 inches high with a base the same size as a single sandwich. Each sandwich is $\frac{5}{8}$ inch thick. How many boxes will they need for 80 sandwiches?
    b) How tall would the box need to be if 40 sandwiches were to be stacked inside?

Q9 Vayun owns 160 farm animals. $\frac{5}{32}$ of them are sheep and $\frac{2}{5}$ of the sheep are lambs. How many lambs does Vayun own?

You can **use your calculator** for questions 10 – 13.

Q10 The amount of sugar in Healthybix cereal has been reduced by $\frac{1}{4}$. There is now 4.8 g of sugar in every 50 g of cereal. Work out the original amount of sugar in 50 g of the cereal.

Q11 Fiza, Kera and Rebekah each buy the same dress at different discounted prices. They get $\frac{7}{15}$, $\frac{4}{9}$ and $\frac{13}{27}$ off the original price, respectively. The dress originally cost £49.95.
    a) Who gets the biggest discount?
    b) Maali later buys the dress from Kera, but gets a further $\frac{1}{5}$ off the price Kera paid. How much does the dress cost Maali?

Q12 Abeeku wants to make a cake. The recipe requires 150 g each of flour, sugar and butter, and 3 eggs. Abeeku only has 2 eggs so he decides to make a smaller cake with the same proportions.
    a) How much flour will Abeeku need to use?
    b) If each egg weighs 25 g, how much will the cake weigh before it goes in the oven?
    c) What fraction of the uncooked weight is flour? Simplify your answer.
    d) If the cake loses $\frac{1}{7}$ of its weight during baking (due to moisture loss), what will it weigh after baking?

Q13 The diagram shows 3 identical trapeziums, each with a different area shaded. Trapezium A has $\frac{1}{9}$ of its area shaded and trapezium B has $\frac{3}{8}$ of its area shaded. What fraction of trapezium C is shaded?

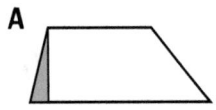
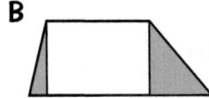
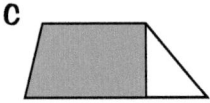

Fractions, Decimals and Percentages

I reckon that converting decimals to percentages is about as easy as it gets — so make the most of it.

Answer questions 1 – 4 **without using your calculator**.

Q1 Express each of the following as a percentage.

a) 0.25 c) 0.75 e) 0.4152 g) 0.06
b) 0.5   d) 0.1   f) 0.8406 h) 0.2828

Q2 Express each percentage as a decimal.

a) 50% c) 40% e) 60.2% g) 43.1%
b) 12% d) 34% f) 8%   h) 6.8%

Q3 Express each of the following as a percentage.

a) $\frac{1}{2}$ c) $\frac{3}{4}$ e) $\frac{2}{5}$ g) $\frac{11}{20}$
b) $\frac{1}{8}$ d) $\frac{5}{4}$ f) $\frac{1}{25}$ h) $\frac{9}{200}$

For f) and g), start by finding an equivalent fraction with denominator 100...

Q4 Express each percentage as a fraction in its simplest form.

a) 25%   e) 7.5%
b) 60%   f) 49.6%
c) 45%   g) 88.6%
d) 30%   h) 32.4%

Best thing to do with e)-h) is to put them over 100, then get rid of the decimal point by multiplying top and bottom by 10. Then just cancel down as normal.

You can **use your calculator** for questions 5 – 7.

Q5 Express each of the following as a percentage. Give your answers to 2 decimal places.

a) $\frac{6}{13}$ c) $\frac{4}{15}$ e) $\frac{3}{11}$
b) $\frac{1}{6}$ d) $\frac{9}{7}$ f) $\frac{11}{3}$

Q6 119 out of 140 houses on an estate have DVD players. What percentage is this?

Q7 In an exam Tina scored 52/80. The grade she receives depends on the percentage scored. What grade will Tina get?

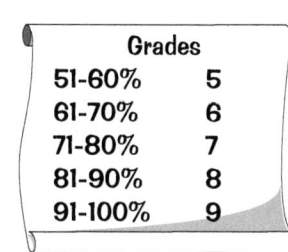

Grades	
51-60%	5
61-70%	6
71-80%	7
81-90%	8
91-100%	9

Fractions, Decimals and Percentages

 This page gets a bit tricky towards the end. Make sure you know the methods for converting between recurring decimals and fractions — then you won't get in a tizz.

Answer these questions **without using a calculator**.

Q8 Write the following fractions as decimals.

a) $\frac{3}{10}$ b) $\frac{37}{100}$ c) $\frac{2}{5}$ d) $\frac{3}{8}$

e) $\frac{14}{8}$ f) $\frac{17}{25}$ g) $\frac{24}{40}$ h) $\frac{4}{80}$

You should cancel down fractions as far as possible before converting to a decimal.

Q9 Fill in the gaps in the following conversion table.

Decimal	0.5		0.125	1.6				0.45	
Fraction	$\frac{1}{2}$	$\frac{1}{5}$			$\frac{1}{4}$	$\frac{7}{2}$	$\frac{3}{20}$		

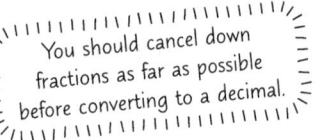

Q10 Write the following fractions as recurring decimals.

a) $\frac{5}{6}$ b) $\frac{7}{9}$ c) $\frac{7}{11}$ d) $\frac{47}{99}$

e) $\frac{10}{11}$ f) $\frac{29}{33}$ g) $\frac{478}{999}$ h) $\frac{5891}{9999}$

Q11 Write the following decimals as fractions in their simplest form.

a) 0.6 b) 0.75 c) 0.95 d) 0.128

e) $0.\dot{3}$ f) $0.\dot{6}$ g) $0.\dot{1}$ h) $0.\dot{1}\dot{6}$

Q12 Write the following recurring decimals as fractions in their lowest terms.

a) 0.222... b) 0.444... c) 0.888... d) 0.808080...

e) 0.121212... f) 0.545545545... g) 0.753753753... h) 0.156156156...

Q13 Convert the following recurring decimals to fractions in their simplest form.

a) $0.1\dot{3}$ b) $0.7\dot{8}$ c) $0.0\dot{8}$ d) $0.13\dot{4}$

e) $0.8\dot{6}\dot{4}$ f) $0.00\dot{6}\dot{0}$ g) $0.21\dot{3}$ h) $0.6\dot{4}0\dot{3}$

Rounding Numbers

 With all these rounding methods, you need to identify the last digit — e.g. if you're rounding 23.41 to 1 decimal place the last digit is 4. Then look at the next digit to the right. If it's 5 or more you round up, if it's 4 or less you leave the last digit as it is.

Q1 Round these numbers to the required number of decimal places.

    a) 62.1935 (1 d.p.)   d) 19.624328 (5 d.p.)   g) 739.995 (2 d.p.)
    b) 62.1935 (2 d.p.)   e) 6.2999 (3 d.p.)   h) 54.0505 (3 d.p.)
    c) 62.1935 (3 d.p.)   f) π (3 d.p.)   i) $5.\dot{8}$ (3 d.p.)

Q2 Round these numbers to the required number of significant figures.

    a) 1329.62 (3 s.f.)   d) 120 (1 s.f.)
    b) 1329.62 (4 s.f.)   e) 0.024087 (1 s.f.)
    c) 1329.62 (5 s.f.)   f) 0.024087 (4 s.f.)

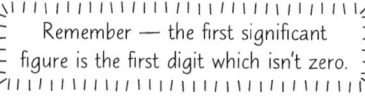 Remember — the first significant figure is the first digit which isn't zero.

Q3 $K = 456.9873$
Write K correct to:

    a) one decimal place   d) three significant figures
    b) two decimal places   e) two significant figures
    c) three decimal places   f) one significant figure

Q4 Round these prices to the nearest pound.

    a) £1100.45   d) £2.55
    b) £87.61   e) £376.49
    c) £299.50   f) £44.19

Q5 A bumper bag of icing sugar weighs 23.4 kg.
What is this correct to the nearest kilogram?

Q6 Priya measured the length of her bedroom as 2.345 metres. Round this measurement correct to the nearest centimetre. Give your answer in metres.

Q7 Jessy jumps 4.65 m in the long jump. What is this to the nearest ten centimetres? Give your answer in metres.

Q8 Kabir's company pays his travel expenses.
They round the distance he drives to the nearest mile, and then pay 20p for every mile. In one week, Kabir drives 95.45 miles. How much money can Kabir claim back?

Q9 A pack of three model cars costs £14.30. John wants to work out the cost per car. What is the answer correct to the nearest penny?

Q10 A baby sea turtle weighs 1815.56 g.
How much does it weigh to 3 significant figures?

Estimating

Get your thinking cap on — you'll need to do this page <u>without a calculator</u>.

Q1 Zawar wants to buy some tropical fish.
The pet shop owner tells him that he will need
a tank with a volume of at least 7000 cm³.
Estimate whether Zawar's tank will be big enough.

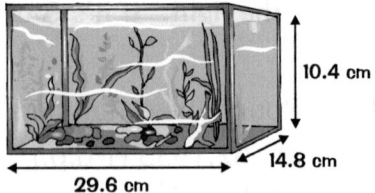

Q2 Find approximate answers to the following:

a) 6560×1.97

b) $38.45 \times 1.4237 \times 5.0002$

c) $45.34 \div 9.345$

d) $34504 \div 7133$

e) $\dfrac{55.33 \times 19.345}{9.23}$

f) $\dfrac{149.5 + 49.1}{153.2 - 48.2}$

g) $\dfrac{821.43 - 219.86}{0.98 + 8.91}$

h) $\dfrac{78.9 \times 304.8}{58.39 \div 21.66}$

i) $\dfrac{1318.46 \div 2.164}{5.138 \times 11.421}$

j) $\pi \div 3$

Round these to nice easy numbers that you can deal with without a calculator.

Q3 At the start of the week, a shop had approximately 15 000 cartons of broccoli juice in stock. The shop sold 1483 cartons on Monday, 2549 on Tuesday, 1539 on Wednesday, 1478 on Thursday and 2958 on Friday. Estimate the number of cartons remaining.

Q4 Showing all your working, estimate the value of the following:

a) $\dfrac{18.2 \times 10.7}{\sqrt{398.6}}$

b) $\dfrac{(9.7)^2 \div 10.3}{4.306 \times 5.011}$

c) $\dfrac{6.42 \times 8.803}{0.321}$

d) $\dfrac{\sqrt{98.6}}{0.3301 + 0.192}$

Q5 Joan needs to estimate the size of her bedroom so that she can buy enough paint to cover the walls. Two of the walls measure 2.86 m by 3.16 m, and the other two walls measure 2.86 m by 3.42 m.
a) Estimate the area that Joan needs to paint in m².
b) If one tin of paint will cover 15 m², how many tins of paint will Joan need to paint her bedroom?

Q6 For each diagram below, estimate the volume shown. Explain whether your estimate will be larger or smaller than the actual volume.

a)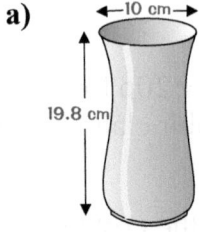

b)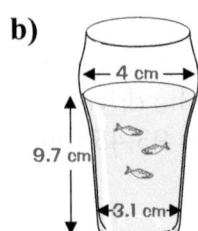

For this, you'll need the formula for the volume of a cylinder: $V = \pi r^2 h$

Q7 Estimate the following roots, to 1 decimal place.

a) $\sqrt{48}$

b) $\sqrt{118}$

c) $\sqrt{84}$

d) $\sqrt{17}$

e) $\sqrt[3]{10}$

f) $\sqrt[3]{25}$

Start with roots that you know — and use them to make an educated <u>guess</u>.

Section One — Number

Bounds

Bounds are useful when you're dealing with rounded numbers — they tell you the range of values that the original unrounded number lies in. Remember, when a number's been rounded to a given unit, the actual value can be up to half a unit bigger or smaller.

Q1 Elliah weighs herself on some scales that are accurate to the nearest 10 grams. The digital display shows her weight as 64.78 kg.
  a) What is the maximum that she could weigh?
  b) What is the minimum that she could weigh?

Q2 A rectangular rug is 1.8 metres long and 0.7 metres wide. Both measurements are given correct to one decimal place.
  a) State the minimum possible length of the rug.
  b) Calculate the maximum possible area of the rug.

Truncating is different from rounding — the number is just cut off.

Q3
  a) The height, h, of the Eiffel Tower is 300.6 m truncated to 1 decimal place. Express the possible values of the height as an inequality.
  b) The width of the base of the Eiffel Tower, when truncated to a whole number, is 125 m. What is the minimum possible width of the base?

Q4 It's Pancake Day and Rua is making a large batch of pancakes to share with friends. Her recipe tells her to add 2.5 litres of milk, but her measuring jug only measures up to 500 ml and is accurate to the nearest 10 ml.
  a) What is the maximum volume of milk Rua could measure out, assuming she is as accurate as she can be?
  b) What is the minimum volume of milk Rua could measure out?

Q5 Sandra has a parcel to post. She weighs it to find out the cost of postage.
  a) A set of kitchen scales, that weigh to the nearest 10 g, show that the weight of the parcel is 90 g. Find the interval in which the actual weight, p, of the parcel lies.
  b) Next she weighs the parcel on a different set of kitchen scales, which are accurate to the nearest 5 g. The parcel weighs 95 g. Give the interval in which p lies according to these scales.
  c) The post office weighs the parcel on some electronic scales to the nearest gram. It weighs 98 g. Can all the scales be right? Explain your answer.

Q6 A village hall contains 125 chairs to the nearest 5.
  a) What are the upper and lower bounds for the number of chairs?
  b) A meeting is going to take place in the village hall. The number of people expected to attend is 130 to the nearest 5. Is it possible that everyone expected will be able to sit down at the meeting? Explain your reasoning.

Bounds

Q7 Jimmy, Siddhi and Douglas are comparing their best times for running the 1500 m.
Jimmy's best time is 5 minutes 30 seconds measured to the nearest 10 seconds.
Siddhi's best time is also 5 minutes 30 seconds, but measured to the nearest 5 seconds.
Douglas' best time is 5 minutes 26 seconds measured to the nearest second. 
   a) What are the upper and lower bounds for Siddhi's best time?
   b) Douglas thinks that he is the quickest at running the 1500 m.
      Explain why this may not be the case.

To find the upper or lower bound of a **calculation**, you've just got to decide which version of the values involved (max or min) to use to get the biggest or smallest overall answer. And remember — you don't always get the maximum value by using the biggest input values.

Q8 $A = 13$, correct to 2 significant figures.
$B = 12.5$, correct to 3 significant figures.
   a) For the value of A, write down the upper bound and the lower bound.
   b) For the value of B, write down the upper bound and the lower bound.
   c) Calculate the upper bound and lower bound for C when $C = AB$.
      Using these values, express the interval in which C lies as an inequality.

Q9 Ash wants to put a new carpet in his living room. He has measured the floor as being 3.4 m × 5.2 m to the nearest 10 cm. There is a discount available at the local carpet shop for anyone who buys more than 18.5 m² of carpet. If Ash buys enough carpet to be sure he can cover the whole floor, will he receive the discount? Explain your answer.

Q10 a) The length of a rectangle is measured as 12 ± 0.1 cm. The width of the same rectangle is measured as 4 ± 0.1 cm. Calculate the perimeter of the rectangle, giving also the maximum possible error.
   b) A rectangle measures $A \pm x$ cm in length and $B \pm y$ cm in width. The formula $P = 2(A + B)$ is used to calculate the perimeter, P, of the rectangle. What is the maximum possible error in P?

You need to add the errors for all the sides together.

Q11 A lorry travelled 125 kilometres in 1 hour and 50 minutes. If the time was measured to the nearest 10 minutes and the distance to the nearest 5 kilometres, what is the maximum value of the average speed of the lorry, in kilometres per hour?

Q12 $R = \dfrac{S}{T}$ is a formula used by stockbrokers.

$S = 940$, correct to 2 significant figures and $T = 5.56$, correct to 3 significant figures.
   a) For the value of S, write down the upper bound and the lower bound.
   b) For the value of T, write down the upper bound and the lower bound.
   c) Calculate the upper bound and the lower bound for R.
   d) Write down the value of R correct to an appropriate number of significant figures.

Section One — Number

Standard Form

Writing very big (or very small) numbers gets a bit messy if you don't use standard form — because of all those zeros. But of course, the main reason for knowing about standard form is... you guessed it — it's in the Exam.

Q1 Delilah is doing some calculations for her science homework.
She needs to give her answers as ordinary numbers.
How should she write the following answers?

a) 3.56×10
b) 3.56×10^3
c) 3.56×10^{-1}
d) 3.56×10^4
e) 0.082×10^2
f) 0.082×10^{-2}
g) 0.082×10
h) 0.082×10^{-1}
i) 157×10
j) 157×10^{-3}
k) 157×10^3
l) 157×10^{-1}

Q2 Write in standard form:

a) 2.56
b) 25.6
c) 0.256
d) 25 600
e) 95.2
f) 0.0952
g) 95 200
h) 0.000952
i) 4200
j) 0.0042
k) 42
l) 420

Q3 Write in standard form:

a) 34.7×10
b) 73.004
c) 0.005×10^3
d) 9183×10^2
e) 15 million
f) 937.1×10^4
g) 0.000075
h) 0.05×10^{-2}
i) 534×10^{-2}
j) 621.03
k) 149×10^2
l) 0.003×10^{-4}

Q4 A tissue sample is three cells thick. Each cell has a thickness of 0.000004 m.
What is the thickness of the tissue sample in mm? Give your answer in standard form.

Q5 This table gives the diameter and distance from the Sun of some planets.

Planet	Distance from Sun (km)	Diameter (km)
Earth	1.5×10^8	1.3×10^4
Venus	1.085×10^8	1.2×10^4
Mars	2.28×10^8	6.8×10^3
Mercury	5.81×10^7	4.9×10^3
Jupiter	7.8×10^8	1.4×10^5
Neptune	4.52×10^9	4.9×10^4
Saturn	1.43×10^9	1.2×10^5

From the table write down which planet is:
a) smallest in diameter
b) largest in diameter
c) nearest to the Sun
d) furthest from the Sun

Write down which planets are:
e) nearer to the Sun than the Earth is
f) bigger in diameter than the Earth

Q6 The following numbers are <u>not</u> written in standard form.
Rewrite them correctly using standard form.

a) 42×10^6
b) 38×10^{-5}
c) 10×10^6
d) 11.2×10^{-5}
e) 843×10^3
f) 42.32×10^{-4}
g) 17×10^{17}
h) 28.3×10^{-5}
i) 10×10^{-3}

Section One — Number

Standard Form

I know you enjoyed that last page on standard form, so here's another. I'm so kind...

Answer questions 7, 9 and 13 to 16 **without using a calculator**.

Q7 Work out the answers to these calculations. Write your answers in standard form.
   a) $(3 \times 10^4) \times (6.3 \times 10^2)$
   b) $(2.8 \times 10^5) \div (1.4 \times 10^3)$
   c) $800\,000 \times (9.2 \times 10^7)$
   d) $(8.9 \times 10^3) + (3.1 \times 10^4)$
   e) $50\,000 + (3.6 \times 10^5)$
   f) $(1.8 \times 10^4) - (5.2 \times 10^3)$

Q8 Evaluate the following, writing your answers in standard form.
   a) $(2.85 \times 10^3) \times (3.2 \times 10^6)$
   b) $(4.93 \times 10^6) \div (8.5 \times 10^4)$
   c) $(9.63 \times 10^5) + (2.4 \times 10^6)$
   d) $(4.35 \times 10^6) - (2.7 \times 10^3)$

Q9 If $x = 4 \times 10^5$ and $y = 6 \times 10^4$ work out the value of the following.
Give your answers in standard form.
   a) xy b) $4x$ c) $3y$

Q10 Which is greater, 4.62×10^{12} or 1.04×10^{13}, and by how much?

Q11 Which is smaller, 3.2×10^{-8} or 1.3×10^{-9}, and by how much?

Q12
   a) The surface area of the Earth is 5.1×10^8 km². Write this <u>without</u> using standard form.
   b) The area of the Earth covered by sea is $362\,000\,000$ km². Write this in standard form.
   c) What is the area of the Earth covered by land? Write your answer <u>without</u> using standard form.

Q13 Write the following in standard form.

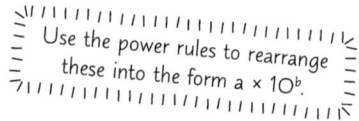
Use the power rules to rearrange these into the form $a \times 10^b$.

   a) $2^{15} \times 5^{17}$
   b) $2^{-20} \times 5^{-21}$
   c) $\dfrac{1}{2 \times 5^{-2}}$

Q14 Find values of x, y and z that satisfy the following calculation:
$$(8 \times 10^x) + (6 \times 10^y) + (2 \times 10^z) = 80\,620$$

Q15 Work out the answers to these calculations. Write your answers in standard form.
   a) $\dfrac{(6.3 \times 10^8) \times (2 \times 10^4)}{(2 \times 10^6) \times (1.5 \times 10^3)}$
   b) $\dfrac{(8.5 \times 10^{12}) \times (3 \times 10^{14})}{(1.6 \times 10^{10}) \div (3.2 \times 10^9)}$
   c) $\dfrac{(3 \times 10^{12}) \times (6 \times 10^{-8})}{(2 \times 10^{-2}) \times (3 \times 10^3)}$
   d) $\dfrac{(3.12 \times 10^{-6}) \div (2 \times 10^{-10})}{(2.95 \times 10^{27}) + (5 \times 10^{25})}$

Q16 There are 6.02×10^{23} carbon atoms in 12 g of carbon.
   a) Estimate the mass of one atom of carbon.
   b) State whether the actual mass of one carbon atom is greater or smaller than your answer to a).

Section One — Mixed Questions

Mixed Questions

What's that? You're enjoying Section One so much you don't want it to end? Well luckily for you these mixed questions are basically a "Greatest Hits" CD of all your favourite topics. Ah, nostalgia...

Try to work out the answers to the following questions **without using a calculator**.

Q1 Using any or all of the figures **2**, **3**, **4**, **7** and **8**, and the symbol $\sqrt{}$, write down:
 a) the largest two-digit odd integer
 b) an irrational number that is less than 2
 c) a prime number between 20 and 30
 d) a square number and a cube number whose sum is 31
 e) two integers that divide to give a rational number, but not an integer

Q2 Calculate the following:
 a) $(2 + 7) \div 3 \times 4$
 b) $8 + 4 \times 9 - 5$
 c) $(9 - 3) \times 5 + 6^2$
 d) $9 \div 3 \times (2^3 + 7)$
 e) $9 \times (4 + 15 \div 5)$
 f) $(3 + \sqrt{16 + 9}) \div 4$
 g) $(17 - (13 + 9) \div 2)^2$
 h) $\sqrt{(19 - 7) \times 8 + 5^2}$

Q3 a) Write down each number below as a product of its prime factors.
  i) 144   iii) 240   v) 400
  ii) 63   iv) 84   vi) 324
 b) Use your answers to part a) to find the LCM of:
  i) 240 and 400   ii) 63 and 84
 c) Use your answers to part a) to find the HCF of:
  i) 144 and 240   ii) 84, 144 and 324

Q4 A party shop sells balloons in packs. Blue balloons come in packs of 30, red balloons come in packs of 50 and white balloons come in packs of 75.
 a) Gina buys one pack of each colour and makes bunches of balloons to hand out. She splits each pack evenly across the bunches. What is the greatest number of bunches she can make if she uses all the balloons?
 b) Romesh wants to make a giant balloon display using an equal number of red, white and blue balloons. What is the smallest number of packs of each colour he needs to use in order to have no balloons left over?

Q5 Evaluate the following, giving your answers in their lowest terms.
Give any answers that are larger than one as improper fractions.
 a) $\dfrac{1}{3} + \dfrac{5}{12}$
 b) $\dfrac{8}{10} - \dfrac{3}{5}$
 c) $\dfrac{2}{6} \times \dfrac{3}{4}$
 d) $\dfrac{14}{12} \div \dfrac{2}{9}$
 e) $\dfrac{4}{15} - \dfrac{1}{5} + \dfrac{2}{3}$
 f) $\dfrac{3}{8} \times \dfrac{5}{9}$
 g) $\left(\dfrac{15}{14} - \dfrac{3}{7}\right) \div \left(\dfrac{6}{5} \times \dfrac{2}{3}\right)$
 h) $2 - \dfrac{11}{16}$
 i) $1\dfrac{1}{7} \times \left(\dfrac{3}{4} + 1\dfrac{1}{5}\right)$

Q6 Write the following fractions as recurring decimals.
 a) $\dfrac{1}{3}$
 b) $\dfrac{5}{12}$
 c) $\dfrac{8}{11}$
 d) $\dfrac{2}{9}$
 e) $\dfrac{50}{66}$
 f) $\dfrac{12}{99}$
 g) $\dfrac{35}{999}$

More mixed practice on the next page...

Mixed Questions

Q7 Write the following recurring decimals as fractions in their simplest form.
    a) 0.777...   **b)** 0.090909...   **c)** 0.424242...   **d)** 0.255255255...

Q8 Fill in the gaps in the following conversion table. Give your answers in their lowest terms and write any fractions that are larger than one as mixed numbers.

Fraction				$\frac{3}{5}$		$\frac{5}{8}$		$\frac{11}{20}$
Decimal	0.8		0.75				0.375	
Percentage		70%		120%	95%			

Q9 A fishing rod is 213.365 cm long. Write the length of the fishing rod correct to:
    a) one decimal place, in centimetres   **d)** one significant figure, in metres
    b) two decimal places, in metres   **e)** two significant figures, in centimetres
    c) three decimal places, in metres   **f)** two decimal places, in centimetres

Q10 Estimate the answers to the following calculations.
    a) $2237 \times 3.053 \times 8.941$ **e)** $\dfrac{6023.756}{49.74 \times 2.852}$
    b) $1164 \div 3.853$ **f)** $\dfrac{32.04 \times 78.22}{52.95 + 66.4}$
    c) $30.63 \times 2.727 \div 11.02$ **g)** $\dfrac{3.878 \times 21.1}{138.7 \div 7.10}$
    d) $\dfrac{191.1 - 62.75}{7.103 + 4.28}$ **h)** $(10.63 + 28.55) \div 18.42 - 9.965$

Q11 A company produces shipping containers that are 2.4 m wide and 2.6 m tall. Both measurements are correct to one decimal place.
    a) What is the minimum possible height of a shipping container?
    b) The containers are exactly 2.99 m long. Estimate the volume of a single shipping container.
    c) The deck of a large cargo ship is 50 m wide and containers are lined up next to each other in rows across the ship. What is the greatest number of containers that could definitely fit in one row?

Q12 Trisha and Araf each time themselves swimming 10 metres.
Trisha records her time as 12.1 s correct to 3 significant figures.
Araf records his time as 12.08 s correct to 2 decimal places.
Araf claims that this means his time was definitely faster than Trisha's.
Is he correct? Explain your answer.

Q13 Work out the answers to these calculations. Write your answer in standard form.
    a) $(6.3 \times 10^8) \div (3 \times 10^4)$ **d)** $4\,000\,000 + (5.7 \times 10^6)$
    b) $90\,000 \times (1.1 \times 10^5)$ **e)** $(3.35 \times 10^8) - (4 \times 10^7)$
    c) $(7.2 \times 10^3) \times (5 \times 10^5)$ **f)** $(2.2 \times 10^2) + (9.9 \times 10^3)$

Section Two — Algebra

Algebra Basics

Make sure you've got to grips with these questions before you get on with the rest of the section — they'll give you a bit of practice at the basic algebra skills you'll need...

Q1 Work out the following temperature changes.
- **a)** 20 °C to -7 °C
- **b)** -10 °C to -32 °C
- **c)** -17 °C to -5 °C
- **d)** -3 °C to 15 °C
- **e)** -31 °C to -16 °C
- **f)** -5 °C to -17 °C

Q2 Which is larger and by how much?
- **a)** -12 + 7 − -4 + 6 − 2 + 7   or   **b)** -30 + 26 − 3 − -7 + 17

Q3 Simplify: **a)** $4x − -5x + 3x − x + 2x − 7x$ **b)** $30y − 10y + 2y − 3y + 4y − -5y$

Q4 Find the value of xy and $\frac{x}{y}$ for each of the following:
- **a)** $x = -100$, $y = 10$
- **b)** $x = 24$, $y = -4$
- **c)** $x = -48$, $y = -3$
- **d)** $x = 0$, $y = -4$

Q5 Find the value of $(a - b) \div (c + d)$ when $a = 10$, $b = -26$, $c = -5$ and $d = -4$.

Q6 Simplify the following:
- **a)** $2x \times -3y$
- **b)** $-8a \times 2b$
- **c)** $-4x \times -2x$
- **d)** $4p \times -4p$
- **e)** $-30x \div -3y$
- **f)** $50x \div -5y$
- **g)** $10x \div -2y$
- **h)** $-30x \div -10x$
- **i)** $40ab \div -10ab$
- **j)** $70x^2 \div -7x^2$
- **k)** $-36x^2 \div -9x$
- **l)** $40y^2 \div -5y$

Q7 Simplify the following by collecting like terms together.
- **a)** $3x^2 + 4x + 12x^2 − 5x$
- **b)** $14x^2 − 10x − x^2 + 5x$
- **c)** $12 − 4x^2 + 10x − 3x^2 + 2x$
- **d)** $20abc + 12ab + 10bac + 4b$
- **e)** $8pq + 7p + q + 10qp − q + p$
- **f)** $15ab − 10a + b − 7a + 2ba$
- **g)** $4pq − 14p − 8q + p − q + 8p$
- **h)** $13x^2 + 4x^2 − 5y^2 + y^2 − x^2$
- **i)** $11ab + 2cd − ba − 13dc + abc$
- **j)** $3x^2 + 4xy + 2y^2 − z^2 + 2xy − y^2 − 5x^2$

Q8 For each of the diagrams below, write down the area of each of the small rectangles and hence find an expression for the area of each large rectangle.

a)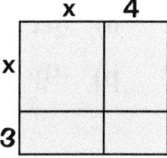

b)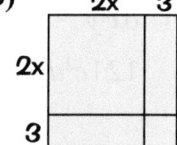

c)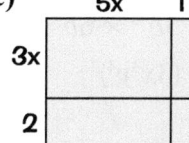

Eeeek — loads of questions...

Powers and Roots

Hang on there. Before you try this page, make sure you know all the rules for dealing with powers.

Remember, 2^4 means 'two to the power four'.

Q1 Complete the following:
a) $2^4 = 2 \times 2 \times 2 \times 2 =$
b) $10^3 = 10 \times 10 \times 10 =$
c) $3^5 = 3 \times \ldots \quad =$
d) $1^9 = 1 \times \ldots \quad =$

Q2 Simplify the following:
a) $2 \times 2 \times 2 \times 2 \times 2 \times 2 \times 2 \times 2$
b) $12 \times 12 \times 12 \times 12 \times 12$
c) $m \times m \times m$
d) $z \times z \times z \times z \times z \times z \times z$

Q3 Complete the following (the first one has been done for you):
a) $10^2 \times 10^3 = (10 \times 10) \times (10 \times 10 \times 10) = 10^5$
b) $10^3 \times 10^4 = \quad =$
c) $10^5 \times 10^3 = \quad =$
d) What is the quick method for writing down the final result in **b)** and **c)**?

Easy — you'll have learnt this from your power rules.

Q4 Complete the following (the first one has been done for you):
a) $2^4 \div 2^2 = \dfrac{(2 \times 2 \times 2 \times 2)}{(2 \times 2)} = 2^2$
b) $2^5 \div 2^2 = \quad =$
c) $4^5 \div 4^3 = \dfrac{(4 \times 4 \times 4 \times 4 \times 4)}{} =$
d) $8^5 \div 8^2 = \quad =$
e) What is the quick method for writing down the final result in **b)**, **c)** and **d)**?

Q5 **Without using a calculator**, decide which of the following are true.
a) $2^4 \times 2^6 = 2^{10}$
b) $2^2 \times 2^3 \times 2^4 = 2^9$
c) $2^3 \times 2^2 = 2^6$
d) $4^{10} \times 4^4 \times (4^2)^3 = 4^{18}$
e) $2^1 \times (2^3)^4 \times 2^4 = 2^{17}$
f) $10^4 \times (10^2)^3 = 10^8$
g) $2^{20} \div 2^5 = 2^4$
h) $3^{12} \div 3^4 = 3^8$
i) $4^6 \div 6^4 = 4^2$
j) $10^{20} \div (10^3)^2 = 10^{14}$
k) $4^6 \div (4^2 \times 4^3) = 4^1$
l) $9^2 \times (9^{30} \div 9^{25}) = 9^{10}$

Q6 For each of the following, answer **true** or **false**:
a) When x is a negative number, x^2 is always positive.
b) When x is a positive whole number, x^4 is always greater than x.
c) For all values of x, a and b, $x^a \times x^b = x^{a \times b}$.

Q7 Remove the brackets from the following and express as a single power.
a) $(3^4 \times 3^2) \div (3^6 \times 3^3)$
b) $(4^{10} \times 4^{12}) \times 4^3$
c) $10^2 \div (10^3 \times 10^{12})$
d) $(3^6)^{-2}$
e) $4^2 \times 4^{-1} \times 4^6 \times (4^2 \div 4^3)$
f) $(5^2 \times 5^3) \div (5^6 \div 5^4)$
g) $(2^7 \times 2^{-1}) \times (2^2 \div 2^5)$
h) $(10^3 \div 10^{-5}) \times (10^4 \div 10^2)$
i) $(7^4 \div 7^{-3}) \div (7^{-8} \times 7^{-5})$
j) $(3^{\frac{1}{5}} \times 3^{\frac{3}{5}}) \div 3^{\frac{2}{5}}$
k) $(4^{-\frac{3}{4}} \times 4^{\frac{1}{4}}) \div 4^{-\frac{1}{4}}$
l) $(2^{\frac{2}{3}} \times 2^{-\frac{1}{3}}) \div (2^{-\frac{5}{3}} \times 2^{\frac{1}{3}})$

Q8 Simplify the following:
a) $x^2 \times x^3$
b) $y^5 \div y^4$
c) $(a^4)^3$
d) $f^1 \times f^4$
e) z^0
f) $\left(\dfrac{2x}{y}\right)^3 \times x^4$
g) $5b^{-3} \times 6b^{-2}$
h) $(3x^3y^4)^2$
i) $3a^3b^2 \times 2a^5b^3$
j) $4p^{-10}q^4 \times 2p^8q^{-15}$
k) $8x^5y^7 \div 4x^3y^4$
l) $121c^2d^3 \div 11c^7d^9$
m) $7a^5b^{-3} \times 4a^{-2}b^4$
n) $(16x^4)^{\frac{1}{2}} \times (27x^6)^{\frac{1}{3}}$
o) $(4x^2)^{\frac{3}{2}} \div (2x^{\frac{1}{3}})^3$
p) $(9y^{-\frac{2}{5}})^{\frac{3}{2}} \div (3y^{-\frac{1}{5}})^2$

Powers and Roots

Use your **calculator** to evaluate the expressions in questions 9 to 13.
Give your answers as decimals to 3 s.f. where necessary.

Q9
a) $(6.5)^3$
b) $(0.35)^2$
c) $(15.2)^4$
d) $(0.04)^3$
e) $\sqrt{5.6}$
f) $\sqrt[3]{12.4}$
g) $\sqrt{109}$
h) $\sqrt[3]{0.6}$
i) $(1\frac{1}{2})^2$
j) $\sqrt{4\frac{3}{4}}$
k) $(\frac{5}{8})^3$
l) $\sqrt[3]{\frac{9}{10}}$

Q10
a) $(2.4)^2 + 3$
b) $5.9 - (1.2)^3$
c) $\sqrt[3]{5.6} + (4.2)^2$
d) $(6.05)^3 - \sqrt[3]{8.4}$
e) $6.1[35.4 - (4.2)^2]$
f) $95 - 3(\sqrt[3]{48} - 2.6)$
g) $1\frac{1}{2}[4 + (2\frac{1}{4})^2]$
h) $19 - 4\left[\left(\frac{1}{4}\right)^2 + \left(\frac{5}{8}\right)^3\right]$
i) $15\frac{3}{5} - 2\frac{1}{2}\left[\left(1\frac{3}{4}\right)^3 - \sqrt[3]{1\frac{1}{2}}\right]$

Q11
a) 1.7^{-3}
b) 2.5^{-2}
c) 16^{-4}
d) $(1.5)^{-1}$
e) $5^{\frac{1}{2}}$
f) $6^{\frac{1}{3}}$
g) $9^{\frac{1}{5}}$
h) $(4.2)^{\frac{2}{3}}$
i) $(1\frac{1}{4})^{-3}$
j) $(2\frac{3}{5})^{\frac{1}{5}}$
k) $(5\frac{1}{3})^{-2}$
l) $(10\frac{5}{6})^{\frac{5}{6}}$

Remember — fractional powers mean roots.

Q12
a) $\sqrt{(1.4)^2 + (0.5)^2}$
b) $5.9\left[(2.3)^{\frac{1}{4}} + (4.7)^{\frac{1}{2}}\right]$
c) $2.5 - 0.6[(7.1)^{-3} - (9.5)^{-4}]$
d) $(8.2)^{-2} + (1.6)^4 - (3.7)^{-3}$
e) $\dfrac{3\sqrt{8} - 2}{6}$
f) $\dfrac{15 + 3\sqrt{4.1}}{2.4}$
g) $3\sqrt{4.7} - 4\sqrt{2.1}$
h) $\dfrac{(2\frac{1}{4})^{-2} - (3\frac{1}{2})^{\frac{1}{2}}}{4.4}$

Q13
a) $(2\frac{1}{4})^3 - (1.5)^2$
b) $(3.7)^{-2} + (4\frac{1}{5})^{\frac{1}{4}}$
c) $\sqrt[3]{5\frac{1}{3}} \times (4.3)^{-1}$
d) $(7.4)^{\frac{1}{3}} \times (6\frac{1}{4})^3$
e) $\dfrac{\sqrt{22\frac{1}{2}} + (3.4)^2}{(6.9)^3 \times 3.4}$
f) $\dfrac{(15\frac{3}{5})^2 \times (2.5)^{-3}}{3 \times 4\frac{1}{4}}$
g) $5[(4.3)^2 - (2.5)^{\frac{1}{2}}]$
h) $\dfrac{3.5(2\frac{1}{6} - \sqrt{4.1})}{(3.5)^2 \times (3\frac{1}{2})^{-2}}$
i) $\dfrac{1\frac{1}{2} + \frac{1}{4}[(2\frac{2}{3})^2 - (1.4)^2]}{(3.9)^{-3}}$
j) $\sqrt[3]{2.73} + 5\sqrt{2}$

Q14 Evaluate the following **without using a calculator**:

a) $8^{\frac{1}{3}}$
b) $49^{\frac{1}{2}}$
c) 3^{-2}
d) 4^{-3}
e) $64^{\frac{3}{2}}$
f) $16^{\frac{3}{4}}$
g) $27^{-\frac{1}{3}}$
h) $\left(\dfrac{81}{25}\right)^{-\frac{1}{2}}$

When a fractional power has a numerator bigger than 1, it's often easier to do the root part before the power part, like this:
$$4^{\frac{3}{2}} = \left(4^{\frac{1}{2}}\right)^3 = \left(\sqrt{4}\right)^3 = 2^3 = 8$$

Multiplying Out Brackets

Q1 Multiply out the brackets and simplify where possible:
- a) $4(x + y - z)$
- b) $x(x + 5)$
- c) $-3(x - 2)$
- d) $7(a + b) + 2(a + b)$
- e) $3(a + 2b) - 2(2a + b)$
- f) $4(x - 2) - 2(x - 1)$
- g) $4e(e + 2f) + 2f(e - f)$
- h) $14(2m - n) + 2(3n - 6m)$
- i) $4x(x + 2) - 2x(3 - x)$
- j) $3(2 + ab) + 5(1 - ab)$
- k) $(x^2 - 2y)z - 2x^2(x + z)$
- l) $4(x^2 - 2y) - (5 + x^2 - 2y)$
- m) $a - 4(a + b)$
- n) $4pq(2 + r^3) + 5qr^3(2p + 7)$
- o) $x^2(x + 1)$
- p) $4x^2\left(x + 2 + \dfrac{1}{x}\right)$
- q) $8ab(a^3 + 3 + b)$
- r) $7pq\left(p + q - \dfrac{1}{p}\right)$
- s) $4[(x + y) - 3(y - x)]$

Remember FOIL for multiplying double brackets — you don't want to miss any terms now, do you...

Q2 Multiply out the brackets and simplify your answers where possible:
- a) $(x - 3)(x + 1)$
- b) $(x - 3)(x + 5)$
- c) $(x + 10)(x + 3)$
- d) $(x - 5)(x - 2)$
- e) $(x + 2)(x - 7)$
- f) $(4 - x)(7 - x)$
- g) $(2 + 3x)(3x - 1)$
- h) $(3x + 2)(2x - 4)$
- i) $(x - \sqrt{2})(4x + \sqrt{2})$
- j) $2(2x + y)(x - 2y)$
- k) $4(x + 2y)(3x - 2y)$
- l) $(3x + 2y)^2$
- m) $(2a - b)^2$
- n) $(t - 2\sqrt{2})(t + 2\sqrt{2})$
- o) $(3p + \sqrt{2})^2$

Q3 Find the product of $5x - 2$ and $3x + 2$.

Q4 Find the square of $2x - 1$.

For triple brackets, use FOIL on two of the brackets, then multiply the result by the third bracket.

Q5 Multiply out the brackets and simplify your answers where possible.
- a) $(x + 1)(x - 2)(x + 2)$
- b) $(x + 3)(x + 2)(x + 5)$
- c) $(x - 2)(2x - 1)(x - 5)$
- d) $(3 - x)(2 + x)(5 + x)$
- e) $(1 - 2x)(1 + x)(3 + x)$
- f) $(x + 10)(4 + 2x)(1 + 3x)$
- g) $(3 + x)^2(3 - x)$
- h) $(x - 1)(2x + 1)^2$
- i) $(x + 3)^3$

Q6 A rectangular pond has length $(3x - 2)$ m and width $(5 - x)$ m. Write down a simplified expression for:
- a) the pond's perimeter
- b) the pond's area

Q7 A rectangular bar of chocolate consists of 20 small rectangular pieces. The size of each small rectangular piece is 2 cm by x cm.

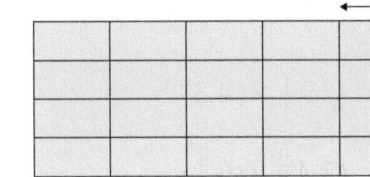

- a) The bar is broken up into its 20 separate pieces. Write down an expression for the perimeter of one piece.
- b) Write down an expression for the sum of the perimeters of all 20 pieces. Give your answer in the form $(ax + b)$ cm.

Q8 Find a simplified expression for the perimeter and the area of the following shapes.

a)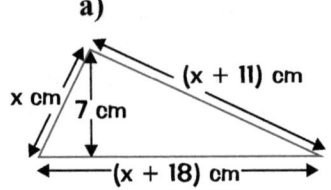
b)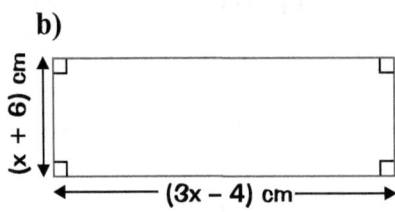
c)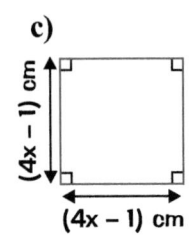
d)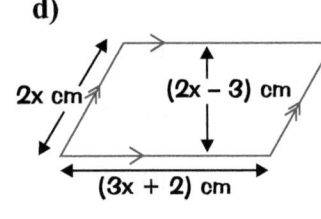

Factorising

Factorising means putting brackets in — you need to look for common factors in all the terms and put them outside a bracket, then put whatever's left inside the bracket.

Q1 All the expressions below have a^2 as a common factor. Factorise each of them.
  a) $a^2b + a^2c$
  b) $5a^2 + 13a^2b$
  c) $2a^2b + 3a^2c$
  d) $a^3 + a^2y$
  e) $2a^2x + 3a^2y + 4a^2z$
  f) $a^2b^2 + a^3c^2$

Q2 Factorise the following expressions.
  a) $x^2 - 5x$
  b) $2x + 6$
  c) $3x^2 + 12x$
  d) $4x^2 - 6x$
  e) $3xy + 12x^2y$
  f) $9x + 15$
  g) $15x^2y - 25x$
  h) $4pq^2 - 20pq + 8p^2q$
  i) $10x^4 + 6x$
  j) $15x^3 - 20x^2$
  k) $21x^2 + 14x$
  l) $5xyz + 20uxy$

Q3 Factorise the following:
  a) $4x + 8xyz$
  b) $8x^3y + 12x^2z$
  c) $8xyz + 16x^2yz$
  d) $20x^2y^2z^2 + 16xyz^2$

Q4 Using the fact that $a^2 - b^2 = (a + b)(a - b)$, factorise the following expressions.
  a) $x^2 - 9$
  b) $y^2 - 16$
  c) $25 - z^2$
  d) $36 - a^2$
  e) $4x^2 - 9$
  f) $9y^2 - 4$
  g) $25 - 16z^2$
  h) $1 - 36a^2$
  i) $x^4 - 36$
  j) $x^4 - y^4$
  k) $1 - (ab)^2$
  l) $100x^2 - 144y^2$

Q5 Factorise:
  a) $x^2 - 4$
  b) $144 - y^4$
  c) $1 - 9x^2y^2$
  d) $49x^4y^4 - 1$
  e) $3x^2 - 12$
  f) $90 - 10y^2$
  g) $50x^2 - 32$
  h) $20 - 45x^2y^2$

Q6 Factorise the following expressions, giving each answer in the form $(a + b)(a - b)$.
  a) $x^2 - 3$
  b) $9x^2 - 5$
  c) $x^2 - 7y^2$
  d) $2 - (xy)^2$

Remember, you can rewrite a non-square number like this: $11 = (\sqrt{11})^2$

These questions are a mixed bunch so look out for which ones are D.O.T.S. and which ones aren't.

Q7 Factorise the following expressions.
  a) $64a^2b^3 - 16b^2a^3$
  b) $pq + qr - pq^2r$
  c) $3m^2 - 24$
  d) $b^4 - ab^3 + b^2c$
  e) $a^4 - 169$
  f) $9ab^2 - 3abc$
  g) $81 - z^2$
  h) $121p^2 - 9q^2$
  i) $m^2n + 3mn - 2mn^3$
  j) $72m^2 - 50n^2$
  k) $144x^2 - 108y^2 - 60z^2$
  l) $64a^2b^2 - 49c^2d^2$

Manipulating Surds

Do these questions <u>without</u> using a calculator.
They're actually not as bad as they might look because you can leave √ or π in your answer.

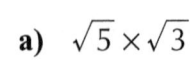

Q1 Simplify:

a) $\sqrt{5} \times \sqrt{3}$
b) $\dfrac{\sqrt{20}}{\sqrt{5}}$
c) $(\sqrt{x})^2$
d) $\sqrt{x^2}$
e) $\sqrt{8} \times \sqrt{8}$
f) $\dfrac{\sqrt{30}}{\sqrt{6}}$

Remember... no calculators on this page.

Q2 A circle has radius $\sqrt{3}$ cm. What is its exact area? (Area of circle = πr^2.)

Q3 Simplify these expressions:

Remember — $\sqrt{a} \times \sqrt{b} = \sqrt{(ab)}$.

a) $\sqrt{4} - \sqrt{1}$
b) $2\sqrt{3} + 3\sqrt{3}$
c) $\sqrt{8}$
d) $(2+\sqrt{3})^2$
e) $4\sqrt{5} - \sqrt{5}$
f) $\sqrt{50}$
g) $\sqrt{8} - \sqrt{2}$
h) $\sqrt{18} - \sqrt{9}$

Q4 Rationalise the denominators of the following expressions, and then simplify if necessary.

a) $\dfrac{2}{\sqrt{8}}$
b) $\dfrac{a}{\frac{\sqrt{40}}{2}}$
c) $\dfrac{x}{\sqrt{xy}}$
d) $\dfrac{6}{3+\sqrt{3}}$
e) $\dfrac{2}{1+\sqrt{6}}$
f) $\dfrac{5+\sqrt{5}}{5-\sqrt{5}}$
g) $\dfrac{2+3\sqrt{3}}{3-\sqrt{3}}$
h) $\dfrac{1-2\sqrt{6}}{2-3\sqrt{6}}$

Remember: rationalising the denominator means getting rid of any square root signs on the bottom of the fraction.

Q5 Simplify these expressions:

a) $\sqrt{28} + \sqrt{63} + \sqrt{7}$
b) $\sqrt{2} \times (\sqrt{6})^3 - \sqrt{48}$
c) $\sqrt{135} + \sqrt{3} \times (\sqrt{5})^5$
d) $\dfrac{2}{\sqrt{3}} + \dfrac{5}{\sqrt{27}}$
e) $\dfrac{6}{\sqrt{28}} - \dfrac{9}{\sqrt{63}}$
f) $\dfrac{60}{\sqrt{20}} + \dfrac{90}{\sqrt{45}} - \sqrt{80}$
g) $(4-3\sqrt{3})(2+\sqrt{3})$
h) $(1+2\sqrt{2})^2$
i) $\dfrac{2}{1+\dfrac{1}{\sqrt{3}}}$

Q6 Are the following expressions rational or irrational?

a) $(1+\sqrt{5})(1-\sqrt{5})$
b) $\dfrac{1+\sqrt{5}}{1-\sqrt{5}}$

Q7 If $x = 1$ and $y = \sqrt{2}$, are the following expressions rational or irrational?

a) $(x+y)(x-y)$
b) $\dfrac{x+y}{x-y}$

Section Two — Algebra

Solving Equations

Q1 When 1 is added to a number and the answer then trebled, it gives the same result as doubling the number and then adding 4. Find the number.

Q2 Solve the following.
- **a)** $3x + 1 = 2x + 6$
- **b)** $4x + 3 = 3x + 7$
- **c)** $5x - 1 = 3x + 19$
- **d)** $x + 2 = \frac{1}{2}x - 1$
- **e)** $11 - 3x = 3 - 5x$
- **f)** $3x - 15 = 15 - 2x$

Q3 Solve the following.
- **a)** $3x - 8 = 7$
- **b)** $2(x - 3) = -2$
- **c)** $4(2x - 1) = 60$
- **d)** $2x - 9 = 25$
- **e)** $\frac{24}{x} + 2 = 6$
- **f)** $5x - 2 = 6x - 7$

Q4 A square has sides of length $(x + 1)$ cm. Find the value of x if:
- **a)** the perimeter of the square is 66 cm
- **b)** the perimeter of the square is 152.8 cm.

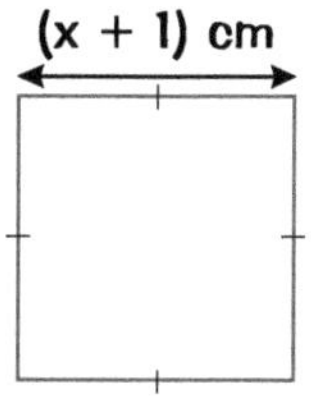

With these wordy ones, you just have to write your own equation from the information you're given.

Q5 Miss Khan took her car to the local garage. She spent £x on new parts, four times this amount on labour and finally £29 for an MOT test. If the total bill was £106.50, find the value of x.

Q6 Solve:
- **a)** $2(x - 3) - (x - 2) = 5$
- **b)** $5(x + 2) - 3(x - 5) = 29$
- **c)** $2(x + 2) + 3(x + 4) = 31$
- **d)** $10(x + 3) - 4(x - 2) = 7(x + 5)$
- **e)** $5(4x + 3) = 4(7x - 5) + 3(9 - 2x)$
- **f)** $3(7 + 2x) + 2(1 - x) = 19$
- **g)** $\frac{x}{3} + 7 = 12$
- **h)** $\frac{x}{10} + 18 = 29$
- **i)** $41 - \frac{x}{11} = 35$
- **j)** $\frac{x}{100} - 3 = 4$
- **k)** $\frac{120}{x} = 16$

Q7 Joan, Kate and Linda win £2400 between them on the National Lottery. Joan gets a share of £x, whilst Kate gets twice as much as Joan. Linda's share is £232 less than Joan's amount.
- **a)** Write down an expression for the amounts Joan, Kate and Linda win.
- **b)** Write down an equation in terms of x, and solve it.
- **c)** Write down the amounts Kate and Linda receive.

Q8 The shape opposite is made up of two rectangles.
- **a)** Write down an expression for the perimeter of the shape.
- **b)** Write down an expression for the area of the shape.
- **c)** For what value of x will the perimeter and area be numerically equal?

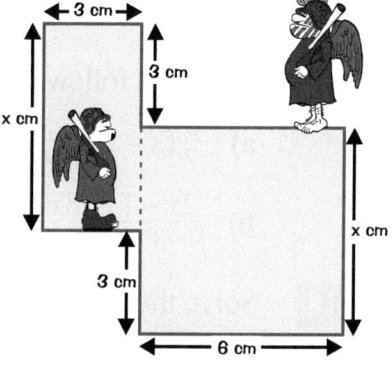

Q9 Solve the following:
- **a)** $5(x - 1) + 3(x - 4) = -11$
- **b)** $3(x + 2) + 2(x - 4) = x - 3(x + 3)$
- **c)** $\frac{3x}{2} + 3 = x$
- **d)** $3(4x + 2) = 2(2x - 1)$
- **e)** $\frac{5x + 7}{9} = 3$
- **f)** $\frac{2x + 7}{11} = 3$

Solving Equations

Q10 For what value of x is the expression $14 - \frac{x}{2}$ equal to the expression $\frac{3x-4}{2}$?

It's easy — you just put the 2 bits together and there's your equation. Then all you've got to do is solve it...

Q11 Two men are decorating a room. One has painted 20 m² and the other only 6 m². They continue painting and manage to paint another x m² each. If the first man has painted exactly three times the area painted by the second man, find the value of x.

Q12 Carol's father was 24 years old when Carol was born. Now he is four times as old as Carol. How old is Carol?

Q13 Mr Ananth is 4 years older than his wife and 31 years older than his son. All three ages add up to 82 years. If Mr Ananth is x years old, find the value of x and find the ages of his wife and son.

Q14 A triangle has the side lengths shown below. Find the length of each side, if the length of AC exceeds that of AB by ½ cm.

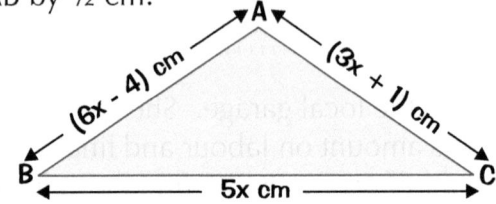

Triangle with sides: AB = $(6x - 4)$ cm, AC = $(3x + 1)$ cm, BC = $5x$ cm.

Q15 Solve the following:

a) $\frac{y}{2} + 2 = 13$

b) $\frac{3x}{4} - 2 = 4$

c) $\frac{2z}{5} - 3 = -5$

d) $\frac{1}{5}(x - 4) = 3$

e) $\frac{2}{3}(x + 1) = 16$

f) $\frac{3}{5}(4x - 3) = 15$

g) $\frac{3x + 2}{2} = 4x - 9$

h) $\frac{4x - 5}{7} = 10 - 3x$

i) $\frac{13x + 4}{10} = \frac{11x + 5}{9}$

Q16 A train travels at 70 mph for x hours and then at 80 mph for $3\frac{3}{4}$ hours. If the train covers 405 miles of track, find the value of x.

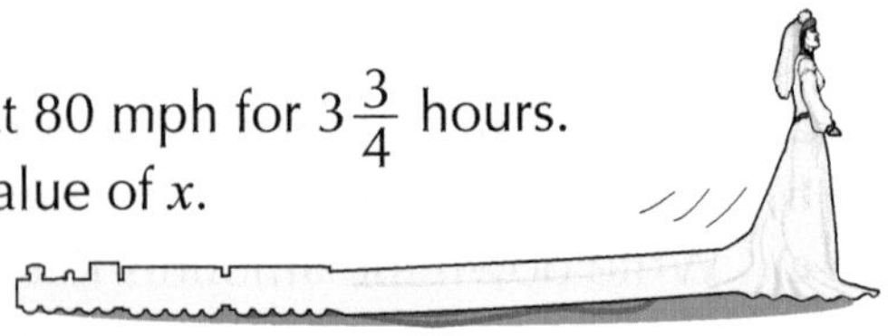

Q17 Solve the following:

a) $\frac{5}{7}(x - 2) - \frac{3}{4}(x + 3) = -4$

b) $\frac{2x - 1}{3} - \frac{3x + 5}{2} = -7$

Remember to do the same to the top and the bottom.

c) $\frac{4x + 7}{5} + \frac{5x + 2}{4} = 6$

d) $\frac{4x + 3}{2} + x = \frac{5x + 41}{4}$

Q18 Solve the following:

a) $2x^2 = 18$
b) $2x^2 = 72$
c) $3x^2 = 27$
d) $4x^2 = 36$
e) $5x^2 = 5$

f) $2x^2 + 1 = 9$
g) $9x^2 - 3 = 1$
h) $16x^2 - 5 = 4$
i) $30 - \frac{x^2}{2} = 28$

j) $17 - \frac{x^2}{3} = 5$

k) $\frac{8}{x^2} = \frac{32}{36}$

l) $\frac{12}{5x^2} = \frac{3}{20}$

m) $\frac{14}{3x^2} = \frac{2}{21}$

Rearranging Formulas

Rearranging is getting the letter you want out of the formula and making it the subject. And it's (almost) the same method as for solving equations, which can't be bad.

Q1 Rearrange the following formulas to make the letter in brackets the new subject.

a) $g = 10 - 4h$ (h)
b) $d = \frac{1}{2}(c + 4)$ (c)
c) $j = -2(3 - k)$ (k)
d) $a = \frac{2b}{3}$ (b)
e) $f = \frac{3g}{8}$ (g)
f) $y = \frac{x}{2} - 3$ (x)
g) $s = \frac{t}{6} + 10$ (t)
h) $p = 4q^2$ (q)

Q2 Jason is saving up to go travelling next year and has got a temporary job selling cars. He is paid a basic wage of £500 a month, plus a bonus of £50 for each car he sells. He has a spreadsheet to keep track of his money, which calculates his wages (£w) after working for m months and selling c cars, using the following formula:
$$w = 500m + 50c$$
a) Rearrange the formula to make c the subject.
b) Find the number of cars Jason needs to sell in 11 months to earn £12 100.

Q3 The cost of hiring a car is £28 per day plus 25p per mile.
a) Find the cost of hiring the car for a day and travelling:
    i) 40 miles
    ii) 80 miles 
b) Write down a formula to give the cost (£c) of hiring a car for one day and travelling n miles.
c) Rearrange the formula to make n the subject.
d) Find the number of miles you can travel during one day if you have a budget of:
    i) £34   ii) £50   iii) £56.50

You can get rid of square root signs by squaring both sides of the equation.

Q4 Rearrange the following formulas to make the letter in brackets the new subject.

a) $y = x^2 - 2$ (x)
b) $y = \sqrt{(x + 3)}$ (x)
c) $r = \left(\frac{s}{2}\right)^2$ (s)
d) $f = \frac{10 + g}{3}$ (g)
e) $w = \frac{5 - z}{2}$ (z)
f) $v = \frac{1}{3}x^2 h$ (x)
g) $v^2 = u^2 + 2as$ (a)
h) $v^2 = u^2 + 2as$ (u)
i) $t = 2\pi\sqrt{\frac{l}{g}}$ (g)

Q5 Mrs Smith buys x jumpers for £J each and sells them in her shop for a total price of £T.
a) Write down an expression for the amount of money she paid for all the jumpers.
b) Using your answer to a), write down a formula for the profit £P Mrs Smith makes selling all the jumpers.
c) Rearrange the formula to make J the subject.
d) Given that Mrs Smith makes a profit of £156 by selling 13 jumpers for a total of £364, find the price she paid for each jumper originally.

Section Two — Algebra

Rearranging Formulas

Q6 A website offering digital photo printing charges 12p per print plus 60p postage.
  a) Find the cost of ordering:
    i) 12 prints
    ii) 24 prints
  b) Write down a formula for the cost C, in pence, of ordering x prints.
  c) Rearrange the formula to make x the subject.
  d) A regular customer is looking through old receipts to check she has been charged the right amount. Find the number of prints she should have received in each of her last three transactions if she was charged:
    i) £4.92
    ii) £6.36
    iii) £12.12

Q7 Rearrange the following to make x the subject.
  a) $xy = z - 2x$
  b) $ax = 3x + b$
  c) $4x - y = xz$
  d) $xy = 3z - 5x + y$
  e) $xy = xz - 2$
  f) $2(x - y) = z(x + 3)$
  g) $xyz = x - y - wz$
  h) $3y(x + z) = y(2z - x)$

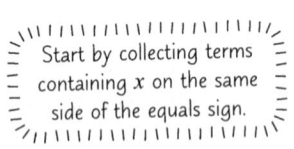
Start by collecting terms containing x on the same side of the equals sign.

Q8 Use the formula $s = ut + \frac{1}{2}at^2$.
  a) Find the distance travelled in metres when the acceleration is 2 m/s², the initial velocity is 3 m/s, and the time taken is 5 seconds.
  b) Rearrange the formula make the a the subject.

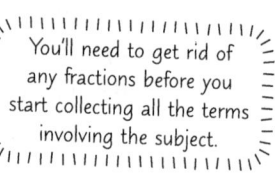
You'll need to get rid of any fractions before you start collecting all the terms involving the subject.

Q9 Rearrange the following to make y the subject.
  a) $x(y - 1) = y$
  b) $x(y + 2) = y - 3$
  c) $x = \dfrac{y + 3}{2y - 5}$
  d) $x + 1 = \dfrac{3y + 7}{5y + 2}$
  e) $x = \dfrac{y^2 + 1}{2y^2 - 1}$
  f) $x = \dfrac{2y^2 + 1}{3y^2 - 2}$

Q10 Rearrange the following to make the letter in brackets the subject.
  a) $pq = 3p + 4r - 2q$ (p)
  b) $fg + 2e = 5 - 2g$ (g)
  c) $a(b - 2) = c(b + 3)$ (b)
  d) $pq^2 = rq^2 + 4$ (q)
  e) $4(a - b) + c(a - 2) = ad$ (a)
  f) $\dfrac{x^2}{3} - y = x^2$ (x)
  g) $\sqrt{hk^2 - 14} = k$ (k)
  h) $2\sqrt{x} + y = z\sqrt{x} + 4$ (x)
  i) $\dfrac{a}{b} = \dfrac{1}{3}(b - a)$ (a)
  j) $\dfrac{m + n}{m - n} = \dfrac{3}{4}$ (m)
  k) $\sqrt{\dfrac{(d - e)}{e}} = 7$ (e)
  l) $\dfrac{x - 2y}{xy} = 3$ (y)

Factorising Quadratics

Q1 Solve these quadratic equations by factorising.
a) $x^2 + 3x - 10 = 0$
b) $x^2 - 5x + 6 = 0$
c) $x^2 - 2x + 1 = 0$
d) $x^2 - 4x + 3 = 0$
e) $x^2 - x - 20 = 0$
f) $x^2 + 14x + 49 = 0$
g) $-x^2 - x + 12 = 0$
h) $-x^2 - 7x + 8 = 0$
i) $-x^2 + 2x + 35 = 0$

Q2 Solve the following quadratic equations by factorising.
a) $2x^2 - 3x - 5 = 0$
b) $3x^2 + 4x - 7 = 0$
c) $2x^2 - 7x - 15 = 0$
d) $4x^2 + 12x + 9 = 0$
e) $4x^2 + 7x - 2 = 0$
f) $5x^2 - 31x + 6 = 0$
g) $-3x^2 - x + 2 = 0$
h) $-2x^2 + 9x - 10 = 0$
i) $-9x^2 - 3x + 2 = 0$

Q3 Rearrange into the form "$ax^2 + bx + c = 0$", then solve by factorising.
a) $x^2 + 6x = 16$
b) $x^2 + 5x = 36$
c) $x^2 + 4x = 45$
d) $x^2 = 5x$
e) $x^2 = 11x$
f) $x^2 - 21 = 4x$
g) $x^2 - 300 = 20x$
h) $x^2 + 48 = 26x$
i) $x^2 + 36 = 13x$
j) $x + 5 - \frac{14}{x} = 0$
k) $x + 4 - \frac{21}{x} = 0$
l) $x(3x + 1) = 10$
m) $2x^2 - 9(x + 2) = 0$
n) $4x + \frac{25}{x} = 20$
o) $6x - 1 = \frac{12}{x}$

Q4 Solve $x^2 - \frac{1}{4} = 0$.

Q5 The area of a rectangular swimming pool is 28 m². The width is x m. The difference between the length and the width is 3 m. Find the value of x.

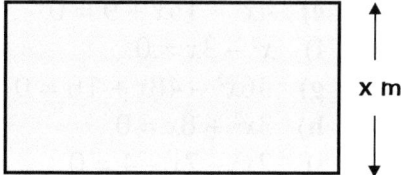

Q6 A rectangular rug has length x m. The width is exactly 1 m less than the length.

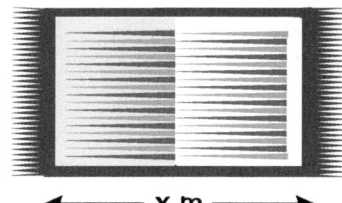

a) Write down an expression for the area of the rug.
b) If the area of the rug is 6 m², find the value of x.

Q7 A triangle has height $(x + 1)$ cm and a base of $2x$ cm.
a) Write down an expression for the area of the triangle and simplify it.
b) If the area of the triangle is 12 cm², find the value of x.

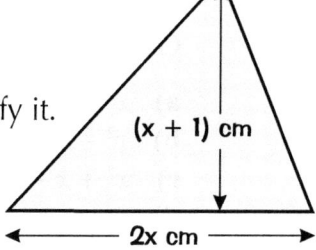

Q8 A square room has a floor with sides measuring x metres. The height of the walls is 3 m.
a) Write down an expression for:
  i) the floor area
  ii) the total area of all four walls
b) If the total area of the floor and the four walls is 64 m², form a quadratic equation and solve it to find x.

Section Two — Algebra

The Quadratic Formula

Oh, go on then, I'll tell you the quadratic formula just this once, but only because I'm so kind — it's $x = \dfrac{-b \pm \sqrt{b^2 - 4ac}}{2a}$.
You won't be given the formula in the exam though, so get it learnt.

Q1 Find the two values, to 2 decimal places, given by each of the following expressions:

a) $\dfrac{2 \pm \sqrt{3}}{2}$

b) $\dfrac{4 \pm \sqrt{10}}{3}$

c) $\dfrac{-2 \pm \sqrt{27}}{2}$

d) $\dfrac{-3 \pm \sqrt{42}}{3}$

e) $\dfrac{-10 \pm \sqrt{160}}{5}$

f) $\dfrac{-27 \pm \sqrt{10}}{2}$

g) $\dfrac{-8 \pm \sqrt{9.5}}{2.4}$

h) $\dfrac{10 \pm \sqrt{88.4}}{23.2}$

Q2 The following quadratics can be solved by factorisation, but practise using the formula to solve them.

Don't forget to rearrange the equation into the form $ax^2 + bx + c = 0$ if necessary.

a) $x^2 + 8x + 12 = 0$
b) $6x^2 - x - 2 = 0$
c) $x^2 - x - 6 = 0$
d) $x^2 - 3x + 2 = 0$
e) $4x^2 - 15x + 9 = 0$
f) $x^2 - 3x = 0$
g) $36x^2 - 48x + 16 = 0$
h) $3x^2 + 8x = 0$
i) $2x^2 - 7x - 4 = 0$
j) $x^2 + x - 20 = 0$
k) $4x^2 + 8x - 12 = 0$
l) $3x^2 - 11x - 20 = 0$
m) $x + 3 = 2x^2$
n) $5 - 3x - 2x^2 = 0$
o) $1 - 5x + 6x^2 = 0$
p) $3(x^2 + 2x) = 9$
q) $x^2 + 4(x - 3) = 0$
r) $x^2 = 2(4 - x)$

Step number 1...
Write out the formula.

Step number 2...
Write down values for a, b and c.

Step number 3...
Sub a, b and c into the formula. Make sure you divide the whole of the top line by 2a — not just half of it.

Q3 Solve the following quadratics using the formula. Give your answers to two decimal places.

a) $x^2 + 3x - 1 = 0$
b) $x^2 - 2x - 6 = 0$
c) $x^2 + x - 1 = 0$
d) $x^2 + 6x + 3 = 0$
e) $x^2 + 5x + 2 = 0$
f) $x^2 - x - 1 = 0$
g) $3x^2 + 10x - 8 = 0$
h) $x^2 + 4x + 2 = 0$
i) $x^2 - 6x - 8 = 0$
j) $x^2 - 14x + 11 = 0$
k) $x^2 + 3x - 5 = 0$
l) $7x^2 - 15x + 6 = 0$
m) $2x^2 + 6x - 3 = 0$
n) $2x^2 - 7x + 4 = 0$
o) $3x^2 + 11x + 9 = 0$

Oops, forgot to mention **step number 4...**
check your answers by putting them **back in the equation.**

The Quadratic Formula

Q4 Rearrange the following into the form "$ax^2 + bx + c = 0$" and then find the **exact** solutions by using the quadratic formula. Simplify your answers where possible.

a) $x^2 = 8 - 3x$

b) $(x + 2)^2 - 3 = 0$

c) $3x(x - 1) = 5$

d) $2x(x + 4) = 1$

e) $x^2 = 4(x + 1)$

f) $(2x - 1)^2 = 5$

g) $3x^2 + 2x = 6$

h) $(x + 2)(x + 3) = 5$

i) $(x - 2)(2x - 1) = 3$

j) $2x + \dfrac{4}{x} = 7$

k) $\left(x - \dfrac{1}{2}\right)^2 = \dfrac{1}{2}$

l) $4x(x - 3) = -3$

m) $3x - \dfrac{3}{x + 1} = -12$

n) $2x - \dfrac{1}{x + 2} = -2$

o) $1 + \dfrac{3}{x + 5} = \dfrac{3}{x + 2}$

'Exact solutions' means give your answers in surd form. Take a look at page 20 if you need some more practice with surds.

Q5 The sides of a right-angled triangle are as shown. Use Pythagoras' theorem to form a quadratic equation in x and then solve it to find x.

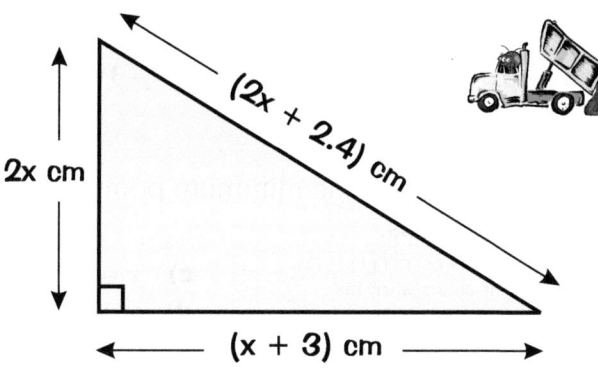

Remember, for right-angled triangles, Pythagoras' theorem is:
$a^2 + b^2 = c^2$

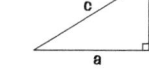

Q6 The area of a rectangle with length $(x + 4.6)$ cm and width $(x - 2.1)$ cm is 134.63 cm².

a) Form a quadratic equation and solve it to find x to two decimal places.
b) What is the rectangle's perimeter to one decimal place?

Careful here — remember lengths have to be positive.

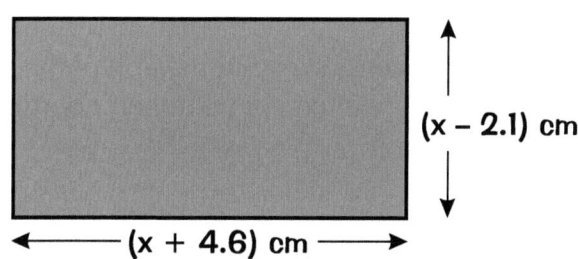

Section Two — Algebra

Completing the Square

All you're doing is writing quadratics in the form "$(x + 4)^2 + 2$" instead of "$x^2 + 8x + 18$" — don't let the name put you off.

Q1 Complete the square for the following expressions.
- a) $x^2 - 4x - 5$
- b) $x^2 - 2x + 1$
- c) $x^2 + x + 1$
- d) $x^2 - 6x + 9$
- e) $x^2 - 6x + 7$
- f) $x^2 - 4x$
- g) $x^2 + 3x - 4$
- h) $x^2 - x - 3$
- i) $x^2 - 10x + 25$
- j) $x^2 - 10x$
- k) $x^2 + 8x + 17$
- l) $x^2 - 12x + 35$

Q2 Solve the following quadratic equations by completing the square. Write down your answers correct to 2 d.p.
- a) $x^2 + 3x - 1 = 0$
- b) $x^2 - x - 3 = 0$
- c) $x^2 + 4x - 3 = 0$
- d) $x^2 + x - 1 = 0$
- e) $x^2 - 3x - 5 = 0$
- f) $2x^2 - 6x + 1 = 0$
- g) $3x^2 - 3x - 2 = 0$
- h) $3x^2 - 6x - 1 = 0$

If you've got an ax^2, take out a factor of 'a' before completing the square, like this: $3x^2 + 12x + 1 = 3(x^2 + 4x) + 1$

Q3 Solve the following quadratic equations by completing the square. Give your answers as surds, simplifying where possible.
- a) $x^2 - 8x - 13 = 0$
- b) $x^2 - 2x - 5 = 0$
- c) $x^2 + 6x - 11 = 0$
- d) $x^2 + 8x + 4 = 0$
- e) $x^2 + 3x - 2 = 0$
- f) $x^2 + 7x + 3 = 0$
- g) $x^2 - 5x - 25 = 0$
- h) $x^2 - 9x + 9 = 0$
- i) $2x^2 + 4x - 7 = 0$
- j) $3x^2 - 6x - 1 = 0$
- k) $-2x^2 + 7x + 3 = 0$
- l) $-3x^2 + 5x - 1 = 0$

Q4 By completing the square, find the coordinates of the minimum point on the graph of each of the following equations.
- a) $y = x^2 - 10x - 3$
- b) $y = x^2 - 7x - 15$
- c) $y = 3x^2 + 12x + 2$
- d) $y = 4x^2 - 5x - 1$

The minimum point occurs when the bracket in the completed square equals 0.

Q5 By completing the square, find the coordinates of the turning point on the graph of each of the following equations. In each case, state whether the turning point is a maximum or a minimum.
- a) $y = x^2 + 4x - 1$
- b) $y = -x^2 + 11x - 6$
- c) $y = -x^2 - 3x + 8$
- d) $y = 2x^2 + 8x - 11$
- e) $y = 2x^2 + 5x - 1$
- f) $y = -3x^2 - 6x + 2$

Q6 For each of the following, sketch the graph of the equation and label the turning point and y-intercept with their coordinates.
- a) $y = x^2 + 2x - 1$
- b) $y = -x^2 + 3x + 2$
- c) $y = 2x^2 - x - 5$

Q7 The turning point of the graph of $y = x^2 + mx + n$ is at $(1, -5)$. What are the values of m and n?

Algebraic Fractions

Multiplying and dividing algebraic fractions is just the same as multiplying and dividing normal fractions — to multiply you just multiply the tops and bottoms separately and to divide you just turn the second fraction upside down and then multiply. Simple.

Q1 Simplify the following by cancelling down where possible:

a) $\dfrac{27x^4y^2z}{9x^3yz^2}$
b) $\dfrac{48a^2b^2}{(2a)^2c}$
c) $\dfrac{3xyz}{9x^2y^3z^4}$
d) $\dfrac{4p^3q^3}{(2pr)^3}$

Q2 Multiply out the following, leaving your answers as simplified as possible:

a) $\dfrac{x^2}{y} \times \dfrac{2}{x^3}$
c) $\dfrac{30a^2b^2c^2}{7} \times \dfrac{21c^2}{ab^3}$
e) $\dfrac{2a^2}{3} \times \dfrac{9b}{a} \times \dfrac{2a^2b}{5}$

b) $\dfrac{10z^3}{xy} \times \dfrac{4x^3}{5z}$
d) $\dfrac{4}{x} \times \dfrac{x^3}{2} \times \dfrac{x}{10}$
f) $\dfrac{400d^4}{51e^5} \times \dfrac{102d^2e^4}{800e^2f}$

It helps if you can cancel some factors before multiplying.

Q3 Divide the following, leaving your answers as simplified as possible:

a) $\dfrac{4x^3}{y} \div \dfrac{2x}{y^2}$
c) $\dfrac{5x^3}{y} \div \dfrac{1}{y}$
e) $\dfrac{4x}{y^4z^4} \div \dfrac{2}{y^2z^3}$

b) $\dfrac{30x^3}{y^2} \div \dfrac{10x}{y}$
d) $\dfrac{16xyz}{3} \div \dfrac{4x^2}{9}$
f) $\dfrac{3m}{2n^2} \div \dfrac{m}{4n}$

Q4 Simplify the following:

a) $\dfrac{(p+q)}{r} \times \dfrac{3}{2(p+q)}$
b) $\left(\dfrac{a}{b} \div \dfrac{c}{d}\right) \times \dfrac{ac}{bd}$
c) $\left(\dfrac{mn}{l} \times \dfrac{m-l}{n^2}\right) \div \left(\dfrac{m}{l+m} \div \dfrac{l}{n}\right)$

Q5 Simplify the following expressions:

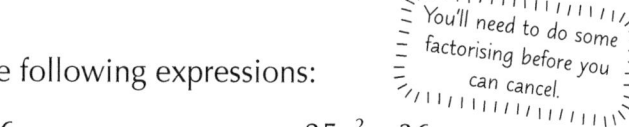

You'll need to do some factorising before you can cancel.

a) $\dfrac{9a^2-16}{6a+8}$
c) $\dfrac{25x^2-36}{15x-18}$
e) $\dfrac{30a-5b}{36a^2-b^2}$

b) $\dfrac{4x^2-y^2}{8x+4y}$
d) $\dfrac{12x+21}{16x^2-49}$
f) $\dfrac{20x-12}{25x^2-9}$

Q6 Simplify the following:

a) $\dfrac{x^2-4}{x^2+x-6}$
b) $\dfrac{x^2+4x+3}{x^2-9}$
c) $\dfrac{x^2-25}{x^2+3x-10}$
d) $\dfrac{2x^2+9x+7}{4x^2-49}$

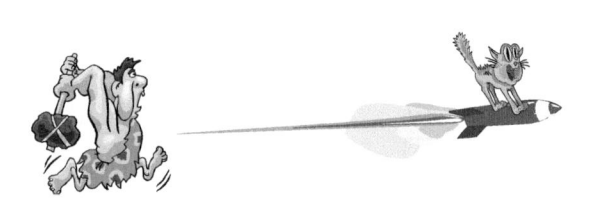

Section Two — Algebra

Algebraic Fractions

OK, I guess it gets a bit tricky here — you've got to get everything over a common denominator before you can get anywhere with adding or subtracting.

Q7 Express each of the following as a single fraction in its simplest form:

a) $\dfrac{6x}{3} + \dfrac{2x+y}{6}$

b) $\dfrac{x}{10} + \dfrac{y-1}{5}$

c) $\dfrac{x}{6} + \dfrac{5x}{7}$

d) $\dfrac{x}{8} + \dfrac{x+y}{4} + \dfrac{x-y}{2}$

e) $\dfrac{zx}{4} + \dfrac{x+z}{y}$

f) $\dfrac{m^2 n}{p} + \dfrac{mn}{p^2}$

g) $\dfrac{2x+y}{x^2} + \dfrac{y}{x^3}$

h) $\dfrac{3}{x-4} + \dfrac{1}{x+2}$

i) $\dfrac{1}{x+y} + \dfrac{1}{x-y}$

j) $\dfrac{a+b}{a-b} + \dfrac{a-b}{a+b}$

k) $\dfrac{2x-9}{x+5} + \dfrac{x+1}{3x+4}$

l) $\dfrac{3x+1}{2x-3} + \dfrac{x-2}{2x+5}$

Q8 Express each of the following as a single fraction in its simplest form:

a) $\dfrac{z}{5} - \dfrac{2z}{15}$

b) $\dfrac{2b}{a} - \dfrac{b}{7}$

c) $\dfrac{p-2q}{4} - \dfrac{2p+q}{2}$

d) $\dfrac{2}{x} - \dfrac{3}{2x} - \dfrac{4}{3x}$

e) $\dfrac{3x}{y} - \dfrac{4-x}{3}$

f) $\dfrac{4}{a^2} - \dfrac{3b}{a+2}$

g) $\dfrac{x}{x+3} - \dfrac{1}{x-3}$

h) $\dfrac{3y}{x-1} - \dfrac{2y}{x+4}$

i) $\dfrac{y+1}{y^2} - \dfrac{y^2+1}{2y^3}$

j) $\dfrac{2}{3x-4} - \dfrac{4}{7x-2}$

k) $\dfrac{9}{4x-1} - \dfrac{2}{2x+3}$

l) $\dfrac{2x+3}{x-2} - \dfrac{x+2}{x+5}$

Q9 Simplify the following: *You'll need to factorise these before multiplying.*

a) $\dfrac{2x+2}{y^2} \times \dfrac{xy}{x+1}$

b) $\dfrac{a^2}{a^2 b + b^2} \times \dfrac{b^3 + 2b^2}{a^2 b}$

c) $\dfrac{x+3}{x^2+3x-4} \times \dfrac{x-1}{x^2-9}$

d) $\dfrac{4x^2-25}{2x-8} \times \dfrac{2x+2}{2x^2-3x-5}$

e) $\dfrac{7x+21}{3x-3} \times \dfrac{2x^2-13x+11}{x^2+5x+6} \times (x^2-3x-10)$

f) $\dfrac{5x^2+30x+40}{3x^2+31x+36} \times \dfrac{7x+63}{x-1} \times \dfrac{3x^2+x-4}{4x^2+18x+8}$

Q10 Simplify the following:

a) $\dfrac{x-3}{y^2} \div \dfrac{2x^2 y - 6xy}{3}$

b) $\dfrac{4y^2}{x+1} \div \dfrac{1}{xy+y}$

c) $\dfrac{2x^2+x-3}{3x-3} \div \dfrac{4x^2 y + 8xy + 3y}{5y}$

d) $\dfrac{7y}{2x^2 y^2 - 5xy^2 - 12y^2} \div \dfrac{2}{2x^3 + 5x^2 + 3x}$

e) $\left(\dfrac{4x+24}{3x^2+36x+60} \div \dfrac{x-9}{2x+4}\right) \times (x^2+x-90)$

f) $\left(\dfrac{2x^2+14x+20}{x-1} \div \dfrac{x^2+2x-15}{x-2}\right) \div \dfrac{1}{x^2-4x+3}$

Sequences

Ahhh, sequences — you really need to know all about them and their nth terms.
They're a doddle once you figure out what's happening in each gap...

Q1 Write down the next three terms in each of these sequences and describe the sequence.

    a) 2, 4, 6, 8, ...   **c)** 1, 4, 9, 16, ...

    b) 1, 3, 5, 7, ...   **d)** 1, 8, 27, 64, ...

Q2   6   11   16   21   26 ...

    a) What are the next three terms in this sequence?

    b) What is the difference between each term?

    c) Write down a formula for the nth term of this sequence.

    d) Use the formula to find the 20th term of the sequence.

It's easy to check your nth term formula — just put in a few values of n and check it gives you the sequence you started with.

Q3 Write down an expression for the nth term of the following sequences:

    a) 2, 4, 6, 8, ...   **b)** 1, 3, 5, 7, ...   **c)** 5, 10, 15, 20, ...   **d)** 5, 8, 11, 14, ...

Q4 For the following sequences, write down the next three terms and the nth term:

    a) 7, 10, 13, 16,...   **b)** 12, 17, 22, 27,...   **c)** 36, 26, 16, 6,...   **d)** 75, 68, 61, 54,...

Q5 A sequence is given by the rule **6n – 5**.
Is 53 a term in this sequence? Explain your answer.

Q6   1   5   9   13 ...

    a) Find an expression for the nth term of this sequence.

    b) Is 75 a term in this sequence? Explain your answer.

Q7 $\dfrac{1}{3}$ $\dfrac{2}{5}$ $\dfrac{3}{7}$ $\dfrac{4}{9}$ ...

    a) What are the next three terms of this sequence?

    b) Find an expression for the nth term of this sequence.

Treat the numerators and denominators as separate sequences.

Q8   10, 20, 15, 17½, 16¼ ...

    a) Write down the next four terms.   **b)** Explain how you would work out the 10th term.

Section Two — Algebra

Sequences

Q9 3 3 6 9 15 24 ...
  a) What is the rule for this sequence?
  b) Find the next three terms in the sequence.

Q10 2 10 8 −2 −10 −8 ...
  a) What are the next three terms of this sequence?
  b) What do you notice about how the sequence is behaving?
  c) What is the 20th term?

Q11 A sequence is given by the rule $u_{n+1} = u_n^2 - 5$.
Given that $u_1 = 2$, find u_2 and u_3.

Remember, u_n means the nth term and u_{n+1} means the term after u_n.

Q12 Write down the next three terms of the following sequences:
  a) 5, 10, 20, 40, ...
  b) 1, 6, 36, 216, ...
  c) 0.1, 0.4, 1.6, 6.4, ...
  d) 729, 243, 81, 27, ...
  e) 31 250, 6250, 1250, 250, ...
  f) 12 288, 3072, 768, 192, ...
  g) 5103, 1701, 567, 189, ...
  h) $1, \sqrt{3}, 3, 3\sqrt{3}, ...$
  i) $3, 3\sqrt{2}, 6, 6\sqrt{2}, ...$

Q13 State whether each of the following sequences is an arithmetic or geometric progression. Give the common difference or common ratio in each case.
  a) 1, 5, 9, 13, ...
  b) −25, −15, −5, 5 ...
  c) 2, 6, 18, 54, ...
  d) 9.6, 8.4, 7.2, 6, ...
  e) 20, 5, 1.25, 0.3125, ...
  f) 987, 876, 765, 654, ...

Q14 The nth term of a sequence is $5n + 10$. The sum of two consecutive terms is 145. Find the values of these terms.

Q15 Write down the next three terms and the nth term of:
  a) 3, 9, 17, 27, ...
  b) 2, 3, 6, 11, ...
  c) 8, 16, 26, 38, ...
  d) 5, 21, 41, 65, ...
  e) 6, 11, 20, 33, ...
  f) 5, 18, 37, 62, ...

Q16 The nth term of a sequence is $3n^2 - 5$.
Is 43 a term in this sequence? Explain your answer.

Q17

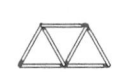

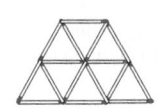

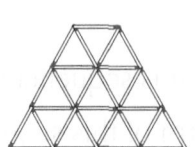

The pattern above is based on individual triangles.
  a) Work out the number of individual triangles that would be in each of the next three groups.
  b) Find an expression for the number of triangles in the nth group.

Section Two — Algebra

Inequalities

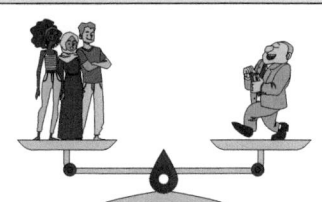

Yet another one of those bits of Maths that looks worse than it is — these are just like equations, really, except for the symbols.

Q1 Write down the inequality represented by each diagram below.

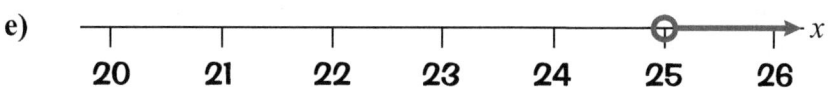

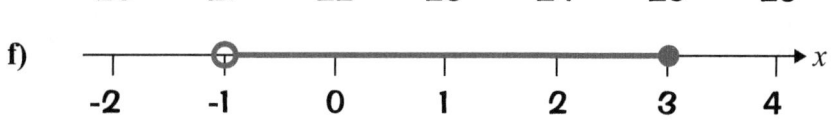

a) [number line: closed circle at 9, open circle at 13]

b) [number line: closed circle at -4, open circle at 1]

c) [number line: closed circle at -4, extending right]

d) [number line: open circle at 5, extending left]

e) [number line: open circle at 25, extending right]

f) [number line: open circle at -1, closed circle at 3]

Q2 Represent each of the following inequalities on a number line.
- a) $x > 5$
- b) $x \leq 2$
- c) $-5 < x < 2$
- d) $-2 \leq x < 3$
- e) $-2 < x \leq 3$
- f) $6 < x \leq 7$
- g) $-3 \leq x \leq -2$
- h) $-3 < x \leq 0$

Q3 Given that x is an integer, find all the possible values of x satisfying the following inequalities. Write your answers using set notation.
- a) $2 < x < 7$
- b) $-2 \leq x < 3$
- c) $-5 \leq x \leq 0$

Q4 Solve the following:
- a) $3x + 2 > 11$
- b) $5x + 4 < 24$
- c) $5x + 7 \leq 32$
- d) $3x + 12 \leq 30$
- e) $2x - 7 \geq 8$
- f) $17 + 4x < 33$
- g) $2(x + 3) < 20$
- h) $2(5x - 4) < 32$
- i) $5(x + 2) \geq 25$
- j) $4(x - 1) > 40$
- k) $10 - 2x > 4x - 8$
- l) $7 - 2x \leq 4x + 10$
- m) $8 - 3x \geq 14$
- n) $16 - x < 11$
- o) $16 - x > 1$
- p) $12 - 3x \leq 18$

Q5 Solve the following:
- a) $-2 < x - 3 < 5$
- b) $1 \leq x + 1 \leq 9$
- c) $7 < 2x + 3 < 11$
- d) $7 < 4 - 3x \leq 16$
- e) $2 \leq \frac{x}{5} + 1 \leq 3$
- f) $-2 < \frac{x-3}{2} < 10$
- g) $1 \leq \frac{2x+7}{3} < 5$
- h) $-10 < \frac{x+1}{5} \leq -2$
- i) $-1 \leq \frac{2-x}{3} < 6$

Section Two — Algebra

Inequalities

Q6 Find the largest integer x, such that $2x + 5 \geq 5x - 2$.

Q7 For each of the following pairs of inequalities, find the integer value of x which satisfies both of them.

a) $x - 3 > 2$ and $2x + 1 < 15$

b) $3x - 11 > 19$ and $5x - 23 < 37$

c) $4 - x < 6$ and $\dfrac{x + 12}{3} < 4$

d) $1 - 2x < 17$ and $\dfrac{2 - 3x}{10} > 2$

Q8 When a number is subtracted from 11, and this new number is then divided by two, the result is always less than five. Write this information as an inequality and solve it to show the possible values of the number.

Q9 Two schools are merging and a new school is being built to accommodate all the pupils. There will be 1130 pupils in total in the new school. No class can have more than 32 pupils.

a) Use this information to write down an inequality involving the number of classrooms, x, in the school.

b) What is the minimum number of classrooms that are needed?

Q10 A couple are planning their wedding. For the reception in a local hotel, they have a budget of £900 to spend on their guests. The hotel charges £18 per head.

a) Use this information to write down an inequality involving the number of guests.

b) What is the maximum number of guests that could be invited?

Q11 The shaded region in each of the following graphs satisfies three inequalities. Write down these inequalities.

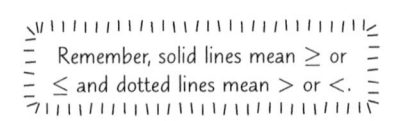

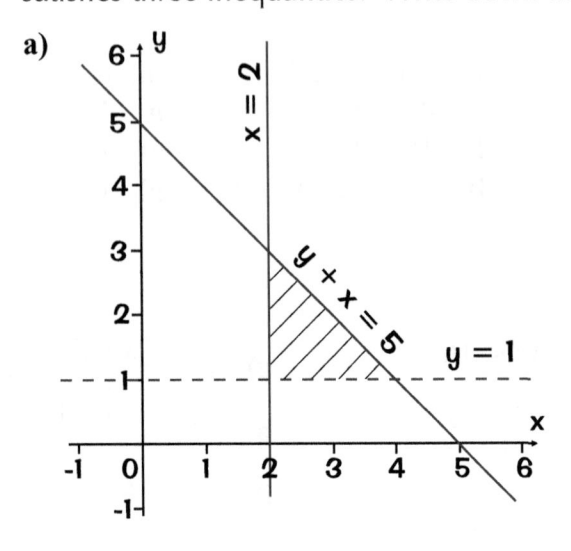

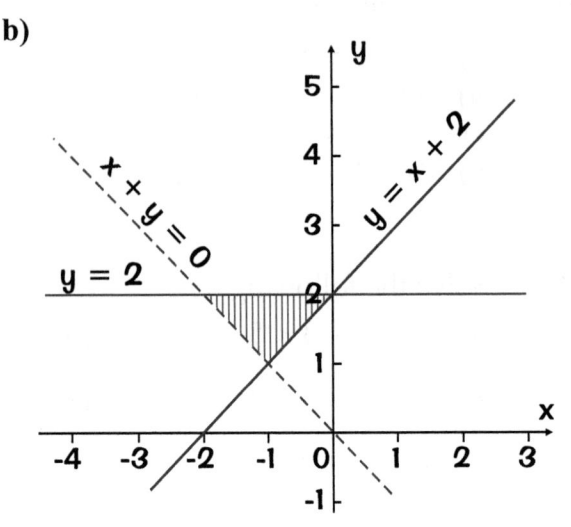

Remember, solid lines mean $\geq$ or $\leq$ and dotted lines mean $>$ or $<$.

a)

b)

Inequalities

Q12 Draw a set of axes with the x-axis from –2 to 6 and the y-axis from –1 to 7. Show on a graph the region enclosed by the following three inequalities.
$$y < 6, \quad x + y \geq 5 \quad \text{and} \quad x \leq 5$$

Q13 Draw a set of axes with the x-axis from –4 to 5 and the y-axis from –3 to 6. Show on a graph the region enclosed by the following.
$$y \leq 2x + 4, \quad y < 4 - x \quad \text{and} \quad y \geq \frac{x}{3} - 1$$

Q14 A company are recruiting new members of staff. All applicants must take two online tests. To get an interview, applicants must score higher than 5 on the first test, at least 7 on the second, and have a total combined score of at least 14.
  a) Write out three inequalities to represent the three criteria for getting an interview. Use x for the score on the first test and y for the score on the second test.
  b) The company want to analyse the quality of applicants by plotting their test scores on a graph and picking out the ones who satisfy the criteria. Using suitable axes, show on a graph the region enclosed by the three inequalities where suitable candidates would be placed.

Q15 Solve the following:
  a) $x^2 < 9$
  b) $x^2 > 16$
  c) $x^2 \leq 4$
  d) $2x^2 \geq 18$
  e) $x^2 \geq 25$
  f) $2x^2 < 32$
  g) $-x^2 < -36$
  h) $-x^2 > -4$
  i) $-3x^2 < -27$
  j) $x^2 + 4 \leq 53$
  k) $2x^2 - 5 > 45$
  l) $17 - \frac{x^2}{3} < 5$

Q16 Write down the inequalities that the shaded region satisfies.

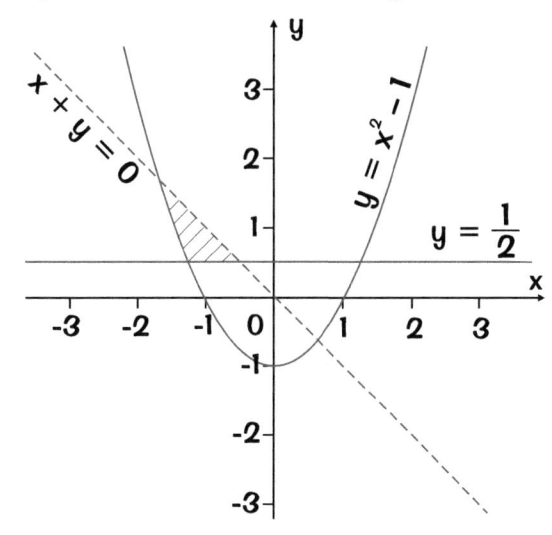

Sketching the graphs will help with these — if you need some practice, have a look at page 46.

Q17 Solve the following:
  a) $x^2 - x - 6 < 0$
  b) $x^2 + 6x + 5 \leq 0$
  c) $x^2 + 3x + 2 > 0$
  d) $x^2 - 10x + 16 \geq 0$
  e) $x^2 - 18 > 7x$
  f) $12x + 35 < -x^2$
  g) $-x^2 + 9x - 20 \leq 0$
  h) $-x^2 - 2x + 3 > 0$
  i) $2x^2 + 7x + 6 \leq 0$
  j) $9x - 2x^2 < 4$
  k) $3x^2 < x + 2$
  l) $4x^2 + 11x \geq 20$

Iterative Methods

Iterative methods aren't as bad as they look (or sound) — all you're doing is repeating the same calculation with different values to home in on the solution.

Q1 The cubic equation $x^3 + x^2 - 4x = 3$ has three solutions. The first solution lies between −3 and −2. The second lies between −1 and 0. The third solution lies between 1 and 2. Copy the table below and use it to find all three solutions to 1 d.p.

Guess (x)	Value of $x^3 + x^2 - 4x$	Too large or Too small
−3	$(-3)^3 + (-3)^2 - 4(-3) = -6$	
−2	$(-2)^3 + (-2)^2 - 4(-2) =$	
−1	$(-1)^3 + (-1)^2 - 4(-1) =$	
0	$(0)^3 + (0)^2 - 4(0) =$	
1	$(1)^3 + (1)^2 - 4(1) =$	
2	$(2)^3 + (2)^2 - 4(2) =$	

Q2 The cubic equation $x^3 - 8x^2 - 3x + 9 = 0$ has three solutions. The first solution lies between −2 and −1. The second lies between 0 and 1. The third solution lies between 8 and 9. By using the decimal search method and a table like the one below, find each solution to 1 d.p.

x	Value of $x^3 - 8x^2 - 3x + 9$	Positive/Negative

Q3 The graph of $y = x^3 + 3x^2 - x - 6$ is shown on the right. It crosses the positive x-axis between $x = 1$ and $x = 2$. Find the value of x where the graph crosses the positive x-axis to 1 d.p.

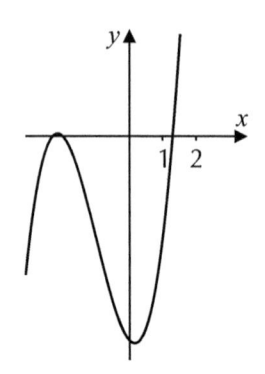

Q4 A cube has a volume of 44 cm³ and side length x cm, where $3 < x < 4$.
  a) Write an equation for the volume of the cube in terms of x.
  b) Use an iterative method to find the value of x to 1 d.p. Show your working.

Section Two — Algebra

Simultaneous Equations

To solve simultaneous equations from scratch, you've got to get rid of either x or y first — to leave you with an equation with just one unknown in it.

Q1 Solve the following simultaneous equations:

a) $4x + 6y = 16$
$x + 2y = 5$

b) $3y - 8x = 24$
$3y + 2x = 9$

c) $3y - 10x - 17 = 0$
$\frac{1}{3}y + 2x - 5 = 0$

d) $\frac{x}{2} - 2y = 5$
$12y + x - 2 = 0$

e) $3x - 4y = 5x - 14$
$2y + x = 11y - 26$

f) $3x + 4y = 10$
$5x - 7y = 3$

g) $2y - 3x = 1$
$4x + 5y = 37$

h) $10x - 7y = -9$
$8x + 9y = 22$

i) $\frac{3}{5}x + 2y = 21$
$2x - \frac{2}{3}y = 4$

Q2 Use the linear equation (the one with no x^2s in it) to find an expression for y. Then substitute it into the quadratic equation (the one with x^2s in it), to solve these equations:

a) $y = x^2 + 2$
$y = x + 14$

b) $y = x^2 - 8$
$y = 3x + 10$

c) $y = 2x^2$
$x - y = -3$

d) $y = x^2 - 2$
$y - 3x = 8$

e) $y = 3x^2 - 10$
$13x - y = 14$

f) $y + 2 = 2x^2$
$2y + 6x = 0$

g) $x + 5y = 30$
$y - x^2 = \frac{4}{5}x$

h) $y = 1 - 13x$
$4x^2 + 4 - y = 0$

i) $2y = 6(x^2 + 3)$
$14x + y = 1$

j) $x^2 + y^2 = 13$
$y = x + 1$

k) $x^2 + y^2 = 18$
$y - x = 6$

l) $y^2 - x^2 = 5$
$4x - 2y = 2$

Q3 Two farmers are buying livestock at a market. Farmer Jill buys 6 sheep and 5 pigs for £430 and Farmer Jacob buys 4 sheep and 10 pigs for £500.

a) If sheep cost £x and pigs cost £y, write down the two purchases as a pair of simultaneous equations.

b) Solve for x and y.

Q4 On Farmer Palmer's farm, the cats have got into the chicken coop and are causing chaos. Farmer Palmer counts, in total, 11 heads and 30 legs. How many cats and how many chickens are in the chicken coop?

Q5 Find the values of x and y for each of the following rectangles by first writing down a pair of simultaneous equations and then solving them.

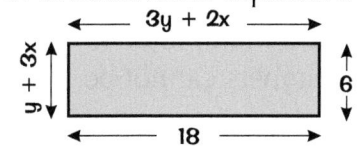

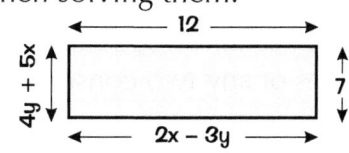

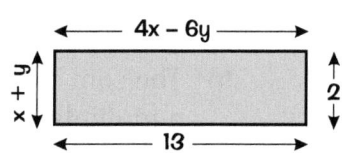

Rectangle 1: width $3y + 2x$ (top), 18 (bottom), height $y + 3x$ (left), 6 (right)

Rectangle 2: width 12 (top), $2x - 3y$ (bottom), height $4y + 5x$ (left), 7 (right)

Rectangle 3: width $4x - 6y$ (top), 13 (bottom), height $x + y$ (left), 2 (right)

Q6 Two customers enter a shop to buy milk and cornflakes. Ms Green buys 5 pints of milk and 2 boxes of cornflakes and spends £3.44. Mr Brown buys 4 pints of milk and 3 boxes of cornflakes and receives £6.03 change after paying with a £10 note. Write down a pair of simultaneous equations and solve them to find the price in pence of a pint of milk (m) and a box of cornflakes (c).

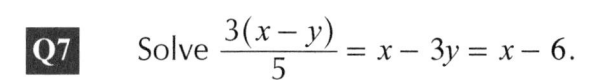

Q7 Solve $\frac{3(x-y)}{5} = x - 3y = x - 6$.

Q8 Find the points of intersection of the curve $y = x^2 - 3x + 2$ and the line $y = 5 - x$.

Proof

Proofs look pretty scary but they're usually alright once you get started. For these first few questions you just need to do some rearranging and make one side of the identity look like the other side.

Q1 Prove that $(n + 3)^2 - (3n + 5) \equiv (n + 1)(n + 2) + 2$

Q2 Prove that $(n - 3)^2 - (n - 5) \equiv (n - 3)(n - 4) + 2$

Q3 Prove that $25 - \frac{(x - 8)^2}{4} \equiv \frac{(2 + x)(18 - x)}{4}$

Q4 Prove that if $3(ax + 7) - 2(x + b) \equiv 4x + 29$, then $a = 2$ and $b = -4$.

Equate the coefficients here — write the coefficients of x equal to each other, and then the constants equal to each other.

Q5 Prove that $(2n + 1)^2 - (2n - 1)^2 - 10$ is not a multiple of 8 for positive integer values of n.

Q6 Prove that the sum of any three consecutive numbers is divisible by 3.

Q7 Prove that an even number multiplied by another even number will always result in an even number.

Q8 Prove that the sum of any three consecutive even numbers is always a multiple of 6.

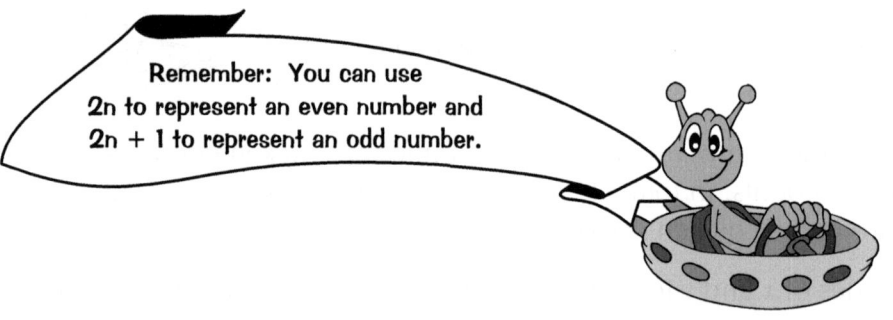

Remember: You can use 2n to represent an even number and 2n + 1 to represent an odd number.

Q9 Prove these statements.
  a) The sum of any two consecutive odd numbers must be a multiple of 4.
  b) The sum of the squares of any two consecutive odd numbers cannot be a multiple of 4.

You might have to prove that a statement isn't true. The best way to do this is to find an example that doesn't work...

Q10 Maisy says "all prime numbers are odd". Prove that Maisy is wrong.

Q11 Prove that these statements are wrong.
  a) If the sum of two integers is even, one of the integers must be even.
  b) If n is an integer and n^2 is divisible by 4, then n is also divisible by 4.

Q12 Christine says "if $a^2 = b^2$, then $a = b$". Prove that Christine is wrong.

Section Two — Algebra

Proof

You'll need all kinds of maths tools to tackle these proofs — power rules, algebraic fractions, sequences... Don't panic if you're feeling stuck — you might need to experiment a bit before you find the right method.

Q13 Prove that $5^{20} - 5^{19}$ is even, without using a calculator.

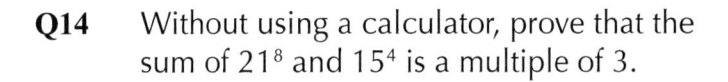

Q14 Without using a calculator, prove that the sum of 21^8 and 15^4 is a multiple of 3.

Q15 Without using a calculator, prove that $3^8 - 1$ is not a prime number.

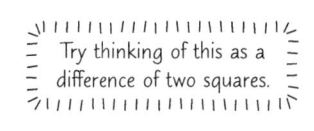

Try thinking of this as a difference of two squares.

Q16 The nth term of a sequence is given by $\frac{1}{2}n^2 - \frac{5}{2}n + 3$.

Prove that the sum of any two consecutive numbers in the sequence is a square number.

Q17 If $a = 5^{99} \times 2^{98}$ and $b = 5^{72} \times 4^{38}$, show that ab has 172 digits when written as an ordinary number.

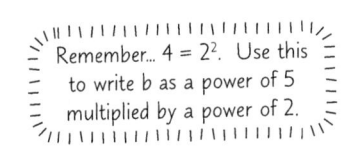

Remember... $4 = 2^2$. Use this to write b as a power of 5 multiplied by a power of 2.

Q18 If $x > 0$, $y > 0$ and $x < y$, prove that $\dfrac{y^2 + 1}{y^2} - \dfrac{x^2 + 1}{x^2} < 0$.

Q19 The mean of a set of 6 numbers is 18. If 1 is subtracted from each number in the set, show that the mean of the new set also decreases by 1.

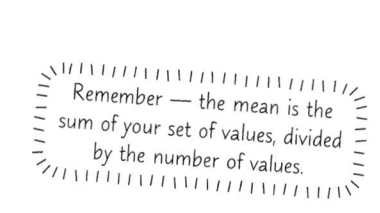

Remember — the mean is the sum of your set of values, divided by the number of values.

Q20 The nth term of a sequence is given by $n^2 - 2n + 2$. Prove that the sum of any two consecutive numbers in the sequence is an odd number.

Q21 Fay claims that $x^2 + 3 > 2x + 1$ for all values of x. Prove that Fay is correct.

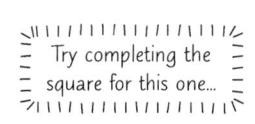

Try completing the square for this one...

Section Two — Algebra

Functions

Functions... functions... functions... what can you say about functions...
Well, one thing you can probably say is that they're not as bad as they look.

Q1 A function is represented by the function machine below.

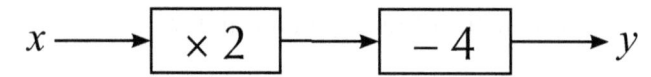

$$x \longrightarrow \boxed{\times 2} \longrightarrow \boxed{-4} \longrightarrow y$$

a) Find the value of y when: **i)** $x = 6$ **ii)** $x = -12$ **iii)** $x = 1.5$
b) Write down the equation that the function machine represents.

Q2 A function machine is shown below.

$$x \longrightarrow \boxed{+6} \longrightarrow \boxed{\div 3} \longrightarrow y$$

a) Find the value of x when: **i)** $y = -6$ **ii)** $y = 18$ **iii)** $y = -0.4$
b) Write down an equation to find the value of x given any value of y.

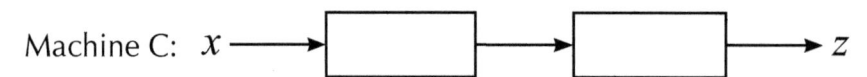

Q3 A function is represented by the following function machine.

$$x \longrightarrow \boxed{\times 2} \longrightarrow \boxed{+3} \longrightarrow y$$

A number is input into the machine. The output is then used as a new input.
What was the original input if the second output is:
a) 5   b) -4

Q4 Machine A and Machine B represent two different functions.

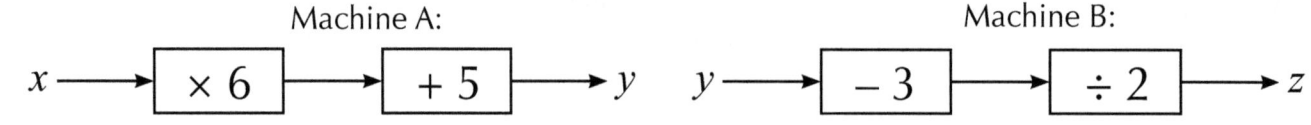

Machine A:
$$x \longrightarrow \boxed{\times 6} \longrightarrow \boxed{+5} \longrightarrow y$$

Machine B:
$$y \longrightarrow \boxed{-3} \longrightarrow \boxed{\div 2} \longrightarrow z$$

a) Find the result when $x = 5$ is put into Machine A and the output is put into Machine B.
b) The combined process of Machine A followed by Machine B can represented by a single two-step function machine which produces an output of z from an input of x. Complete this function machine, Machine C, by filling in the boxes below.

Machine C: $x \longrightarrow \boxed{} \longrightarrow \boxed{} \longrightarrow z$

Q5 A function is represented by the following function machine.

$$x \longrightarrow \boxed{-5} \longrightarrow \boxed{\times 4} \longrightarrow y$$

A number is put into the machine. The result is the same as the input.
What was the number?

Q6 A function is represented by the following incomplete function machine.

$$x \longrightarrow \boxed{} \longrightarrow \boxed{} \longrightarrow y$$

Use the following information to fill in the two boxes.
- When $x = 1$, $y = 2$.
- When $x = -1$, $y = -16$.

Each box can only contain an addition, a subtraction, a multiplication or a division.

Section Two — Mixed Questions

Mixed Questions

Fab work — you've almost reached the end of the section. Give these final mixed questions a go and then relax, maybe even give yourself a reward of a nice cup of tea and a cheeky biscuit.

Q1 Simplify the following:
- a) $-4a \times -8b$
- b) $5c \div 5d$
- c) $7x \times -3x$

Q2 Simplify the following:
- a) $4a^2 \times 3a^3$
- b) $32j^{10} \div 8j^7$
- c) $24x^6y^4 \div 6x^2y^4$
- d) $(4c^4)^2 \times c^3$
- e) $(25d^4)^{\frac{1}{2}} \times (8d^6)^{\frac{2}{3}}$
- f) $n \times \left(\frac{2n}{m}\right)^3$

Q3 Evaluate the following **without using a calculator**:
- a) 5^{-3}
- b) $100^{\frac{3}{2}}$
- c) $36^{-\frac{1}{2}}$
- d) $\left(\frac{7}{8}\right)^2$

Q4 A rectangular garden has length $(6x - 2)$ m and width $(2x + 8)$ m. Half the total area of the garden is a patio. Write down a simplified expression for:
- a) The perimeter of the garden.
- b) The area of the patio.

Q5 Factorise the following expressions:
- a) $6x^2y + 4x^3z$
- b) $32ab^2 - 24ab$
- c) $z^2 - 25$
- d) $16 - x$

Q6 Simplify these expressions:
- a) $\sqrt{16} - \sqrt{12}$
- b) $3\sqrt{6} + 2\sqrt{6}$
- c) $\sqrt{32}$
- d) $\frac{8}{2\sqrt{7}}$
- e) $\sqrt{18} + \sqrt{8}$
- f) $\frac{2 + \sqrt{6}}{2 - \sqrt{6}}$

Q7 Solve the following:
- a) $2x - 7 = 23 - 3x$
- b) $\frac{x}{2} + 6 = 10 + x$
- c) $4(x + 3) = x - 3$
- d) $\frac{2x}{3} - 7 = \frac{x}{5}$
- e) $2(10 + x) = 11 + 3(x + 5)$
- f) $\frac{2x + 9}{5} + \frac{3x + 3}{4} = 6$

Q8 For what value of c is the expression $\frac{c}{4} - 3$ equal to the expression $\frac{2c - 4}{9}$?

Q9 A phone company charges £2.20 to connect a long-distance call, plus 3p for every minute of the phone call.
- a) Find the cost of a 25-minute phone call.
- b) Write down a formula for the cost (£C) of a phone call that lasts for x minutes.
- c) Rearrange the formula to make x the subject.
- d) Geoff made a phone call that cost £5.62. How long did it last?

Q10 Solve these quadratic equations by factorising:
- a) $x^2 + 17x + 60 = 0$
- b) $x^2 + 72 = 17x$
- c) $2x^2 + 5x = 3$
- d) $x - 1 = \frac{12}{x}$

More mixed practice on the next page...

Mixed Questions

Q11 Rearrange the following into the form "$ax^2 + bx + c = 0$" and then find the **exact** solutions by using the quadratic formula. Simplify your answers where possible.

　a) $x(x - 8) = -3$　　**b)** $2(x^2 + 1) = 7x$　　**c)** $10x - x^2 = 17$

Q12 By completing the square, find the coordinates of the minimum point on the graph of each of the following equations.

　a) $y = x^2 - 6x - 23$　　**b)** $y = 5x^2 - 20x + 3$　　**c)** $y = 2x^2 + 6x - 7$

Q13 Express each of the following as a single fraction in its simplest form:

　a) $\dfrac{3a^2}{b} \div \dfrac{3b}{4a}$　　**c)** $\dfrac{2a+6}{a^2 - 3a - 18}$　　**e)** $\dfrac{50x^2 - 18}{20x + 12}$　　**g)** $\dfrac{y}{2x} - \dfrac{y+7}{3x}$

　b) $\dfrac{12p}{q^2} \times \dfrac{q}{6p}$　　**d)** $\dfrac{4x^2 - xy}{3xy + 4x^2 - y^2}$　　**f)** $\dfrac{15}{2m} - \dfrac{3}{m}$　　**h)** $\dfrac{11}{x+6} + \dfrac{2}{x-1}$

Q14 What is the nth term of this sequence: $\dfrac{3}{5}, \dfrac{5}{8}, \dfrac{7}{11}, \dfrac{9}{14}$?

Q15 A sequence is given by the rule $u_{n+1} = 2u_n^2 - 12$. Given that $u_1 = 3$, find u_2 and u_3.

Q16 Billie has £670 to spend on travelling. She has planned a budget of £26 a day.
　a) Use this information to write down an inequality involving the number of days, x, that Billie can travel for.
　b) What is the maximum number of days she can go travelling for?

Q17 The cubic equation $x^3 - 3x^2 - 3x + 6 = 0$ has three solutions. The first solution lies between −1 and −2. The second lies between 1 and 2. The third lies between 3 and 4. By using the decimal search method and a table like the one below, find each solution to 1 d.p.

x	Value of $x^3 - 3x^2 - 3x + 6$	Positive/Negative

Q18 Solve the following simultaneous equations:

　a) $3x + 5y = 31$　　**c)** $3x - 2y = 0$　　**e)** $5x = y - 11$
　　　$y - 2x = 14$　　　　$7x + 2y = 5$　　　　$y = x^2 + x - 1$

　b) $\dfrac{x}{4} - y = 3$　　**d)** $y = x^2 + 2$　　**f)** $\dfrac{y}{2} = 2x^2 - 15$
　　　$3y + x + 2 = 0$　　　$y = x + 14$　　　　$14x = y$

Q19 Joanne says, "I know that $x^2 - 1 = (x + 1)(x - 1)$. So subtracting one from a square number can never give you a prime number." Give an example to show that Joanne is wrong.

Q20 A function is represented by the following function machine.

$$x \longrightarrow \boxed{-4} \longrightarrow \boxed{\times 7} \longrightarrow y$$

　a) Find the value of:　**i)** y when $x = 7$　　**ii)** y when $x = 4$　　**iii)** x when $y = 35$
　b) Write down an equation to find the value of x given any value of y.

Section Three — Graphs

Straight Lines and Gradients

Gradients might seem confusing at first, but remember — they're just 'the change in y' divided by 'the change in x'. Oh, and careful with those signs...

Q1 Which letters represent the following lines:

a) $x = y$
b) $x = 5$
c) $y = -x$
d) $x = 0$
e) $y = -5$
f) $x + y = 0$
g) $y = 5$
h) $x - y = 0$
i) $y = 0$
j) $x = -7$?

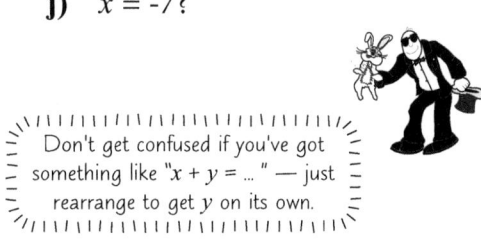

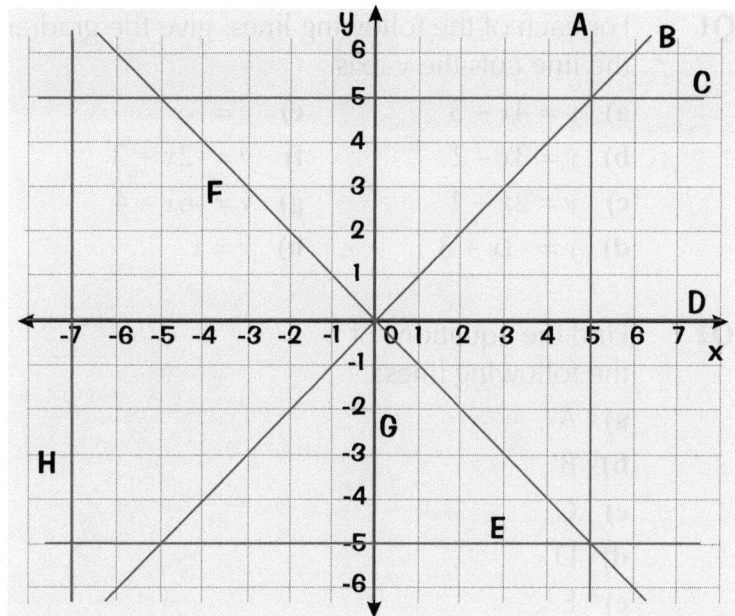

Don't get confused if you've got something like "x + y = ..." — just rearrange to get y on its own.

Q2 Find the gradient of:

a) line A
b) line B
c) line C
d) line D
e) line E
f) line F
g) line G
h) line H
i) line I
j) line J

Q3 What is the gradient of the line joining the points:

a) (3, 5) and (5, 9)
b) (6, 3) and (10, 5)
c) (-6, 4) and (-3, 1)
d) (8, 2) and (4, 10)
e) (8, 5) and (6, 4)
f) (-3, -1) and (1, -4)?

Uphill gradients are always positive, downhill always negative. Impressed? Hmmm....thought not. Can be a bit of an uphill battle, these.

Q4 A straight line has gradient $-\frac{1}{3}$ and passes through the points (2, 3), (a, 2) and (11, b). What are the values of a and b?

y = mx + c

Writing the equation of a line in the form y = mx + c gives you a nifty way of finding the gradient and y-intercept. Remember that — it'll save you loads of time. Anything for an easy life...

Q1 For each of the following lines, give the gradient and the coordinates of the point where the line cuts the y-axis.

a) $y = 4x + 3$
b) $y = 3x - 2$
c) $y = 2x + 1$
d) $y = -3x + 3$
e) $y = 5x$
f) $y = -2x + 3$
g) $y = -6x - 4$
h) $y = x$
i) $y = -\frac{1}{2}x + 3$
j) $y = \frac{1}{4}x + 2$
k) $3y = 4x + 6$

I know these are a bit algebra-ish, but don't worry, they won't bite.

Q2 Find the equations of the following lines:

a) A
b) B
c) C
d) D
e) E
f) F

Yeah, OK, this sounds a bit scary, but just work out the gradient (m) and look at the y-intercept (c) and pop them back into "y = mx + c"... easy lemons.

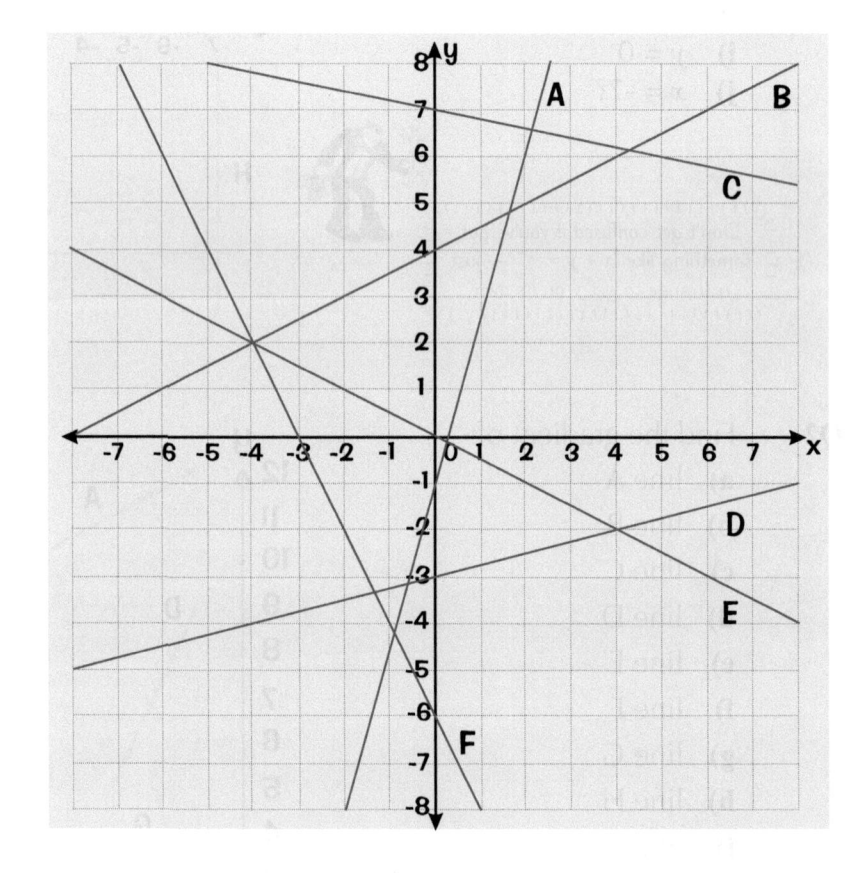

Q3 Find the equation of the straight line which passes through:
a) (3, 7) and has a gradient of 1
b) (2, 8) and has a gradient of 3
c) (4, -4) and has a gradient of -1
d) (-1, 7) and has a gradient of -3.

Q4 Write down the equation of the line which passes through the points:
a) (2, 2) and (5, 5)
b) (1, 3) and (4, 12)
c) (1, 0) and (5, -12)
d) (-5, 6) and (-1, -2).

Q5 Find the value of letters a-d, given that:
a) the point (a, 13) is on the line $y = 3x + 1$
b) the point (b, –2) is on the line $y = \frac{1}{2}x - 6$
c) the point (4, c) is on the line $y = 2x - 1$
d) the point (–3, d) is on the line $y = -3x$?

Q6 Which of the following points lie on the line $y = 3x - 1$?
(7, 20), (6, 15), (5, 14)

Drawing Straight Line Graphs

If you know it's a straight line, you only really need two points, but it's always a good idea to plot three — it's a bit of a safety net, really.

Q1 Complete this table of values for $y = 2x + 3$:

x	0	3	8
y			

Plot these points on graph paper and draw the graph of $y = 2x + 3$.
Use your graph to find:
 a) The value of y when x = 5
 b) The value of y when x = 2
 c) The value of x when y = 11
 d) The value of x when y = 17

Q2 Complete this table of values for $y = \frac{1}{4}x - 3$:

x	-8	-4	8
y			

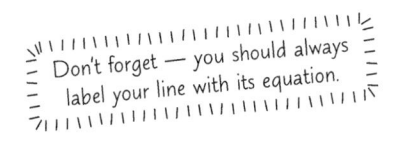

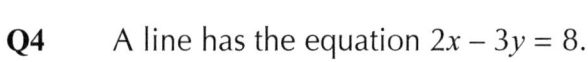

Don't forget — you should always label your line with its equation.

Plot these points on graph paper and draw the graph of $y = \frac{1}{4}x - 3$.
Use your graph to find:
 a) The value of y when x = 2
 b) The value of y when x = 0
 c) The value of x when y = -2
 d) The value of x when y = -1.5

Q3 For each of the following, identify the <u>gradient</u> and <u>y-intercept</u> of the line.
Then use them to draw the graph of the given line on graph paper.
 a) $y = 3x + 1$
 b) $y = \frac{1}{2}x - 5$
 c) $y = -3x + 4$
 d) $y = -x - 1$

Q4 A line has the equation $2x - 3y = 8$.
 a) Rearrange the equation into the form $y = mx + c$.
 b) What are the coordinates of the point where the line cuts the y-axis?
 c) What is the gradient of the line?
 d) Use your answers to **b)** and **c)** to help you draw the line $2x - 3y = 8$ on graph paper.

Q5 Sketch the graphs of the following equations:
 a) $y = 2x - 3$
 b) $2y - x = 1$
 c) $y = 3x - 6$
 d) $4x + y = 8$
 e) $x = 7 - y$
 f) $2 + 2y = 9x$

When you're asked to sketch a line, it doesn't need to be super-accurate (so you <u>don't</u> need graph paper). But try to make the <u>gradient</u> roughly correct, and give the coordinates of <u>key points</u>, such as the x- and y-intercepts.

Q6 Draw the lines $y = \frac{1}{2}x + 1$ and $y = 2x - 2$ on graph paper.
Write down the coordinates of the point where the two lines intersect.

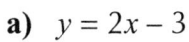

Section Three — Graphs

Coordinates and Ratio

Q1 Find the midpoint of the line AB, where A and B have coordinates:
   a) A(2, 3) B(4, 5)
   b) A(0, 11) B(11, 11)
   c) A(3, 15) B(14, 3)
   d) A(6, 7) B(0, 0)
   e) A(16, 16) B(3, 3)
   f) A(17, 28) B(44, 13)

   Your answers should be coordinates too.

   ahh... nice'n'easy...

Q2 Gowri is designing the plan of a kitchen using some computer aided design software. The coordinates of the room on screen are (0, 10), (220, 10), (0, 260), (220, 260). She needs to enter the coordinates of the ceiling light, which will be exactly in the centre of the room. What will the coordinates of the light be?

Q3 Find the midpoint of each of these lines:
   a) Line PQ, where P has coordinates (-1, 5) and Q has coordinates (5, 6).
   b) Line AB, where A has coordinates (-3, 3) and B has coordinates (4, 0).
   c) Line RS, where R has coordinates (4, -5) and S has coordinates (0, 0).
   d) Line GH, where G has coordinates (10, 13) and H has coordinates (-6, -7).
   e) Line MN, where M has coordinates (-5, -8) and N has coordinates (-21, -17).

Q4 Point Q lies on the line segment RS. Find the coordinates of Q when the coordinates of R and S and the ratio RQ : QS are as follows:
   a) R(2, 4) S(8, 10)   RQ : QS = 1 : 2
   b) R(-4, 2) S(16, 17)   RQ : QS = 3 : 2
   c) R(9, -1) S(-9, 3)   RQ : QS = 1 : 3
   d) R(-21, -45) S(-14, -10) RQ : QS = 6 : 1
   e) R(7, -8) S(21, -7)   RQ : QS = 3 : 1
   f) R(-17, 0) S(7, -17)   RQ : QS = 3 : 5

   Divide the horizontal distance between R and S in the given ratio — this will help you find the x-coordinate of Q. Then do the same thing with the vertical distance to find the y-coordinate of Q.

Q5 Point C lies on the line segment AB, with AC : CB = 2 : 7. Point A has coordinates (5, 3) and point C has coordinates (-1, 0). Find the coordinates of B.

Q6 On the graph on the right, G lies on the line segment DE, with DG : GE = 3 : 1. F and H lie on the circumference of the circle, and FH is a diameter of the circle.
   a) Find the coordinates of G.
   b) Is point G at the centre of the circle? Explain your answer.

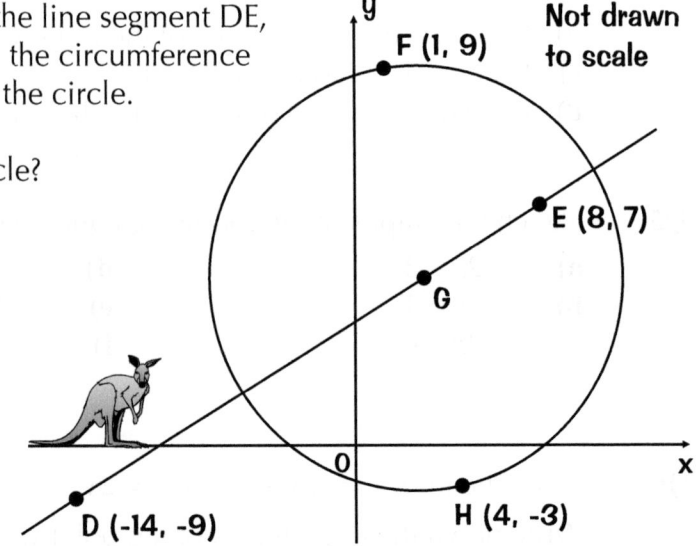

   Don't forget — the diameter of a circle goes through its centre.

   F (1, 9), E (8, 7), D (-14, -9), H (4, -3). Not drawn to scale.

Parallel and Perpendicular Lines

When lines are parallel, their gradients are the same. When lines are perpendicular, their gradients multiply together to give -1. That's it — not much else to it really...

Q1 Identify whether each of the following pairs of straight lines are parallel, perpendicular or neither.

You only need to compare the gradients to answer this question.

- a) $y = 3x + 4$, $y = 3x - 8$
- b) $2y = x - 17$, $y = \frac{1}{2}x + 17$
- c) $y = x - 4$, $y = -2x - 4$
- d) $3y + 3x = 9$, $y = x + \frac{3}{2}$
- e) $2x = y + 8$, $2y = x + 8$
- f) $3 - x = 3y$, $y - 3x = 5$
- g) $4y + 5x = 0$, $2y = 22 - \frac{5}{2}x$
- h) $y = 2x - 8$, $8y + 4x = 9$

Q2 Line A has the equation $y = 3x - 4$.
Line B is parallel to line A and passes through (8, 25).
- a) Find the gradient of line B.
- b) Find the equation for line B.

Q3 Line C is defined by $y = \frac{1}{2}x + 12$.
Line D is perpendicular to line C and passes through (5, -13).
- a) Find the gradient of line D.
- b) Find the equation for line D.

Q4 Find the equation of the line which is:
- a) parallel to $y = 2x - 1$ and passes through (4, 11).
- b) perpendicular to $y = -\frac{1}{4}x + 1$ and passes through (5, 21).
- c) parallel to $y = x$ and passes through (-2, -10).
- d) parallel to $3y + 2x = 1$ and passes through (9, 0).
- e) perpendicular to $10y + 5x = 3$ and passes through (-7, -1).
- f) parallel to $8y - x + 4 = 0$ and passes through $(3, \frac{1}{2})$.
- g) perpendicular to $2x = 8 - y$ and passes through (16, 47).
- h) perpendicular to $6 + 8y = 3x$ and passes through (12, -37)

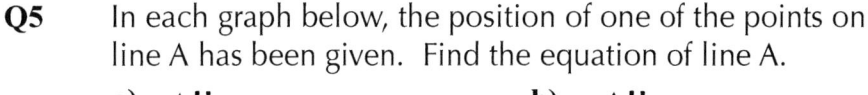

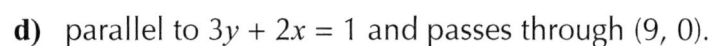

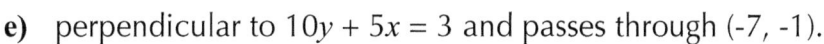

Q5 In each graph below, the position of one of the points on line A has been given. Find the equation of line A.

a) $y = 2x$; point (0, 3) marked on line A

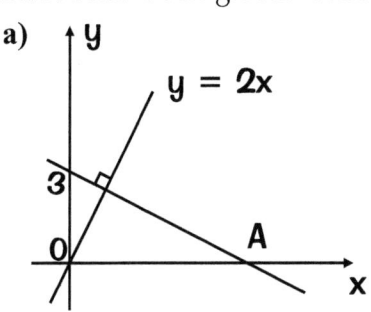

b) $y = \frac{-x}{3} + 3$; point (3, 0) marked on line A

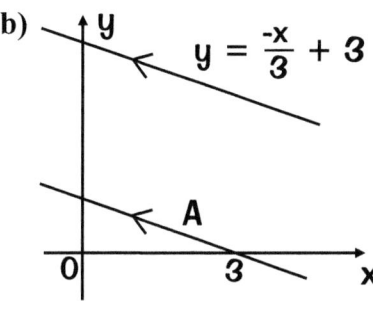

c) $y = -x - 4$; point (1, -5) marked on line A

Section Three — Graphs

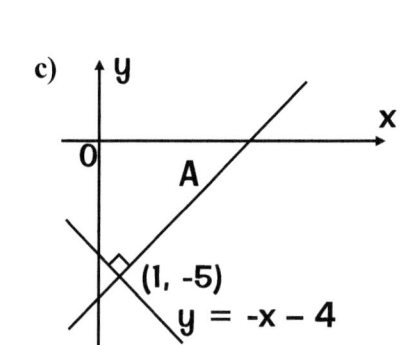

Quadratic Graphs

So, you can spot a quadratic graph at ten paces, but can you draw one...

Q1 Complete this table of values for the quadratic graph $y = 2x^2$.

a) Draw axes with x from -4 to 4 and y from 0 to 32.
b) Plot these 9 points and join them with a smooth curve.
c) Label your graph.

x	-4	-3	-2	-1	0	1	2	3	4
$y = 2x^2$	32	18					8		

Q2 Complete this table of values for the graph $y = x^2 + 3x + 5$.

x	-4	-3	-2	-1	0	1	2	3
x^2	16	9					4	
3x				-3				9
$y = x^2 + 3x + 5$	9				9			

a) Draw axes with x from -4 to 3 and y from 0 to 25.
b) Plot the points and join them with a smooth curve.
c) Draw and label the line of symmetry for the quadratic graph $y = x^2 + 3x + 5$.

If the x^2 term has a <u>minus</u> sign in front of it, the curve will be turned <u>upside down</u>.

Q3 Complete this table of values for the graph $y = 3 - x^2$.

a) Draw the graph $y = 3 - x^2$ for x from -4 to 4.
b) State the maximum y-value of the graph $y = 3 - x^2$.

x	-4	-3	-2	-1	0	1	2	3	4
$-x^2$	-16						-4		
$y = 3 - x^2$	-13						-1		

Q4 The curve on the right has the equation $y = ax^2 + bx + c$.

a) Find the value of c.
b) Write down the coordinates of the turning point.
c) Find the roots of the equation $ax^2 + bx + c = 0$.

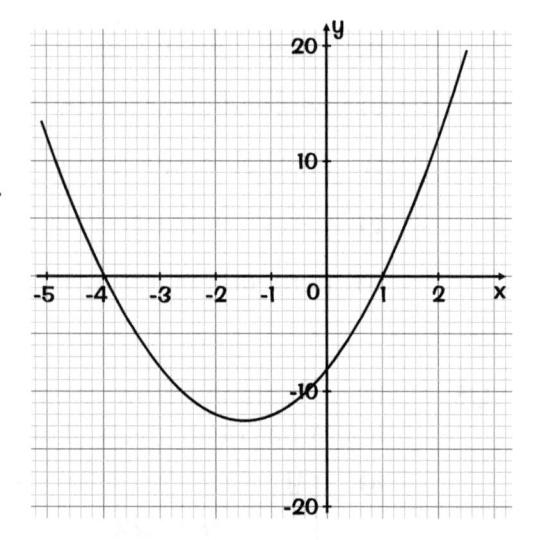

Finding the roots of $ax^2 + bx + c = 0$ is just a fancy way of saying "what values of x give $y = 0$?"

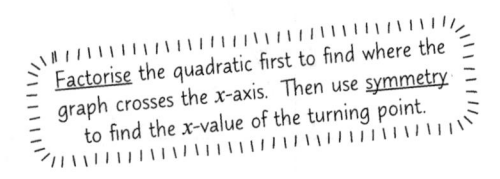

Q5 Sketch the following graphs. Make sure you label each graph with the coordinates of the turning point and the points where the graph crosses the x-axis.

a) $y = x^2 + 8x - 20$
b) $y = x^2 - 5x + 6$
c) $y = -x^2 + 1$
d) $y = -x^2 - 4x - 4$

<u>Factorise</u> the quadratic first to find where the graph crosses the x-axis. Then use <u>symmetry</u> to find the x-value of the turning point.

Section Three — Graphs

Harder Graphs

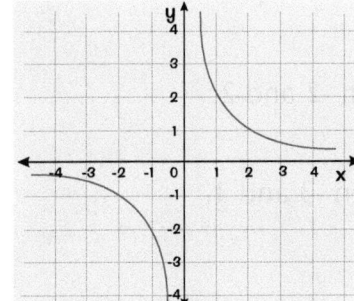

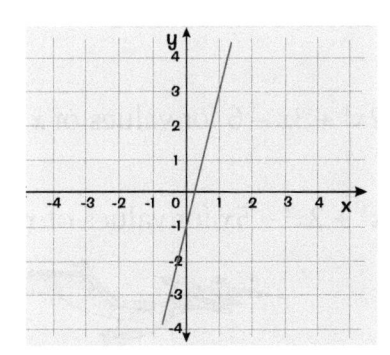

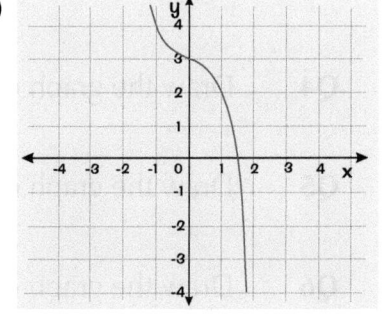

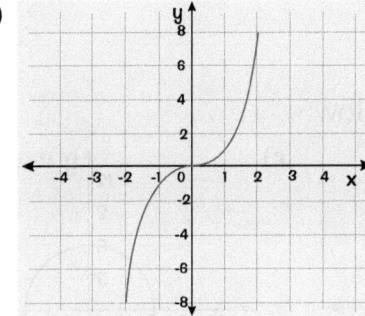

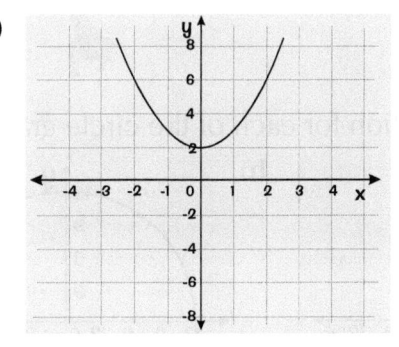

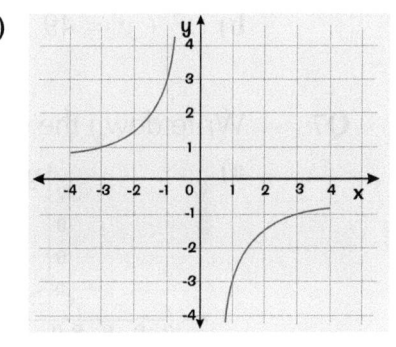

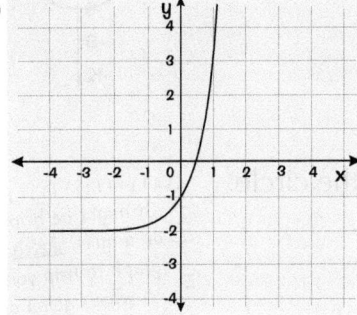

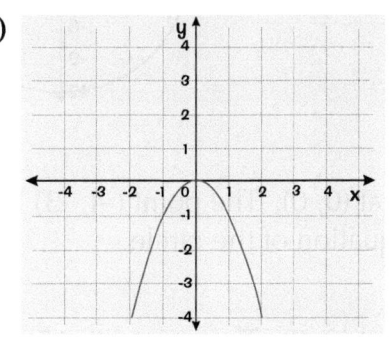

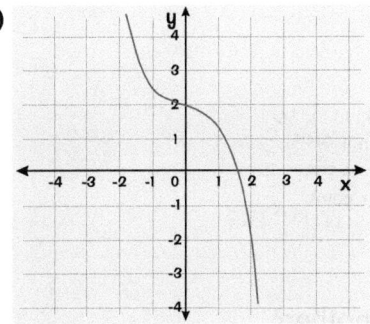

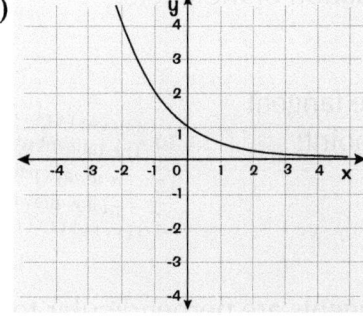

You should know the basic shapes for quadratic, cubic, exponential and reciprocal graphs. They might look complicated at first, but you'll soon be able to spot them a mile away.

Q1 Here are some equations. Match each equation to one of the curves below.

a) $y = 4x - 1$ **e)** $y = -x^2 - 3$ **i)** $y = -x^3 + 3$

b) $y = -x^2$ **f)** $y = 2^{-x}$ **j)** $y = x^3$

c) $y = x^2 + 2$ **g)** $y = 2x^3 - 3$ **k)** $y = 5^x - 2$

d) $y = -\dfrac{3}{x}$ **h)** $y = -\dfrac{1}{2}x^3 + 2$ **l)** $y = \dfrac{2}{x}$

Section Three — Graphs

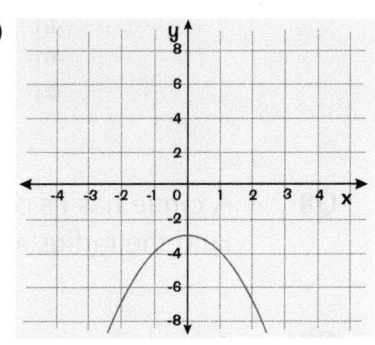

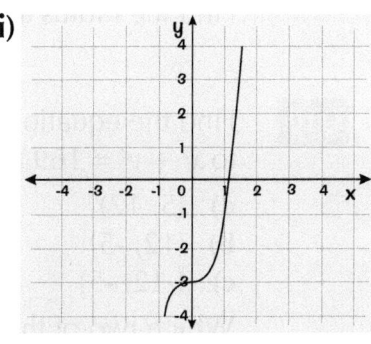

Harder Graphs

Q2 Complete this table of values for $y = x^3 + 4$:

x	-3	-2	-1	0	1	2	3
x^3							
+4							
y							

Draw the graph of $y = x^3 + 4$.

Q3 Complete this table of values for $y = -x^3 - 4$:

x	-3	-2	-1	0	1	2	3
$-x^3$							
-4							
y							

Draw the graph of $y = -x^3 - 4$.

Q4 Draw the graph of $y = 2x^3 + 3x - 6$ for values of x between -2 and 2.

Q5 Draw the graph of $y = x^3 + 2x^2 - 5x$ for values of x between -3 and 3.

Q6 Draw the graph of:
a) $x^2 + y^2 = 4$
b) $x^2 + y^2 = 49$

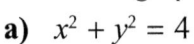

Q7 Write down the equation for each of the circle graphs below:

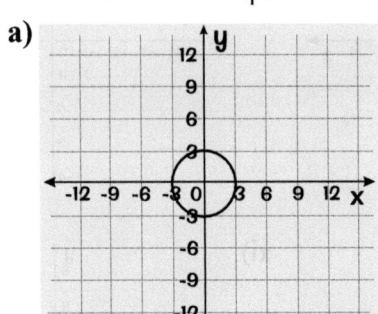

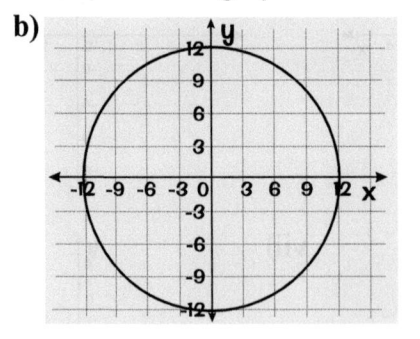

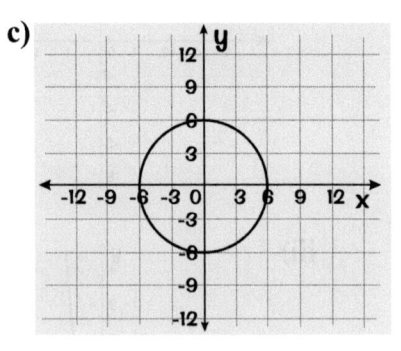

a) b) c)

Q8 A circle has its centre at (0, 0). The point (-4, -3) lies on the circle. Find the radius and equation of the circle.

It might be helpful to do a quick sketch of the graph to help you spot what's going on.

Q9 A circle has its centre at (0, 0). The point (-8, 15) lies on the circle. Find the radius and equation of the circle.

Q10 Find the equation of the tangent to $x^2 + y^2 = 169$ at the point:
a) (5, 12)
b) (12, -5)
c) (-12, -5)

Which two of these tangents are perpendicular to one another?

The tangent at a point on a circle is always perpendicular to the radius drawn from that point.

Section Three — Graphs

Harder Graphs

These equations and shapes are a bit more alien... but just go about plotting them the same way as a cubic or quadratic and you'll be fine. Don't try to skip stages when you're working through it — errors will then become much harder to spot.

The two halves of a 1/x graph never touch and are symmetrical around y = x and y = -x.

Q11 Complete this table of values for the graph $y = 1/x$.

a) Draw axes with x from -4 to 4 and y from -1 to 1.
b) Plot these points and draw the two smooth curves that form the graph.
c) Label your graph.

x	-4	-3	-2	-1	0	1	2	3	4
y=1/x		-0.33			n/a				0.25

The O's just there to fool you — no graph with A/x in its equation will pass through $x = 0$.

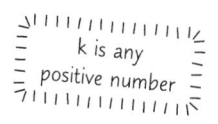

k^x graphs are always above the x-axis and pass through the point (0, 1).

k is any positive number

Q12
a) Complete this table of values for the graph $y = 2^x$.
b) Draw the graph $y = 2^x$ for x from -4 to 4.
c) Why do k^x graphs always pass through (0, 1)?

x	-4	-3	-2	-1	0	1	2	3	4
y=2^x				0.5	1		4		

All these types of equations can be combined — see what shape of graph you get.

Q13
a) Complete this table of values for the graph $y = 3^x - 6/x$.
b) Draw the graph $y = 3^x - 6/x$ for x from -3 to 3.

x	-3	-2	-1	0	1	2	3
3^x			0.33		3		
6/x						3	
y=3^x – 6/x					-3		

Q14 Sketch the following graphs on the same set of axes.
Mark on any points where the lines cross the axes.

a) $y = 3^x$
b) $y = 9^x$
c) $y = 4^{-x}$

Q15 The graph below shows how the number of grey squirrels living in a forest changes over time. The equation for this graph is $S = ab^t$ where S is the number of grey squirrels, t is the time in years and a and b are positive constants.

a) Using the graph, find the constants a and b.
b) $t = 0$ on 1st January 2012. Assuming the population of grey squirrels continues to grow in the same way, how many squirrels will there be on 1st January 2017?

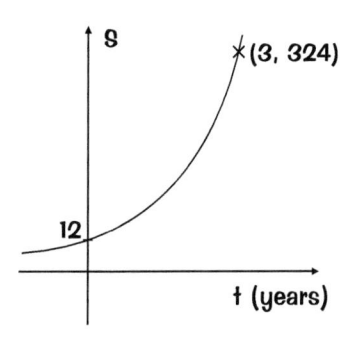

(3, 324)
12

Harder Graphs

Remember — Sin and Cos only have values between −1 and 1 and repeat themselves every 360°. Tan has values between −∞ and ∞ and repeats itself every 180°.

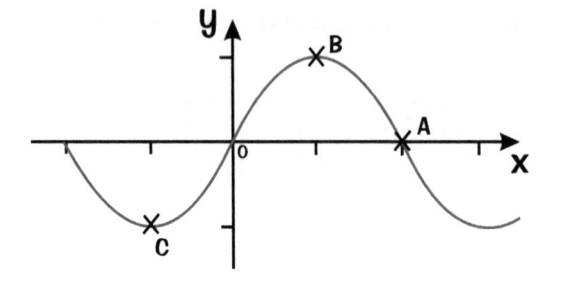

Q16 This is the graph of $y = \sin x$. Write down the coordinates of the points A, B and C.

Q17 This is the graph of $y = \cos x$. Write down the coordinates of the points D, E, F and G.

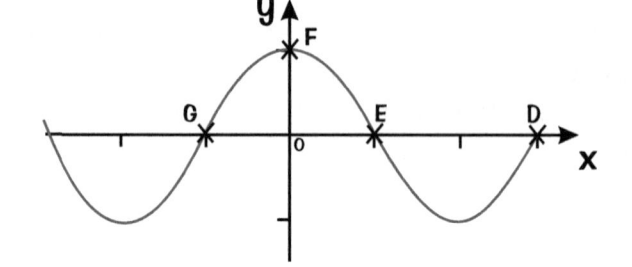

Q18 The points marked with letters all lie on either the $y = \sin x$ or the $y = \cos x$ graph. For each point, state which graph goes through it.

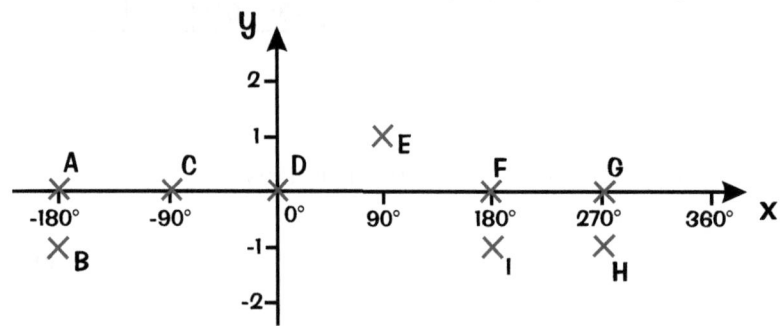

Q19 Sketch the graph of $y = \tan x$ for values of x between -180° and 450°.

Q20 Complete this table of values for $y = \cos x + 1$:

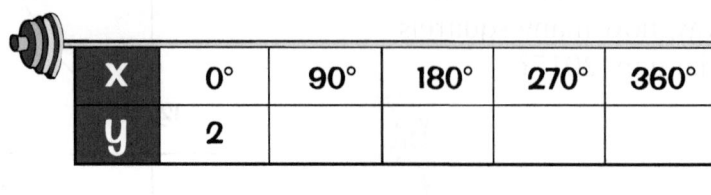

x	0°	90°	180°	270°	360°
y	2				

Solving Equations Using Graphs

Q1 Solve the following simultaneous equations by drawing graphs. Use values $0 \leq x \leq 6$

a) $y = x$
   $y = 9 - 2x$
b) $y = 2x + 1$
   $2y = 8 + x$
c) $y = 4 - 2x$
   $x + y = 3$
d) $y = 3 - x$
   $3x + y = 5$
e) $2x + y = 6$
   $y = 3x + 1$
f) $y = 2x$
   $y = x + 1$
g) $x + y = 5$
   $2x - 1 = y$
h) $2y = 3x$
   $y = x + 1$
i) $y = x - 3$
   $y + x = 7$
j) $y = x + 1$
   $2x + y = 10$

Q2 Use the graphs to find the solutions to the following simultaneous equations to 1 decimal place:

a) $y = x + 2$
   $y = -2x + 4$
b) $y = x^2 - x$
   $y = -2x + 4$

Use this diagram for Q2 and Q3.

Q3 Use the graphs to find the solutions to the following equations. Give your answers to 1 decimal place where appropriate.

a) $x^2 - x = 0$
b) $x^2 - x = x + 2$
c) $x^2 - x - 8 = 0$

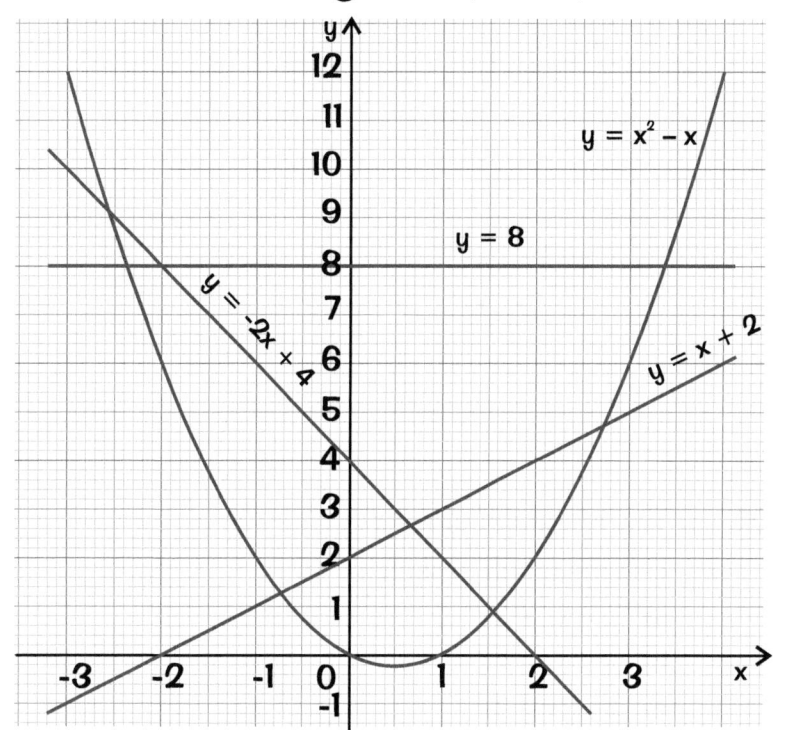

These equations look a bit nasty, but they're just made up of the equations you've got graphs for. And you know how to do the rest of it, don't you...

Q4 Complete this table for $y = -\frac{1}{2}x^2 + 5$:

x	-4	-3	-2	-1	0	1	2	3	4
$-\frac{1}{2}x^2$									
+5									
y									

Draw the graph $y = -\frac{1}{2}x^2 + 5$.

a) Use your graph to solve the following equations (to 1 d.p.):

   i) $-\frac{1}{2}x^2 + 5 = 0$ ii) $-\frac{1}{2}x^2 + 5 = -3$ iii) $-\frac{1}{2}x^2 + 5 = x$

b) Find the equation of the line you could add to your graph to solve $-\frac{1}{2}x^2 - 2x + 3 = 0$.

Section Three — Graphs

Graph Transformations

You've got to learn the rules for these shifts and reflections — it won't take long. And don't forget — "y = function of (x + a)" shifts the graph to the <u>left</u> and "y = function of (x − a)" shifts the graph to the <u>right</u>.

Q1 This is a graph of $y = x^2$.

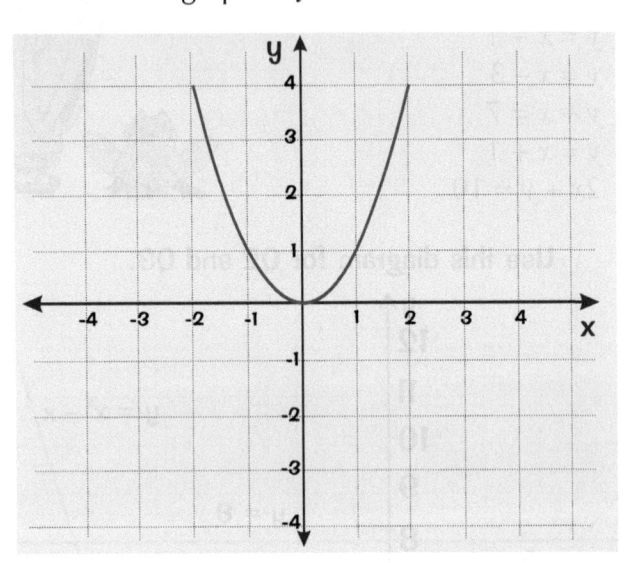

Use the graph to sketch:
a) $y = x^2 + 1$
b) $y = x^2 - 3$
c) $y = (x + 2)^2$
d) $y = (x - 3)^2 + 1$
e) $y = -x^2 + 2$

Q2 This is a graph of $y = x^3$.

Use the graph to sketch:
a) $y = x^3 + 2$
b) $y = x^3 - 4$
c) $y = (x + 3)^3$
d) $y = (x - 4)^3$
e) $y = -x^3 + 2$
f) $y = (-x)^3 - 1$
g) $y = (x + 3)^3 - 1$
h) $y = (x - 1)^3 + 3$

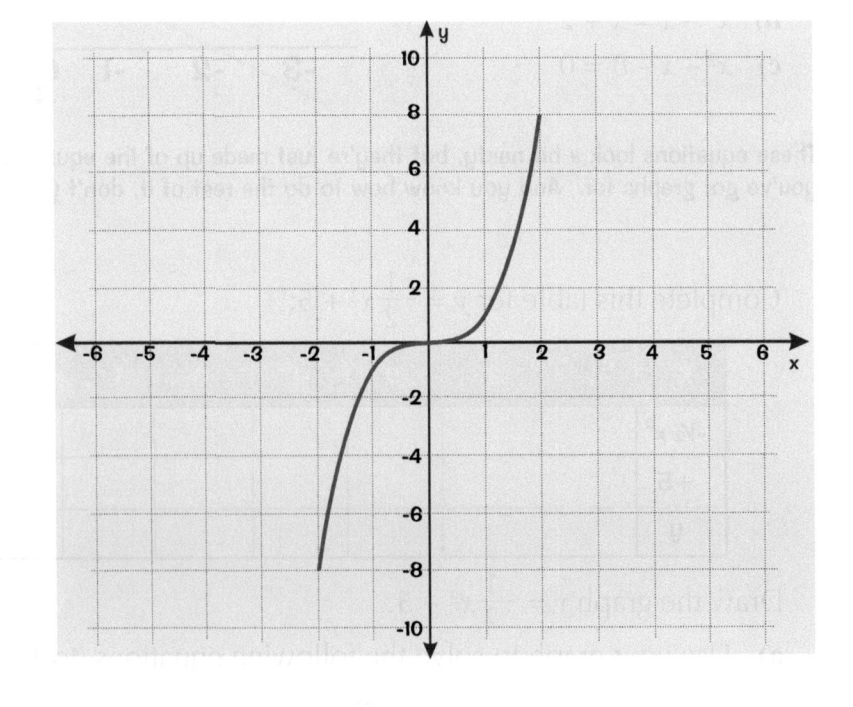

Graph Transformations

Q3 The graph of $y = \sin x$ is shown below.

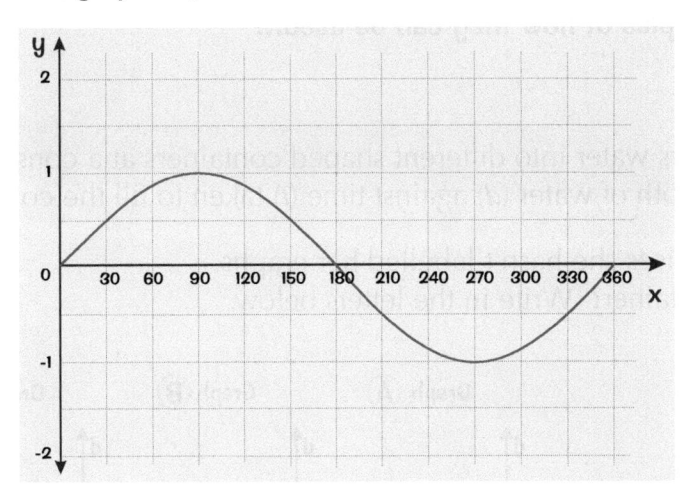

a) On a single set of axes, draw the graphs of:
   i) $y = 2 + \sin x$
   ii) $y = \sin(x + 60)$
   iii) $y = -\sin x$.

b) Write down the coordinates of the points on the graph $y = \sin x$ that are invariant under the transformation in part iii).

Q4 This is the graph of $y = \cos x$:

On a single set of axes, draw the graphs of:
a) $y = 1 + \cos x$
b) $y = \cos(x - 90)$.

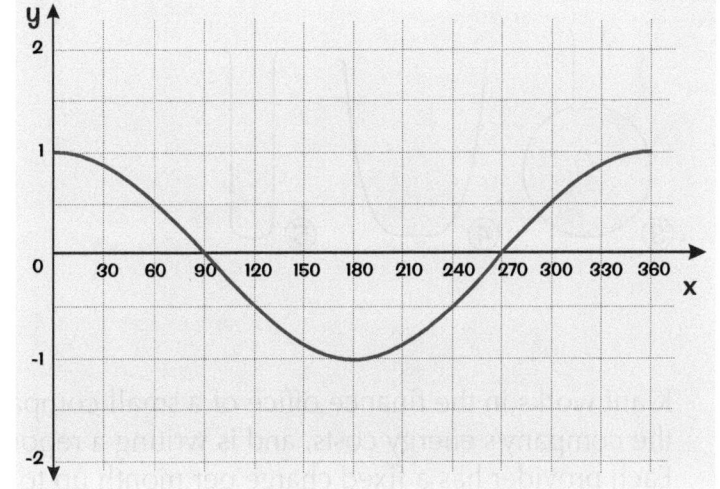

Q5 The graph of $y = x^2 - 3x + 2$ is shown on the right.

Use the graph to write down the coordinates of the turning point of the following, stating whether each turning point is a maximum or a minimum.

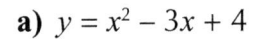

a) $y = x^2 - 3x + 4$
b) $y = x^2 - 3x - 2$
c) $y = -2 + 3x - x^2$ ← Remember... $x^2 = (-x)^2$
d) $y = x^2 + 3x + 2$
e) $y = (x - 2)(x - 3)$ ← Start by factorising $x^2 - 3x + 2$.

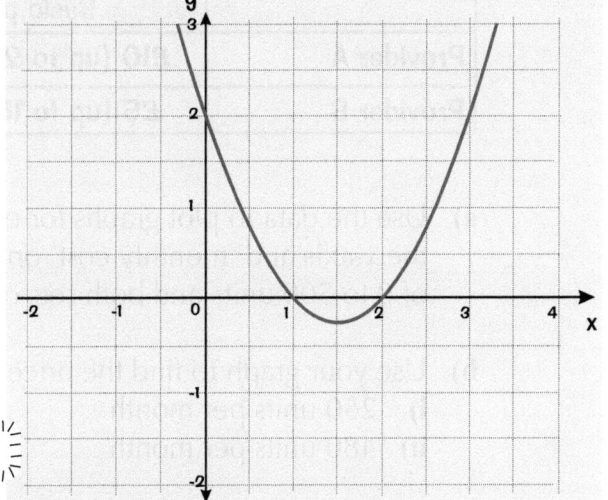

Q6 The curve $y = x^3 + 2x + 4$ is reflected in the y-axis. Write down the equation of the new curve.

Section Three — Graphs

Real-Life Graphs

Graphs are pretty useful even outside of the maths classroom (no, really). Here are a couple of examples of how they can be used...

Q1 In her science lesson, Gaia pours water into different shaped containers at a constant rate, then plots graphs of the depth of water (d) against time (t) taken to fill the container.

At the end of the lesson she realises she hasn't labelled her graphs. Which graph matches each container? Write in the letters below.

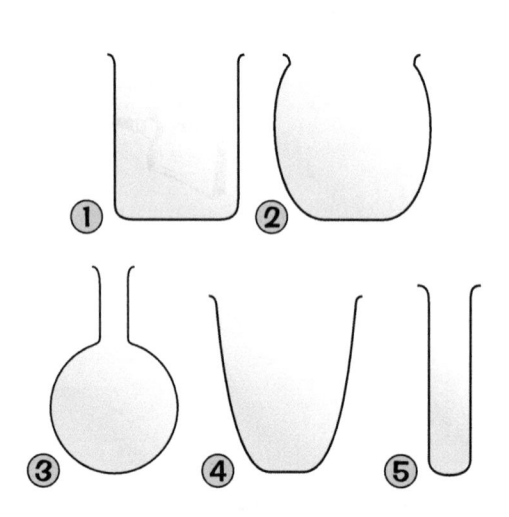

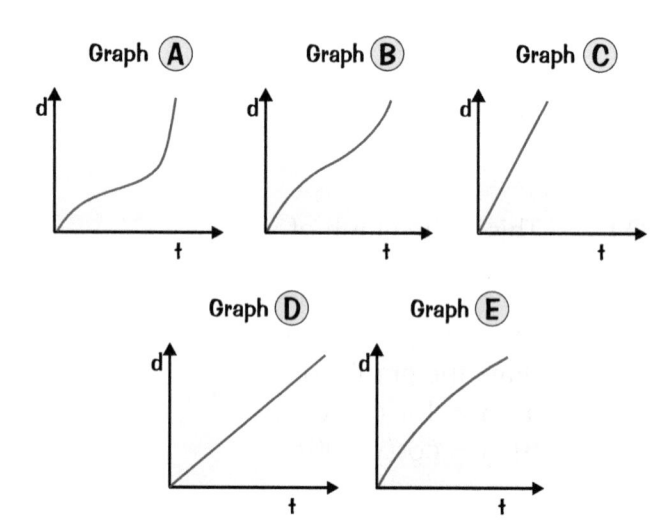

Q2 Kiani works in the finance office of a small company. She has been asked to review the company's energy costs, and is writing a report comparing two energy providers. Each provider has a fixed charge per month up to a certain number of units, and a cost per unit for each additional unit. The table below shows the rates for each provider.

	Basic price	Cost per unit for each additional unit
Provider A	£10 (up to 200 units)	£0.05 per unit
Provider B	£5 (up to 150 units)	£0.06 per unit

a) Use the data to plot graphs for each provider with 'number of units used' on the x-axis and 'monthly cost' on the y-axis. Your x-axis should cover the range of 0 to 500 units and both sets of data should be plotted on the same axes.

b) Use your graph to find the price each energy provider would charge for:
i) 250 units per month
ii) 480 units per month

c) Use the graph to determine the number of units per month the company would need to use for there to be no difference in price between the two providers.

Section Three — Graphs

Distance-Time Graphs

You need to remember what the different bits of a distance-time graph mean — what it looks like when stopped, changing speed and coming back to the starting point.

Q1 Pasha drives a bus from Kendal to Ingleton and back again. The bus company graphed the journey to help them organise their bus schedules.

   a) How long did it take to get to Ingleton?
   b) How much time was spent driving to and from Ingleton excluding stops?
   c) What was the average speed for the journey from Kendal to Ingleton?
   d) What was Pasha's fastest speed?
   e) The transport manager wants to reduce the duration of the stops so that Pasha can still start the journey at the same time but complete the whole route by 1630. Would this be possible?

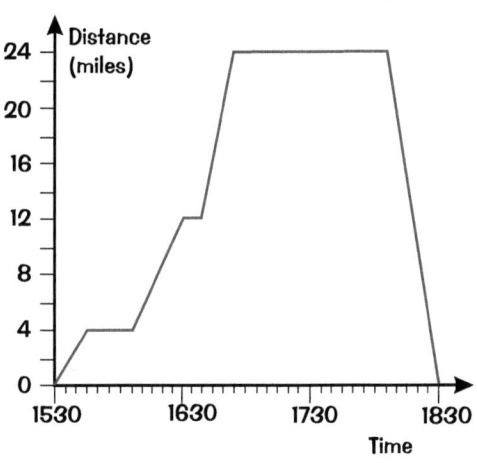

Q2 On sports day the first three in the 1000 m race ran as shown in the graph below.

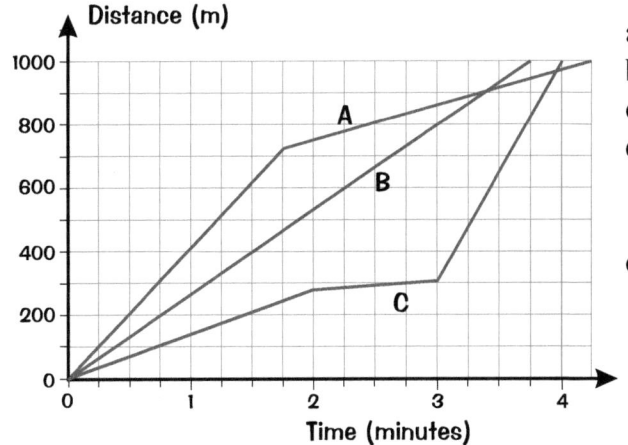

   a) Which runner, A, B or C, won the race?
   b) How long did the winner take?
   c) Which runner kept up a steady speed?
   d) What was that speed
      i) in m/min?
      ii) km/h?
   e) Which runner achieved the fastest speed at any point during the race, and what was that speed?

Q3 Richard and Gabrielle are having a bicycle race. The distance-time graph for Richard is shown on the right.

   a) What is Richard's average speed during the race? Give your answer to 2 decimal places.
   b) Estimate Richard's speed after 60 s.
   c) Gabrielle maintains a constant speed of 5 m/s throughout the race. Draw Gabrielle's distance-time graph on the same axes.
   d) Who is the winner?

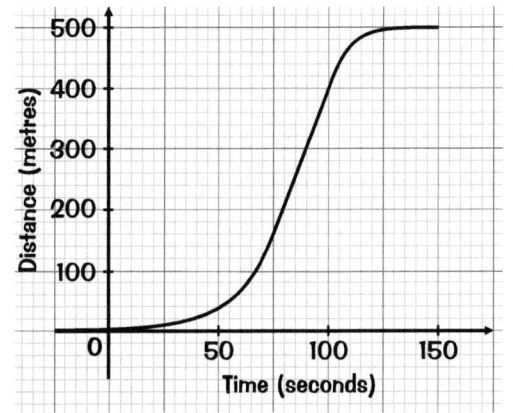

A curved line on a distance-time graph shows acceleration or deceleration — at the beginning Richard is speeding up and at the end he's slowing down.

Velocity-Time Graphs

Speed and velocity have slightly different meanings — but for these types of graphs they are one and the same thing, which is handy. These graphs can also tell you the distance travelled — just work out the area under the graph. Nifty.

Q1 This is a speed-time graph of a train journey.

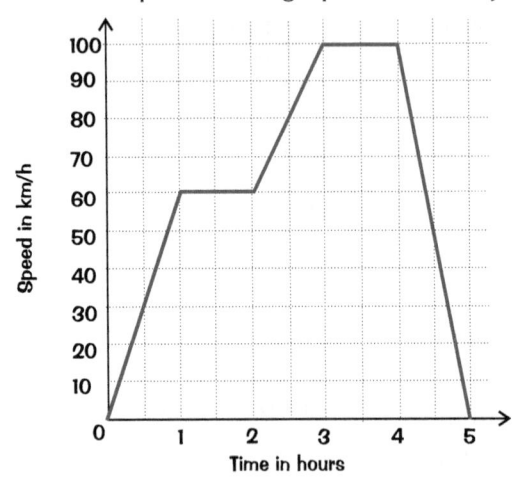

a) What was the maximum speed?
b) How long did the train travel at a constant speed for in total?
c) What was the rate of deceleration?

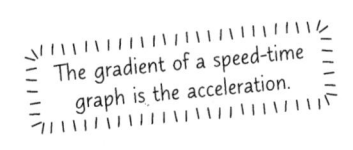

The gradient of a speed-time graph is the acceleration.

Q2 Andrew's cycle computer plots a graph of his journey but only shows his speed.

He wants to know how far he travelled.
a) Calculate the distance travelled in:
  i) the first two hours.
  ii) the last two hours.
b) Calculate the total distance travelled.

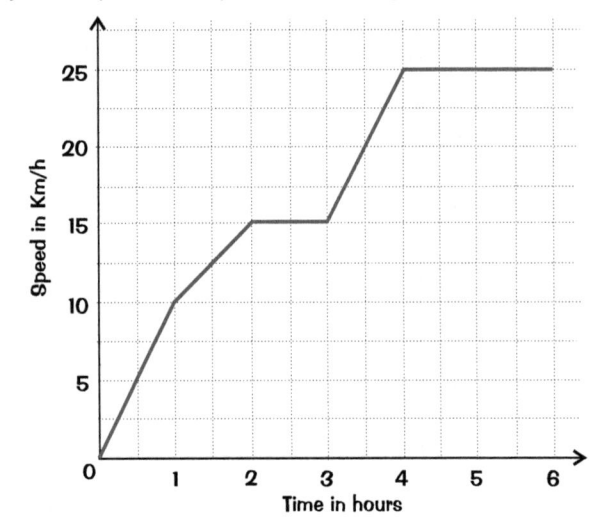

Q3 A racing driver completes one lap of a circuit. The velocity-time graph of the lap is shown below.

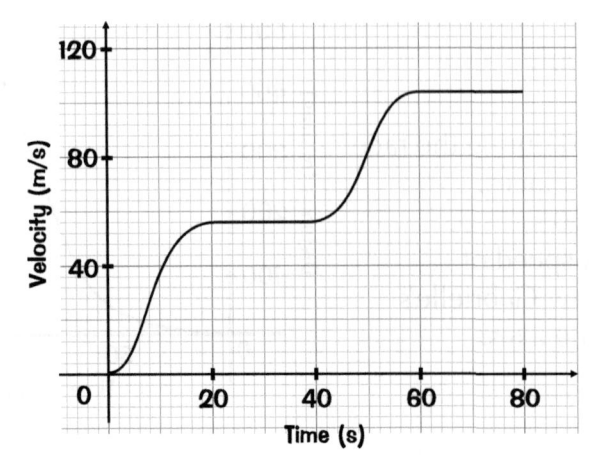

To find the acceleration from a curved graph, you'll need to draw a tangent to the curve.

a) Estimate the length of the circuit.
b) Estimate the acceleration after 50 s.

Section Three — Graphs

Gradients of Real-Life Graphs

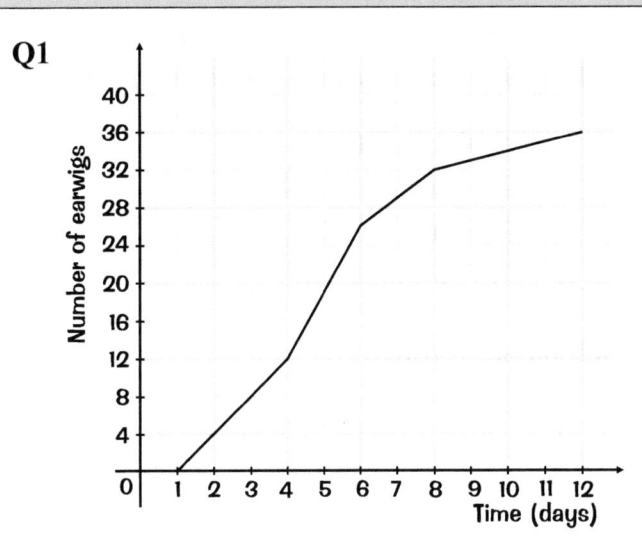

Q1 Fin counts the number of earwigs in a 1 m² area of his garden at the same time each day for 12 days. His results are shown in the graph opposite.

a) At what rate did the number of earwigs increase between day 1 and day 4?
b) Between which days did the number of earwigs increase at the lowest rate?
c) What was the average rate of increase in the number of earwigs between day 4 and day 12?

Q2 The graph shows how the temperature in a desert changes between 2 am and midday.

a) Estimate the rate of temperature change, in °C per hour, at 6 am.
b) What was the average rate of temperature change, in °C per hour, between 9 am and midday? Give your answer to 2 decimal places.

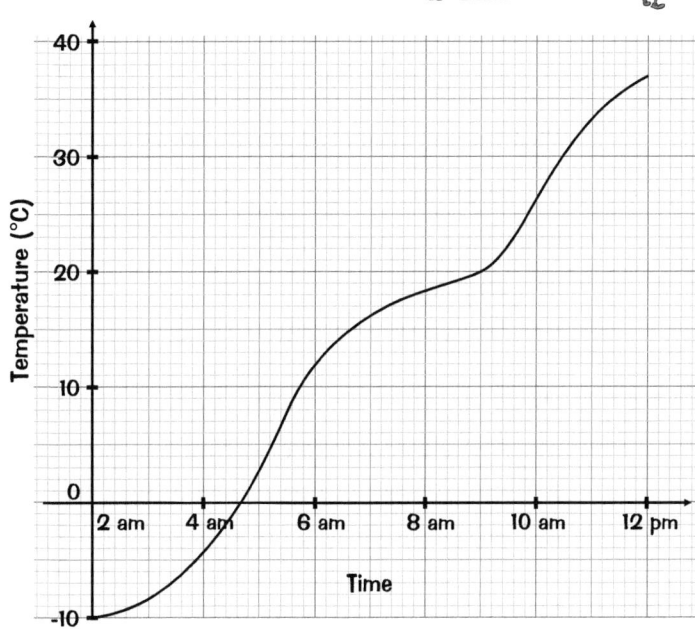

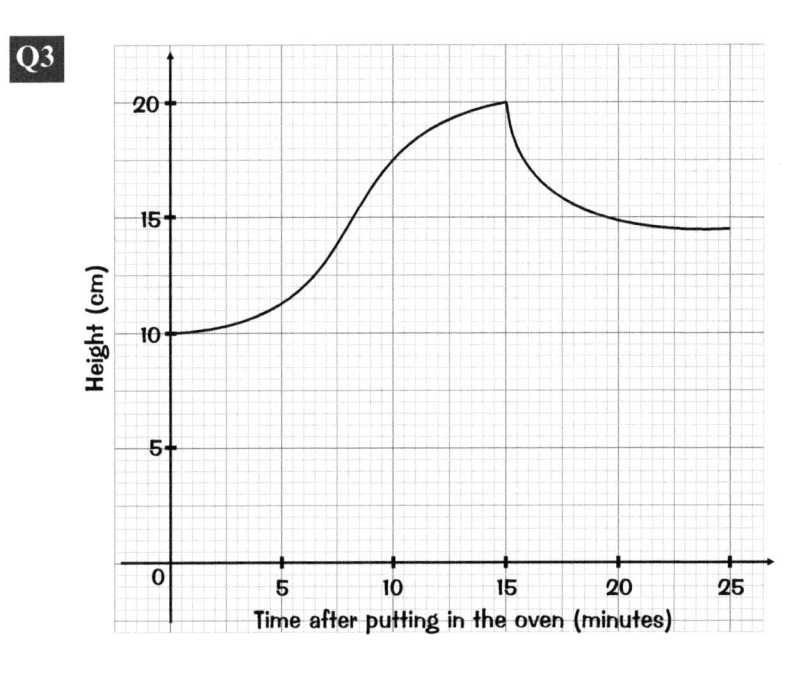

Q3 Bilal is making a soufflé. He bakes it in the oven for 15 minutes and then takes it out and lets it cool for 10 minutes. The graph shows how the height of the soufflé changes during this time.

a) Find an estimate for the soufflé's greatest rate of growth during its time in the oven. Give your answer to 1 decimal place.
b) What was the average rate of change in the height of the soufflé during the first 3 minutes it was out of the oven?

Section Three — Graphs

Section Three — Mixed Questions

Mixed Questions

Right — it's time to mix things up a bit. These pages have got questions on every topic in this section, so by the time you're done with them you can be graph-solutely sure you know your stuff.

Q1 Calculate the gradient of the line which goes through the points:
- a) (7, 2) and (2, 12)
- b) (–6, 2) and (–2, 1)
- c) (3, 7) and (–7, 2)
- d) (2, –10) and (6, –4)
- e) (7, 5) and (6, 1)
- f) (3, 7) and (9, –3)

Q2
- a) Find the equation of the straight line which passes through:
  - i) (6, 8) and (–5, a) and has a gradient of 2
  - ii) (4, –7) and (6, b) and has a gradient of $\frac{1}{2}$
  - iii) (1, 5) and (c, 3) and has a gradient of –1
  - iv) (9, 2) and (d, –2) and has a gradient of $-\frac{1}{3}$
- b) Find the value of the letters a-d for each of the lines in part a).

Q3 Complete this table of values for $y = \frac{5}{4}x - \frac{1}{4}$:

Plot these points on graph paper and draw the graph of $y = \frac{5}{4}x - \frac{1}{4}$ for $-9 \leq x \leq 9$.

x	-3	1	5
y			

Use your graph to find:
- a) The value of y when $x = -5$
- b) The value of y when $x = 3$
- c) The value of x when $y = -9$
- d) The value of x when $y = 11$

Q4 Work out the coordinates of the midpoint of the line segment:
- a) AB where A has coordinates (8, 4) and B has coordinates (4, 0).
- b) MN where M has coordinates (3, 9) and N has coordinates (–5, –1).
- c) PQ where P has coordinates (2, –1) and Q has coordinates (–3, 1).

Q5 Hiroto draws four straight lines on a graph. Line A has the equation $y = 2x + 5$, line B has the equation $3x - y = 6$ and line C has the equation $2y - 6x + 15 = 0$.
- a) Which two of these three lines are parallel?
- b) Line D is perpendicular to line A and goes through the point (2, –11). Write an equation for line D in the form $y = mx + c$.

Q6 Complete this table of values for the graph $y = -x^2 + 3x + 4$.

- a) Draw the graph of $y = -x^2 + 3x + 4$ for x from –2 to 6.
- b) Find the coordinates of the turning point.

x	-2	-1	0	1	2	3	4	5	6
$-x^2$		-1			-4		-16		-36
$3x$	-6			3		9		15	
$y = -x^2 + 3x + 4$			0		6			-6	

- c) Is this turning point a maximum or a minimum? Explain how you could know this without calculating any values or plotting the graph of $y = -x^2 + 3x + 4$.

Q7 A circle has its centre at (0, 0). The point (5, –12) lies on the circle. Find the radius and equation of the circle.

Mixed Questions

Q8 Sketch the graph of $y = 2^{-x}$. Mark on any points where the graph crosses the axes.

Q9 Complete this table of values for $y = (\sin x) - 1$.

x	–180°	–90°	0°	90°	180°
y		–1			

Q10 Solve the following simultaneous equations by drawing graphs. Use the values $0 \leqslant x \leqslant 6$.
a) $y = x + 1$
   $y + 1 = 2x$
b) $2y = x - 1$
   $4y = x + 2$
c) $y - x = 1$
   $3y = 6x + 1$

Q11 This is a graph of $y = x^3 + 2x^2$. Use the graph to sketch:
a) $y = x^3 + 2x^2 - 1$
b) $y = (x + 1)^3 + 2(x + 1)^2$
c) $y = (-x)^3 + 2(-x)^2$
d) $y = -(x^3 + 2x^2)$
e) $y = (x - 1)^3 + 2(x - 1)^2 + 1$

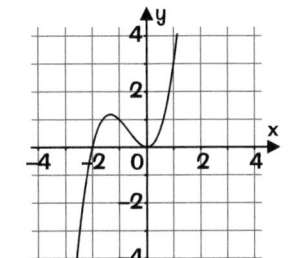

Q12 Zoltan cycles to work every day. The graph shows his journeys on Tuesday and Wednesday last week.
a) Zoltan left the house at the same time each day. How much earlier did he arrive on Tuesday?
b) What speed was Zoltan going at before he first stopped on Wednesday? Give your answer in metres per second.
c) The route Zoltan took on Tuesday went over a hill. How far had Zoltan travelled when he reached the top of the hill? Explain how you know.

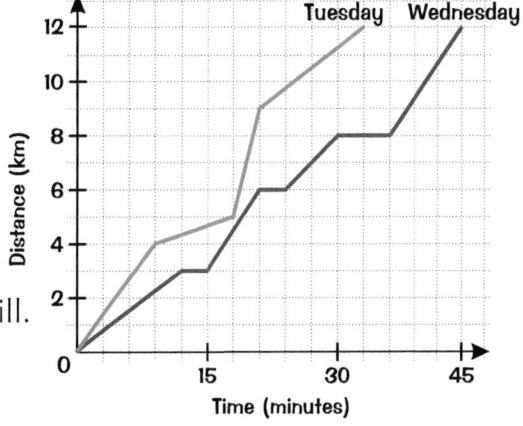

Q13 Marianne uses a GPS device to record the speed of a remote control car on a race track. Her results are shown on this speed-time graph.
a) After how many seconds did the car first reach its maximum speed?
b) How fast was the car going when it started travelling at a constant speed?
c) What was the rate of acceleration of the car before it reached a constant speed?
d) Calculate the total distance travelled by the car on the race track.

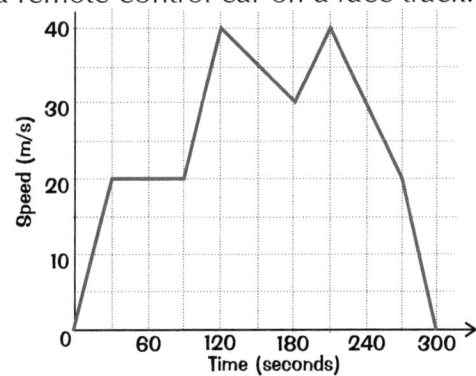

Q14 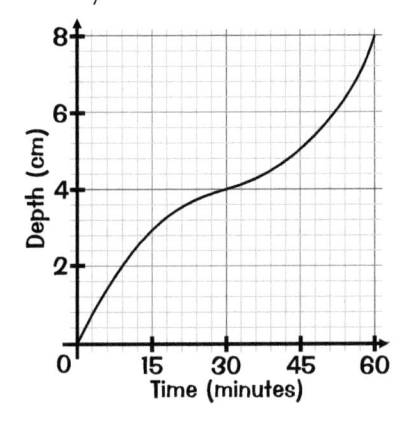 The graph shows the depth of sand in the bottom bulb of an hourglass as it fills up over the course of an hour.
a) The rate of change in depth is faster where the bulb is narrower and slower where the bulb is wider. How far above the base of the bulb is its widest point?
b) Estimate the rate of change in depth, in cm per minute, after 15 minutes.

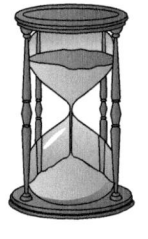

Section Three — Mixed Questions

Ratios

I don't want to spoil the surprise, but you're going to need your calculator for this bit — get your finger on that fraction button...

Q1 For each of the following ratios, complete the statements that describe them by filling each gap with a fraction:

a) Cats and dogs in the ratio 2 : 5.
  i) There are ...... as many cats as dogs.
  ii) There are ...... times as many dogs as cats.

b) Sprouts and peas in the ratio 3 : 4.
  i) There are ...... as many sprouts as peas.
  ii) There are ...... times as many peas as sprouts.

Q2 Write these ratios in their simplest forms:
a) 6 : 8
b) 5 : 20
c) 1.5 : 3
d) 2¼ : 4
e) 2 weeks : 4 days
f) £1.26 : 14p
g) 3 km : 100 m
h) 2.4 : 1.5
i) 27 mm : 8.1 cm

Q3 A rectangle has sides in the ratio 1 : 2. Calculate the length of the longer side if the shorter side is:
a) 3 cm   b) 5.5 cm   c) 15.2 m

Calculate the length of the shorter side if the longer side is:
d) 3 cm   e) 5.5 cm   f) 15.2 m

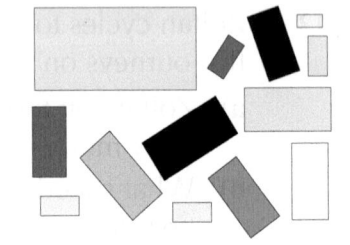

Q4 Divide the following amounts in the ratios given:
a) £20 in the ratio 2 : 3
b) 150 m in the ratio 8 : 7
c) 500 g in the ratio 1 : 2 : 2
d) 8 hrs in the ratio 1 : 2 : 3

For these you add up the ratio numbers to find the total number of parts and divide by this. Then multiply by each number in the ratio separately to find the different amounts.

Q5 Ayomide and Peter share a bar of chocolate marked into 16 squares. They share it in the ratio 1 : 3 respectively. How many squares does each boy get?

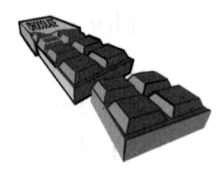

Q6 A 2 litre bottle of cola is to be shared between three girls in the ratio 2 : 3 : 5. How many <u>millilitres</u> will each girl get?

Watch out for your units — you'll have to change them over for this one — and your answer should be in <u>millilitres</u>.

Q7 Oak and ash saplings are planted along a roadside in the ratio 2 : 3 respectively. If there are 20 oak saplings, how many ash saplings are there?

Q8 Tony gives £100 to be shared by Jane, Holly and Rosemary in a ratio according to their age. Jane is 10, Holly is 12 and Rosemary is 3 years old. How much will each child get?

Q9 Sunil and Paul work in a restaurant. As they work different hours, they split their tips in the ratio 3 : 4. One night they got £28 in tips between them. How much did each person get?

Ratios

Q10 A recipe for flapjacks is 250 g of oats, 150 g of brown sugar and 100 g of margarine. What <u>fraction of the mixture</u> is:
  a) oats?
  b) sugar?

Q11 The ratio of girls to boys in a school is 7:6.
If there are 455 pupils in total, how many are
  a) girls?
  b) boys?

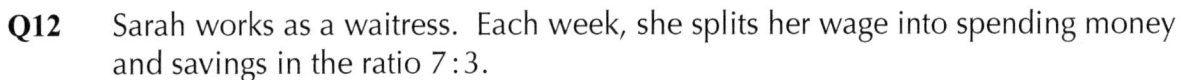

Q12 Sarah works as a waitress. Each week, she splits her wage into spending money and savings in the ratio 7:3.
  a) One week, Sarah earns £130. How much should she put in her savings that week?
  b) The next week, Sarah put £42 into her savings. How much did she earn in total that week?

Q13 An architect is drawing the plan of a house to a scale of 1 cm to 3 m.
  a) Write this ratio in its simplest form.
  b) How wide is a room that appears as 2 cm on the drawing?
  c) The hall is 10 m long. How long will the architect need to make it on the drawing? Give your answer to the nearest 0.1 cm.

Make sure you convert to the same units when you're working out the ratio.

Q14 Concrete is mixed using cement, sand and gravel in the ratio 1:3:6. 
  a) If Dave uses a 5 kg bag of cement, how much:
    i) sand does he need?
    ii) gravel does he need?
  b) If Dave needs 80 kg of concrete, how much of each substance does he need?

Q15 I picked some strawberries after a few wet days. Some were nibbled by snails, some were mouldy and some fine. The ratio was 2:3:10 respectively.
  a) If <u>9 strawberries were mouldy</u> how many:
    i) were fine?
    ii) were not fine?
  b) What fraction of the total amount were fine?

Q16 Salt & Vinegar, Cheese & Onion and Prawn Cocktail flavour snacks were sold in the school tuck shop in <u>the ratio 5:3:2</u>. If 18 bags of Prawn Cocktail were sold, how many bags: 
  a) of Salt & Vinegar were sold?
  b) were sold altogether?

Section Four — Ratio, Proportion and Rates of Change

Ratios

Q17 Reduce each of the following ratios to the form 1 : n.
    a) 2 : 18   **b)** 8 : 5   **c)** 3 : 26   **d)** 12 : 25

Q18 Salim has red and green pens in his stationery cupboard.
The ratio of green pens to the total number of pens is 3 : 11.
What is the ratio of green pens to red pens?

Q19 In a box of chocolates there are 36 strawberry-flavoured chocolates, and the ratio of orange chocolates to strawberry chocolates is 5 : 6. If someone eats 6 of the orange chocolates, what is the new ratio of orange to strawberry chocolates?

Q20 Luiza and Tobiah count the money they each have in their pocket.
Luiza has £17.50, and the ratio of Luiza's money to Tobiah's money is 5 : 4.
Luiza gives £4 to Tobiah. What is the new ratio between their amounts?

Q21 The ratio of fiction to non-fiction books in a library is 7 : 3.
60% of the fiction books are hardback, and 20% of the non-fiction books are hardback.
What percentage of all the books in the library are hardback?

You'll need to set up simultaneous equations for the next three questions.
If you need some more practice at simultaneous equations, see page 41.

Q22 A jacket costs £a and a pair of gloves costs £b.
One day, the price of the jacket goes up by £1 and the price of the gloves goes down by £8. The ratio of the jacket's price to the gloves' price is then 4 : 1. The next day, the price of the jacket goes up again by £4, and the price of the gloves drops by a further £2. The ratio of their prices becomes 10 : 1. How much did the jacket and gloves cost originally?

Q23 Jack's hat collection contains striped hats and spotted hats.
The ratio of spotted hats to the total number of hats is 2 : 7.
    a) Jack picks a hat to wear at random. What is the probability it will be a striped hat?
    b) What is the ratio of spotted hats to striped hats?
    c) Jack throws away 5 striped hats. The ratio of spotted to striped hats is now 1 : 2. How many spotted hats does Jack have?

Q24 Nadia's fruit bowl contains only apples and bananas. If Nadia randomly selects a piece of fruit from the bowl, the probability it will be a banana is $\frac{2}{5}$. However, before she chooses a piece of fruit, Nadia throws away 3 bananas. The probability of her choosing a banana is now $\frac{1}{4}$. How many apples and bananas were originally in the bowl?

Section Four — Ratio, Proportion and Rates of Change

Direct and Inverse Proportion

Remember, for direct proportion, divide for one, then times for all.
And for inverse proportion, times for one, then divide for all.

Chocolate cake
(serves 6)
180 g   flour
240 g   sugar
210 g   butter
3   eggs
60 g   cocoa powder

Q1 Isla is making a chocolate cake using the recipe shown on the right. She wants to make the cake for 10 people.
  a) How much sugar will she need?
  b) How much flour will she need?
  c) Isla only has 320 g of butter. Will this be enough for her cake?

Q2 £12 is worth 33.96 Pentagonia dollars. How much is £19 worth in Pentagonia dollars?

Q3 A recipe for a pasta sauce contains tomatoes and peppers in the ratio 5 : 2. Sketch a graph showing the number of tomatoes against the number of peppers in the sauce. Mark two points on the line.

Q4 Angela pays £408 for 3 months' worth of school dinners for her 4 children. What would the cost of 5 months' worth of school dinners be for 3 children?

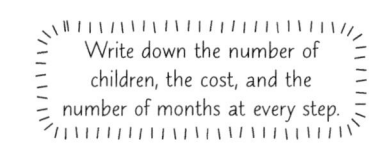

Write down the number of children, the cost, and the number of months at every step.

Q5 30 bags of popcorn costs £8.40. 175 g of popcorn costs £1.96 when bought in these bags. How much does one bag of popcorn weigh?

Q6 It takes 2 people 2 hours to wrap 60 presents. Working at the same rate, how long (in hours and minutes) would it take:
  a) 1 person to wrap 60 presents?
  b) 1 person to wrap 93 presents?
  c) 3 people to wrap 93 presents?

Q7 2 postal workers can deliver letters to 282 houses in 3 hours.
  a) Assuming that each worker has the same delivery rate, how many postal workers would be needed to deliver letters to 376 houses in 2 hours?
  b) If some postal workers had a slower delivery rate, how might your answer to part a) change?

Q8 Working together, Michael and Omolara can paint 12 bikes in 18 hours. Working at the same rate, how many bikes could they paint if:
  a) they worked for 45 hours?
  b) two of their friends helped them and they worked for 24 hours?

Section Four — Ratio, Proportion and Rates of Change

Direct and Inverse Proportion

Q9 y is directly proportional to x. If $y = 5$ when x is 25:
    a) Find an equation for y in terms of x.
    b) Use your equation from part **a)** to find y when x is 100.

Q10 $y \propto x$ and $y = 132$ when $x = 10$.
    a) Find the value of y when $x = 14$.
    b) Sketch the graph of this proportion for $x > 0$ and mark two points on the line.

Q11 $y = 3$ when $x = 8$ and y is inversely proportional to x.
    a) Find an equation for y in terms of x.
    b) Use your equation from part **a)** to find the value of y when $x = 12$.

Q12 $y \propto \dfrac{1}{x}$ and $x = 4$ when $y = 5$.
    a) Find the value of x when $y = 10$.
    b) Sketch the graph of this proportion for positive x, marking two points on the graph.

Q13 Given that $y \propto \dfrac{1}{x}$, complete this table of values.

x	1	2	3	4	5	6
y					9.6	

Put the numbers into the equation $y = k/x$ to find the value of k. Then you can find the rest of the y's.

Q14 In each of the following tables, y varies inversely as the square of x.
Complete each table, given that x is always positive.

a)

x	1	2	5
y		4	1

b)

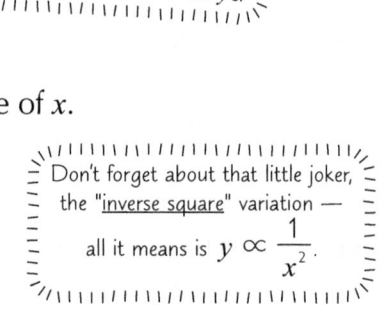

x	2		8
y	24	6	2⅔

Don't forget about that little joker, the "inverse square" variation — all it means is $y \propto \dfrac{1}{x^2}$.

Q15 Two cylindrical containers are filled to the same depth with water. The first container has a radius of 16 cm and the water in it has a mass of 16 kg. If the second container has a radius of 8 cm, find the mass of the water inside it.

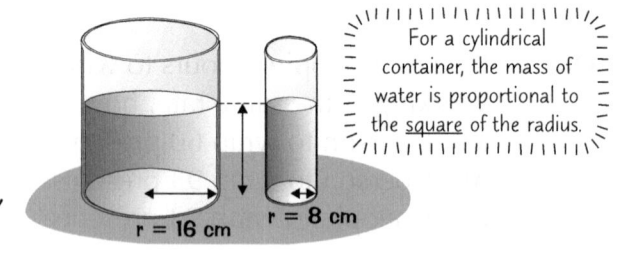

For a cylindrical container, the mass of water is proportional to the square of the radius.

r = 16 cm   r = 8 cm

Q16 Given that r is inversely proportional to s cubed, and $r = 2.4$ when $s = 10$, find the values of:
    a) r when $s = 5$
    b) s when $r = 300$
    c) r when $s = -4$
    d) s when $r = -0.3$

Q17 The gravitational pull of the Earth is inversely proportional to the square of the distance from the centre of the Earth. At the Earth's surface (approx. 6371 km from the centre) the gravitational pull is around 9.8 N/kg. When launching a satellite into space, the gravitational pull helps determine the orbit. What would be the gravitational pull on a satellite at a height of 100 km above the Earth's surface (to 1 d.p)?

Section Four — Ratio, Proportion and Rates of Change

Percentages

Finding "something %" of "something-else" is really quite simple — so you'd better be sure you know how. You also need to be able to give "something" as a percentage of "something else". Try this mix for size...

Q1 Find:

    a) 8% of £16   **b)** 85% of 740 kg   **c)** 40% of 40 minutes

Q2 87 out of 120 pupils at Backwater School have access to a computer. What percentage is this?

Q3 Donald works in South Mathrica, where the currency is the Mathrican pound (£).
He earns an annual wage of £23 500.
He doesn't pay tax on the first £6400 that he earns.
How much income tax does he pay a year if the rate of tax is:
    a) 25%   **b)** 40%?

Q4 There are approximately 6000 fish and chip shops in the UK. On average, a fish and chip shop gets about 160 visitors each day. Given that the population of the UK is roughly 60 million, approximately what percentage of the population visit a fish and chip shop each day?

Q5 At birth, Jeong-Suk was 0.3 m tall. By adulthood she had grown to 1.5 m tall. Calculate her height now as a percentage of her height at birth.

Q6 Amy has 20 pets. 60% of them are dogs and 3 of the dogs have black fur.
Without using a calculator, work out the percentage of Amy's dogs that have black fur.

Q7 At a film festival there are 40 movie stars. Daniel meets 85% of the movie stars, as well as 16 other people. What percentage of the people that Daniel met were <u>not</u> movie stars?

These questions are simple too — you just need to "find the new amount after a % increase or decrease". Once you've worked out the multiplier for the percentage change, just multiply the original value by it and there's your answer.

Q8 John bought a new TV. The tag in the shop said it cost £299 + VAT.
If VAT is charged at 20%, how much did he pay?

Q9 Four friends stay at the Pickled Parrot Hotel for a night and each have an evening meal. Bed and Breakfast costs £37 per person and the evening meal costs £15 per person. How much is the total cost, if a service charge is added at 17½%?

Q10 The owners of a museum are expecting a 14% increase in visitors next year.
This year they had 20 400 visitors.
How many visitors should they expect next year?
Give your answer to 3 significant figures.

Section Four — Ratio, Proportion and Rates of Change

Percentages

Q11 Tim is choosing between two cars to buy.
The first car is priced at £8495 and has 15% off.
The second car is priced at £8195 and has 12% off.
Which car is the cheapest? Show your working.

Q12 Tanya paid £6500 for her new car. Each year its value decreased by 8%.
How much was it worth when it was one year old?

Q13 Akpan wanted a new coffee table for his lounge. A local furniture shop had just what he was looking for — and for only £130.00 + delivery. Akpan had £150 in his bank account. If delivery was charged at 17½%, could Akpan afford the table?

Q14 I wish to invest £5000 for three years and have decided to place my money with the Highrise Building Society. The Silver Account pays 1.895% simple interest per annum. The Gold Account pays 2.3% simple interest per annum on the first £4000, but no interest on any additional money invested in the account.

If I want to invest the entire £5000 into just one account, how much interest would I earn if I choose:
  a) the Silver account?
  b) the Gold account?

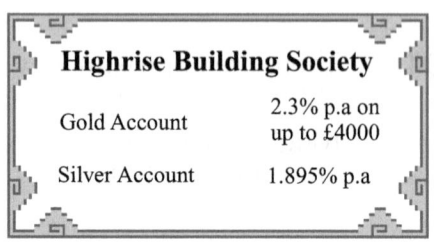

Highrise Building Society
Gold Account — 2.3% p.a on up to £4000
Silver Account — 1.895% p.a

Finding the percentage change is a bit trickier... but you'll be sure to get these questions right if you find the difference in values first, then use the formula:

$$\text{Percentage 'change'} = \frac{\text{'change'}}{\text{original}} \times 100$$

Q15 During a rainstorm, a water butt increased in weight from 10.4 kg to 13.6 kg.
What was the percentage increase (to the nearest percent)?

Q16 An electrical store reduces the price of a particular camera from £90.00 to £78.30.
What is the percentage reduction?

Q17 Desmond's GCSE maths exam is next week. As part of his revision he attempted 31 questions on his least favourite topic of percentages. He got 21 questions fully right on the first attempt. Two days later he tried all 31 questions again and this time got 29 correct.
  a) What percentage of questions did he get correct on his first attempt?
  b) What percentage of questions did he get correct on his second attempt?
  c) What is the percentage improvement in Desmond's results?

Q18 Emma makes wooden furniture. It costs her £10 for the materials to make one chair and £7 a day to rent the workshop where she makes the chairs.

If Emma makes 4 chairs in 5 days and sells them for £120 in total, what is her percentage profit?

Section Four — Ratio, Proportion and Rates of Change

Percentages

Q19 Rob withdraws £340 from his bank account to pay for a telescope, making his account £242 in debit. He then sells the telescope and deposits his takings back into his account, after which it is £176.20 in credit.

If there were no other transactions on Rob's account between him buying and selling the telescope, what was Rob's percentage profit on the telescope?

Finding the <u>original value</u> always looks a bit confusing at first. The bit most people get wrong is deciding whether the value given represents <u>more</u> or <u>less than 100%</u> of the original — so <u>always</u> check your answer <u>makes sense</u>.

Q20 In the new year sales Robin bought a tennis racket for £68.00. The original price had been reduced by 15%. What was the original price?

Q21 There are 360 people living in a village.
The population of the village has grown by 20% over the past year.
a) How many people lived in the village one year ago?
b) If the village continues to grow at the same rate, how many whole years from today will it be before the population is more than twice its current size?

Q22 A shop sells pairs of socks for £3.70 and makes a 48% profit.
a) What is the cost price of a pair of socks?
b) The shop has a sale and makes a 36% loss on the socks. What is the price of the socks during the sale?

Some percentage questions can be a bit weird and wonderful, so you'll need to get your thinking cap on. But don't panic — as long as you remember all your percentage skills, you'll be fine.

Q23 In Sushila's kitchen cupboard, the ratio of drinks to other items in the cupboard is 3:5. $\frac{2}{5}$ of the drinks are bottles of orange squash. **Without using a calculator**, calculate the percentage of items in the cupboard that are bottles of orange squash.

Q24 If $L = MN$, what is the percentage increase in L if M increases by 15% and N increases by 20%?

Q25 The two shorter sides of a right-angled triangle have lengths a and b. a is increased by 33% and b is decreased by 12%. What is the percentage change in the area of the triangle?

Q26 At a running club, 30% of the members are male. 60% of the male members and 50% of the female members are training to run a marathon. **Without using a calculator**, work out what percentage of the members are training for a marathon.

Section Four — Ratio, Proportion and Rates of Change

Compound Growth and Decay

This topic might sound daunting, but it all boils down to the formula, so make sure you get it learnt: $N = N_0 \times$ (percentage change multiplier)^n. N is just the final amount, N_0 is the initial amount, and n is the period of time.

Q1 A financial advisor is asked to predict the future value of his clients' investments. Calculate the amount in each of these accounts if:
  a) £200 is invested for 10 years at 9% compound interest per annum
  b) £500 is invested for 3 years at 7% compound interest per annum
  c) £750 is invested for 30 months at 8% compound interest per annum
  d) £1000 is invested for 15 months at 6.5% compound interest per annum.

Q2 A scientist is investigating a new strain of harmful bacteria. She needs to grow at least 4000 to have a big enough sample to run tests in the lab. The bacteria grows at the compound rate of 12% per hour, and she starts with 200 bacteria in the sample.
  a) How many will there be after 3 hours?
  b) How many will there be after 1 day?
  c) After how many whole hours will there be at least 4000 bacteria?
  (Solve this by trial and error.)

Just make sure you get the <u>increase</u> and <u>decrease</u> the right way round... basically, just check your answer sounds like you'd expect — and if it doesn't, <u>do it again</u>.

Q3 An unknown radioactive element was discovered at the site of a suspected UFO crash. It was observed every day and the mass remaining was measured.
Initially there was 9 kg, but this decreased at the compound rate of 3% per day. How much radioactive element was left after:
  a) 3 days
  b) 6 days
  c) 1 week
  d) 4 weeks?
Give your answers to 3 d.p.

Q4 Money is invested on the stock market. During a recession the value of the shares falls by 2% per week. Find the value of the stock if:
  a) £2000 was invested for a fortnight
  b) £30 000 was invested for four weeks
  c) £500 was invested for 7 weeks
  d) £100 000 was invested for a year.

Q5 Mrs Smith decides to invest £7000 in a savings account. She has the choice of putting all her money into an account paying 5% compound interest per annum or she can put half of her investment into an account paying 6% compound interest per annum and the remaining half into an account paying 4% per annum.
If she left the investment alone for 3 years, which is her best option and by how much?

I'd put my money in Victorian rolling pins, myself...

Section Four — Ratio, Proportion and Rates of Change

Compound Growth and Decay

"Appreciate" and "depreciate" just mean "increase in value" and "decrease in value" — nothing more complicated than that.

Q6 A small clothing company is about to go bust as business has been slow.
When the owner started up four years ago she bought machinery costing £3500.
The depreciation on this machinery is typically 2½% per year.
How much money could the owner raise by selling this machinery now, second-hand?
Give your answer to the nearest £100.

Q7 The activity of a radio-isotope decreases at a compound rate of 9% every hour.
If the initial activity is recorded at 1100 counts per minute, what will it be after:
a) 2 hours
b) 4 hours
c) 1 day?
d) The activity of the same radio-isotope is recorded at just 66 counts per minute. Using trial and error, estimate the length of time elapsed since the recording of 1100 counts per minute.

Q8 A used car salesman is buying stock at an auction. Before the auction, he estimates the value of each car on offer using their original price, their age, and a depreciation of 14% each year. This value is the maximum amount he will bid for each car.
Calculate the maximum amount he should bid on these used cars:
a) a car which cost £13 495 two years ago
b) a car which cost £8495 six months ago
c) a car which cost £34 000 eighteen months ago

Q9 A culture of bacteria increases in number at a compound rate of 0.4% per hour.
If initially there was a culture of 5000 cells, how many cells will there be after:
a) 3 hours?
b) 8 hours 30 minutes?
c) 135 mins?
d) 2 days?

Q10 Property prices in Angletown increase at a rate of 20% per annum.
At the start 2015, the price of a house was £172 800.
a) What was the price of the house at the start of 2012?
b) Show that the price of the house at the start of each year forms a geometric progression.

Q11 An antique vase is worth £463 today. Its value has appreciated by 16% per year since its owner bought it 5 years ago. How much was it worth when it was bought?

Q12 The population of a country is 16 million, and the annual compound growth rate is estimated to be 1.3%. Predict the country's population:
a) in 4 years' time
b) in 20 years' time
c) 6 years ago.

Section Four — Ratio, Proportion and Rates of Change

Unit Conversions

You'll need to know the metric conversions for the exam, so get learning them. You don't need to memorise the conversions involving imperial units though — you'll be given the ones you need in the exam.

METRIC		IMPERIAL	METRIC-IMPERIAL
1 cm = 10 mm	1 tonne = 1000 kg	1 Yard = 3 feet	1 kg ≈ 2.2 pounds
1 m = 100 cm	1 litre = 1000 ml	1 Foot = 12 Inches	1 foot ≈ 30 cm
1 km = 1000 m	1 litre = 1000 cm³	1 Gallon = 8 Pints	1 gallon ≈ 4.5 litres
1 kg = 1000 g	1 cm³ = 1 ml	1 Stone = 14 Pounds	1 mile ≈ 1.6 km
		1 Pound = 16 Ounces	

Q1 Jeremy used a website to calculate his car's efficiency. He needed to enter the engine capacity in cubic centimetres, but only knew that it was 1.4 litres. What capacity should he have entered into the website?

'Ounces' is written as 'oz' and 'pounds' is written as 'lbs'.

Q2 Express the given quantity in the unit(s) in brackets:
   a) 3.3 cm [mm]
   b) 60 g [kg]
   c) 4 ft [in]
   d) 36 in [ft]
   e) 87 in [ft and in]
   f) 43 oz [lb and oz]
   g) 7 g [kg]
   h) 950 g [kg]
   i) 6 ft [in]
   j) 5 lb [oz]
   k) 301 ft [yd and ft]
   l) 0.6 mm [m]

Q3 Convert 147 kg into pounds.

Q4 A horse's drinking trough holds 14 gallons of water. Approximately how many litres is this?

Q5 Deborah is filling in a health questionnaire. She needs to write down her weight in kilograms. She weighs 9 stone 4 pounds. How much does Deborah weigh in kilograms?

Q6 Barbara cycled 51 km in one day while Rasima cycled 30 miles. Who cycled further?

Q7 A seamstress needs to cut an 18 inch strip of finest Chinese silk.
   a) Approximately how many cm is this?
   b) Approximately how many mm is this?

Q8 The priceless Greek statue in my garden is 21 feet tall.
   a) How many inches is this?
   b) How many yards is this?
   c) How many cm is this?
   d) How many km is this?

Q9 At the gym Arnold can lift a barbell weighing 60 kg.
   a) Approximately how many lbs is this?
   b) How many ounces is this?

   Sylvester can lift a barbell weighing 10 stone.
   c) Who can lift the most?

Section Four — Ratio, Proportion and Rates of Change

Unit Conversions

Q10 Dick is making The World's Wobbliest Jelly. The recipe requires 5 lb of sugar. How many 1 kg bags of sugar does Dick need to buy so that he can make the jelly?

Q11 This graph can be used to convert between pounds and euros.

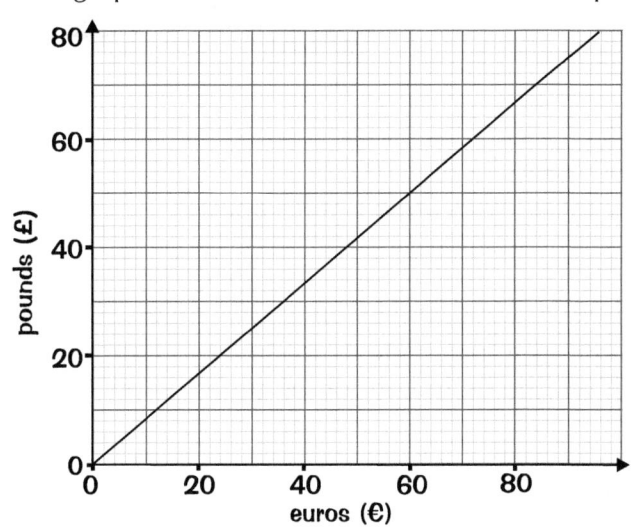

a) How many pounds are equal to €62?

b) Tim has £35. He wants to buy a computer game which costs €40. Does he have enough money to buy the game?

c) Sarah buys some steak that costs €15 per kg. How much will it cost in £ per lb?

Q12 The speed limit on a road is 40 miles per hour.
a) What is the speed limit in km/h?
b) A car is travelling along the road at 18.8 m/s. How much over or under the speed limit is this car?
c) A car is travelling along the road at 1750 cm/s. How much over or under the speed limit is this car?

Q13 Convert these area measurements:
a) 900 mm² to cm²
b) 15 m² to mm²
c) 4 m² to cm²
d) 500 cm² to m²
e) 38 cm² to mm²
f) 860 000 mm² to m²

Q14 A swimming pool has a volume of 2500 m³.
a) Convert this volume to cm³.
b) Convert this volume to mm³.

Q15 A scientist measures the volume of a gorilla's skull to be 549 cm³. She estimates that the gorilla's brain had a volume of 682 000 mm³. Can she be correct?

Q16 A brick has volume 840 cm³ and mass 2058 g. Find the density of the brick in kg/m³.

Q17 Matt is taking part in a 10 mile race. Along the race route, there are water stops at 1 km intervals and at the finish line. Matt drinks 135 ml of water at every water stop.

The organisers of the race paid 95 pence per gallon of water. How much did it cost for the water that Matt drank (to the nearest penny)?

Section Four — Ratio, Proportion and Rates of Change

Speed, Density and Pressure

Speed, density and pressure — just learn the formulas and keep an eye on the units and everything'll be fine and dandy.

Q1 An athlete can run 100 m in 11 seconds.
Calculate the athlete's speed in:
a) m/s
b) km/h.

Q2 A plane flies over city A at 09.55 and over city B at 10.02.
What is its average speed (in mph) if these cities are 63 miles apart?

Q3 The distance from Kendal (Oxenholme) to London (Euston) is 260 miles. The train travels at an average speed of 71 mph (including stops). Pete needs to be in London by 10.30. If he catches the 07.05 from Kendal, will he be in London on time? Show your working.

Q4 In a speed trial a sand yacht travelled a measured mile in 36.4 seconds.
a) Calculate this speed in mph.
b) On the return mile he took 36.16 seconds.
Calculate the average speed over the two runs in mph.

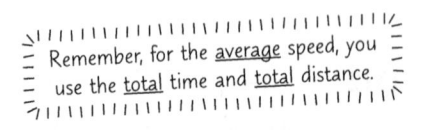

Remember, for the average speed, you use the total time and total distance.

Q5 A motorist drives from Manchester to London. 180 miles is on motorway where she averages 65 mph. 55 miles is on city roads where she averages 28 mph and 15 miles is on country roads where she averages 25 mph.
a) Calculate the total time taken for the journey.
b) Calculate the average speed for the journey.

Q6 Mohammed walks at an average speed of 4 km/h. He needs to walk to Askam-in-Furness, 3 km away. He needs to be there at 3.00pm. What time should he set off?

Q7 The distance between two railway stations is 145 km.
a) How long does a train travelling at 65 km/h on average take to travel this distance?
b) Another train travels at an average speed of 80 km/h, not including a 10 minute stop during the journey. How long does this second train take?
c) If both arrive at 1600, what time did each leave?

Q8 Two athletes run a road race. One ran at an average speed of 16 km/h, the other at 4 m/s. Which was the fastest? How long would each take to run 10 km?

Q9 A plane leaves Amsterdam at 0715 and flies at an average speed of 650 km/h to Paris, arriving at 0800. It takes off again at 0840 and flies at the same average speed to Nice arriving at 1005.
a) How far is it from Amsterdam to Paris?
b) How far is it from Paris to Nice?
c) What was the average speed for the whole journey, including the stop at Paris?

Section Four — Ratio, Proportion and Rates of Change

Speed, Density and Pressure

Q10 A runner covered the first 100 m of a 200 m race in 12.3 seconds.
  a) What was his average speed for the first 100 m?
  b) The second 100 m took 15.1 seconds. What was his average speed for the 200 m?

Q11 A military plane can achieve a speed of 1100 km/h. At this speed it passes over town A at 1205 and town B at 1217.
  a) How far apart are towns A and B?
  b) The plane then flies over village C which is 93 km from B. To the nearest minute, how long does it take from B to C?

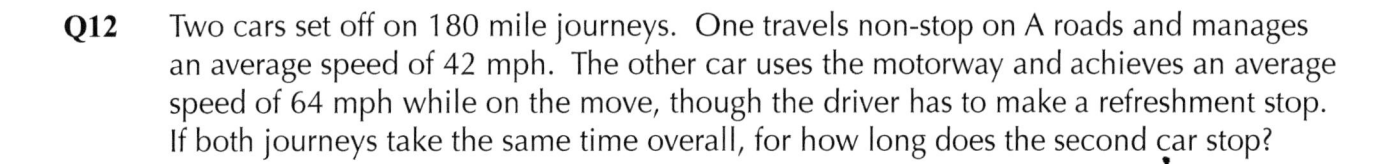

Q12 Two cars set off on 180 mile journeys. One travels non-stop on A roads and manages an average speed of 42 mph. The other car uses the motorway and achieves an average speed of 64 mph while on the move, though the driver has to make a refreshment stop. If both journeys take the same time overall, for how long does the second car stop?

Q13 A stone is dropped from a cliff top. After 1 second it has fallen 4.9 m, after 2 seconds a total of 19.6 m and after 3 seconds a total of 44.1 m. Calculate its average speed:
  a) in the first second;
  b) in the third second;
  c) for all 3 seconds.
  d) Change all the m/s speeds to km/h.

Q14 Three racing cars have top speeds of 236.6, 233.8 and 227.3 km/h. How many seconds (to the nearest 0.1 s) would each take to cover 5 miles at these speeds? (Use 1 km = 0.621 miles.)

Q15 Find the density of each of these pieces of wood, giving your answer in g/cm^3:
  a) Mass 3 g, volume 4 cm^3
  b) Mass 12 kg, volume 20,000 cm^3
  c) Mass 20 g, volume 25 cm^3
  d) Mass 14 kg, volume 0.02 m^3.

Q16 Calculate the mass of each of these objects:
  a) a small marble statue of density 2.6 g/cm^3 and volume 24 cm^3
  b) a plastic cube of volume 64 cm^3 and density 1.5 g/cm^3
  c) a gold ingot measuring 12 cm by 4 cm by 4 cm with density 19.5 g/cm^3
  d) a pebble with volume 30 cm^3 and density 2.5 g/cm^3.

Q17 Work out the volume of each of these items:
  a) a bag of sugar of mass 1 kg and density 0.85 g/cm^3
  b) a packet of margarine with density 0.9 g/cm^3 and mass 250 g
  c) a box of cereal with density 0.2 g/cm^3 and mass 500 g.
  d) a 50 kg sack of coal with density 1.1 g/cm^3

Speed, Density and Pressure

Q18 My copper bracelet has a volume of 3.9 cm³. The density of copper is 8.9 g/cm³. Work out the mass of my bracelet.

Q19 Ice has a density of 0.93 g/cm³. If the mass of a block of ice is 19.5 kg, what is its volume?

Q20 Some petrol in a can has a mass of 4 kg. The density of the petrol is 0.8 g/cm³. How many litres of petrol are in the can?

Q21 A jug holds 1.9 litres of lemonade. The mass of the lemonade is 2 kg. Find the density of the lemonade in g/cm³.

Q22 A 1.5 kg box full of self raising flour measures 12 cm by 18 cm by 6 cm.
A 1 kg box of granary flour measures 10 cm by 14 cm by 6 cm.
 a) Find the density of each sort of flour in g/cm³.
 b) Jake needs to measure out 450 g of granary flour but his scales are broken. Use your answer to part **a)** to work out how much flour he should measure out in his measuring jug. Give your answer in ml.

Q23 A solid piece of aluminium cut in the shape of a square-based pyramid has vertical height 9 cm and base edges of length 10 cm. The mass of the pyramid is 810 g. What is the density of aluminium in g/cm³?

Q24 A solid rubber ball has a diameter of 7 cm. The density of the rubber is 920 kg/m³. What is the mass of the rubber ball? Give your answer in grams to 2 d.p.

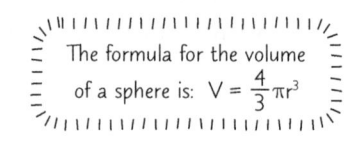

The formula for the volume of a sphere is: $V = \frac{4}{3}\pi r^3$

Q25 A mattress weighing 450 N sits on the floor, which is horizontal. The side of the mattress resting on the floor measures 1.5 m by 2 m. Work out the pressure exerted by the mattress on the floor.

Q26 When a chest of drawers of weight 680 N rests on horizontal ground, it exerts a pressure of 850 N/m². Work out the area of the base of the chest of drawers.

Q27 A large speaker sitting on horizontal ground exerts 640 N/m² of pressure on the ground. The side of the speaker that rests on the ground has an area of 0.7 m². What is the weight of the speaker?

Q28 A chair with a circular base exerts a pressure of 500 N/m² onto the floor it rests on. If the chair weighs 147 N, what is the radius of its base? Give your answer in cm to 2 d.p.

Section Four — Ratio, Proportion and Rates of Change

Section Four — Mixed Questions

Mixed Questions

And just like that, you've almost reached the end of Section Four... have a go at these last few ratio, proportion and rates of change questions while it's all still fresh in your mind.

Q1 Kyle grew some tulips is his garden. They were yellow, red and pink in the ratio $3:7:5$.
   a) If 28 flowers were red, how many:
      i) were yellow?
      ii) were pink?
   b) What fraction of the total number of tulips were yellow?

Q2 Reduce each of the following ratios to the form $1:n$.
   a) $4:24$ b) $12:3$ c) $6:32$ d) $18:63$

Q3 It takes 2 people 12 hours to repaint 2 cars.
Working at the same rate, how long would it take:
   a) 1 person to repaint 3 cars?
   b) 8 people to repaint 6 cars?

Q4 y is directly proportional to x. If $y = 9$, $x = 24$.
   a) Find an equation for y in terms of x.
   b) Find the value of y when $x = 44$.

Q5 Given that $y \propto \dfrac{1}{x}$, complete these tables of values:

a)
x	1	2	3		
y			8	1.5	0.5

b)
x		1	2	3	
y	3			0.5	0.1

Q6 Farah is selling her house for an asking price of £240 000. Her estate agent will get 2% of the sale price of the house. How much will the estate agent get if Farah's house sells for:
   a) 16% below the asking price?
   b) 4% above the asking price?

Q7 Jade bought six tins of paint for £14.50 each, two canvases for £15.00 each and a brush for £3.00. She used these items to create two pieces of artwork which she then sold for £111 each. What is her percentage profit on the artwork?

Q8 Leah bought a sofa in the sales for £468. The original price had been reduced by 35%. What was the original price of the sofa?

Q9 Jacob invests £6000 into a savings account. He has a choice of two accounts:
   - Account A pays 2.45% compound interest per annum.
   - Account B pays 2.6% simple interest per annum.
   a) If his investment is left alone for 3 years, which account is the best option, and how much more interest does it pay?
   b) If his investment is left alone for 6 years, which account is the best option, and how much more interest does it pay?

More mixed practice on the next page...

Mixed Questions

Q10 Angus buys an old car for £1800. For the first three years, the car's value depreciates by 12% each year. After three years, Angus finishes repairing the car, and from this point the value of the car appreciates by 18% each year.
  a) What is the lowest value of the car?
  b) How much is the car worth after 6 years?

See page 76 for a reminder of the unit conversions. Remember, you need to learn the metric ones for the exam.

Q11 Express the given quantity in the unit in brackets:
  a) 5600 ml [litres]
  b) 5.5 gallons [pints]
  c) 76 mm [metres]
  d) 245 pounds [stone]
  e) 3 yards [inches]
  f) 6 stone 2 pounds [ounces]

Q12 Fozia's fish tank can hold 256 pints of water.
  a) How many gallons is this?
  b) Approximately how many litres is this?

  Tyler's fish tank can hold 148 500 cm³ of water.
  c) Who has the bigger fish tank and approximately how many more ml can it hold?

Q13 This graph can be used to convert between Australian dollars (A$) and pounds (£).

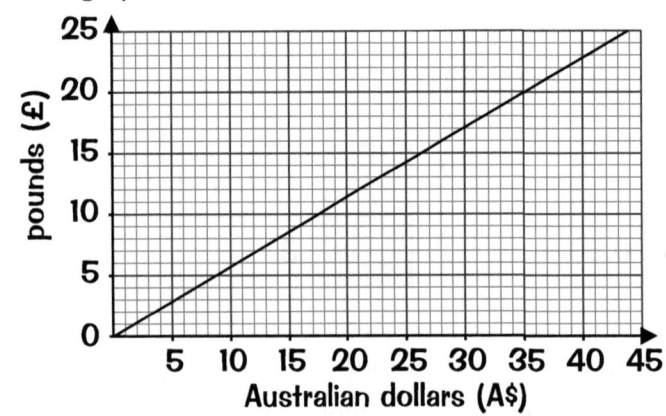

  a) How many pounds are equal to A$28?
  b) Kelvin is paid A$22 per hour. How much will he earn, in pounds, if he works from 9.00 am to 1.30 pm?
  c) The cost of some compost is directly proportional to the quantity bought. 28 gallons of compost costs £40. Approximately how many litres can you buy for A$17.50?

Q14 Irene and Ashaad both drove 132 miles from Sheffield to Newcastle. Irene set off at 10.56 am and arrived at 1.08 pm. Ashaad set off at 4.50 pm and arrived at 7.35 pm. Who had the faster average speed and by how many miles per hour?

Q15 Find:
  a) The volume of an 200 g wooden building block with a density of 0.5 g/cm³.
  b) The density in g/cm³ of a cube with a side length of 7 cm and a mass of 1.715 kg.
  c) The mass of a square-based pyramid with a vertical height of 15 cm, base edges of length 4 cm and a density of 0.6 g/cm³.

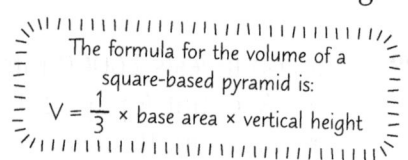

The formula for the volume of a square-based pyramid is:
$V = \frac{1}{3} \times \text{base area} \times \text{vertical height}$

Q16 A bookcase weighing 740 N rests on a floor, which is horizontal. The side of the bookcase resting on the floor is 2.4 m by 0.5 m. What is the pressure exerted by the bookcase on the floor?

Section Five — Geometry and Measures

Geometry

For this page, you'll need to know the sum of the angles in a triangle, on a straight line, in a quadrilateral and around a point. You'll also need to know the properties of isosceles triangles. Good luck.

For the following diagrams, find the <u>lettered</u> angles. LM and PQ are straight lines.

None of these diagrams are drawn accurately — <u>don't</u> try to measure them.

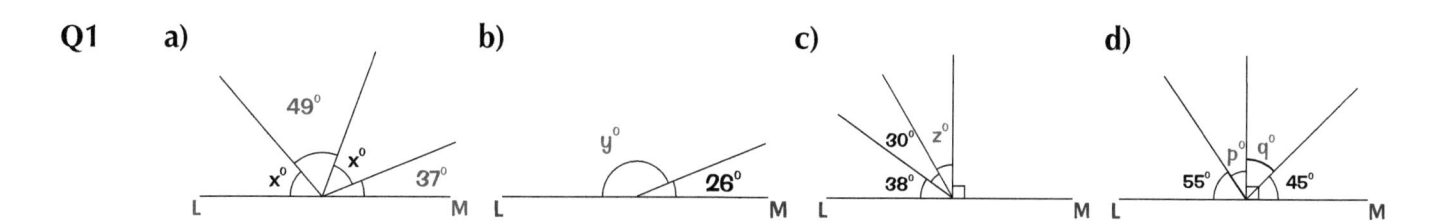

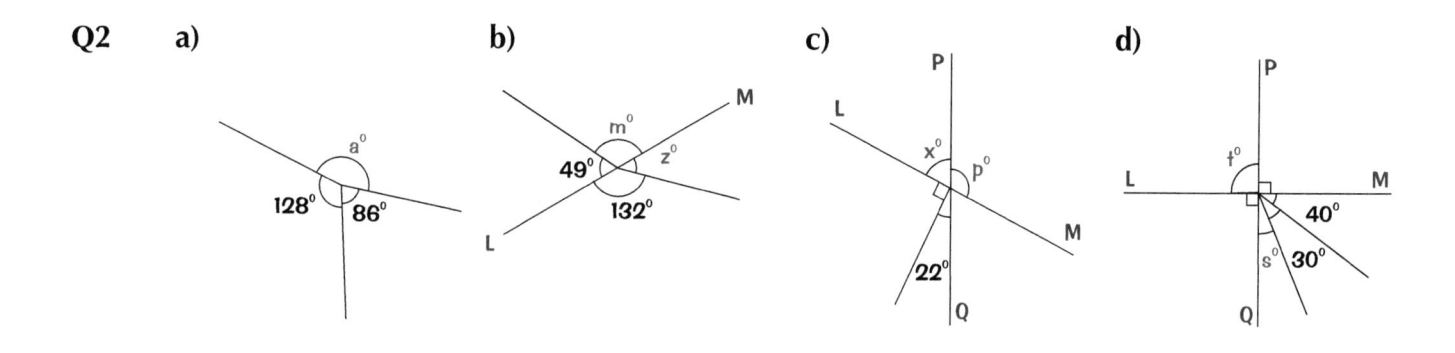

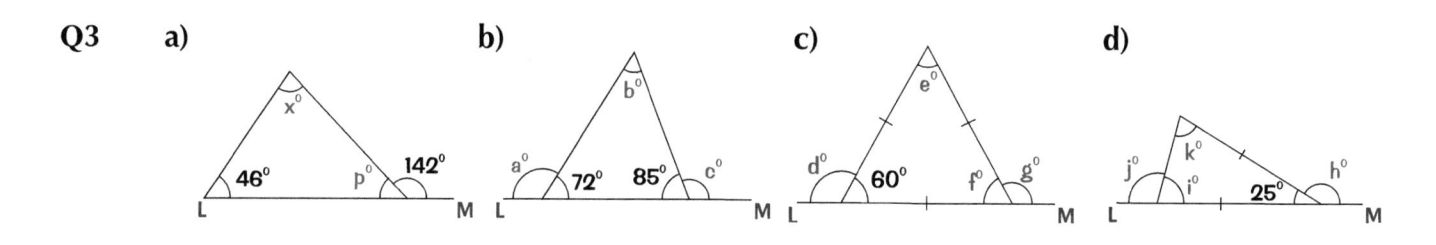

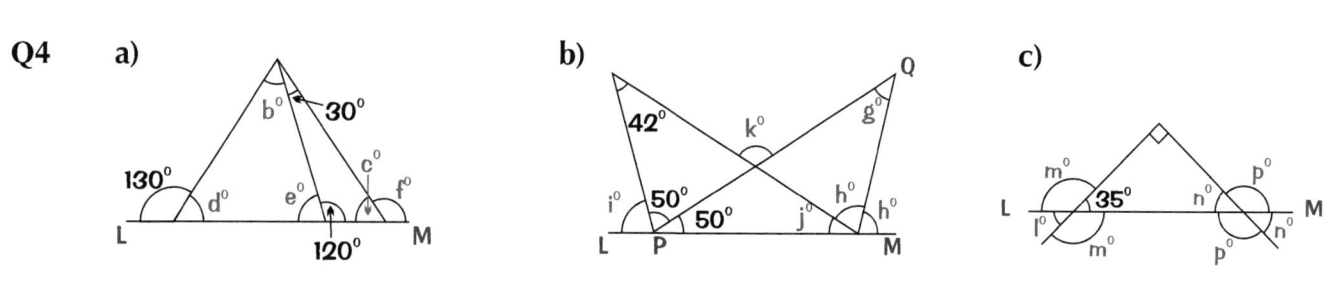

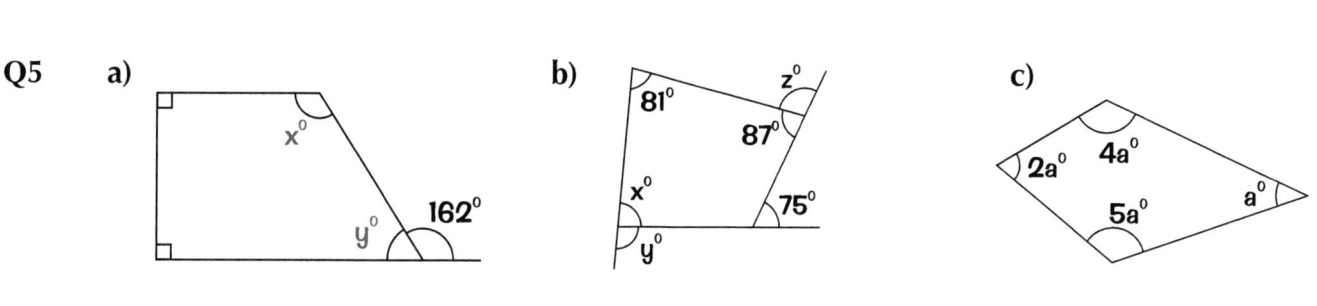

Q1 a) [diagram with 49°, x°, x°, 37° on line LM]
b) [diagram with y°, 26° on line LM]
c) [diagram with 30°, z°, 38° on line LM]
d) [diagram with 55°, p°, q°, 45° on line LM]

Q2 a) [diagram with a°, 128°, 86°]
b) [diagram with m°, 49°, z°, 132°, lines L to M]
c) [diagram with P, L, x°, p°, 22°, Q, M]
d) [diagram with P, L, f°, M, 40°, s°, 30°, Q]

Q3 a) [triangle with x°, 46°, p°, 142° on LM]
b) [triangle with a°, 72°, b°, 85°, c° on LM]
c) [isosceles triangle with d°, e°, 60°, f°, g° on LM]
d) [triangle with j°, k°, i°, 25°, h° on LM]

Q4 a) [diagram with 130°, b°, 30°, c°, d°, e°, f°, 120° on LM]
b) [diagram with 42°, k°, g°, Q, i°, 50°, 50°, j°, h°, h° on LPM]
c) [diagram with L, l°, m°, m°, 35°, n°, n°, p°, p°, M]

Q5 a) [quadrilateral with x°, y°, 162°]
b) [quadrilateral with 81°, z°, 87°, x°, 75°, y°]
c) [quadrilateral with 2a°, 4a°, 5a°, a°]

Parallel Lines

This page is a bit dull — just lots of boring angles... still, that's geometry for you. Oh and by the way, you've got to work the angles out — don't try and sneakily measure them, they're probably drawn wrong anyway...

Q1 Find the sizes of the angles marked by letters in these diagrams.

a) 130°, a
b) b, 124°
c) 48°, c

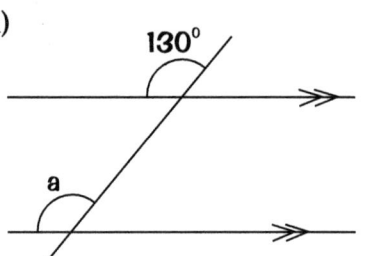

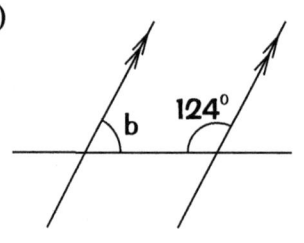

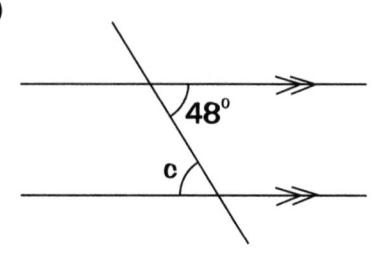

Q2 Find the sizes of the angles marked by letters in these diagrams.

a) d, e, 72°, 50°
b) 65°, 134°, f, g
c) h, 75°, 61°, i, j

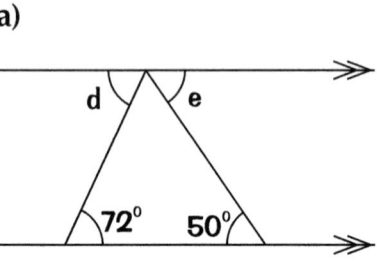

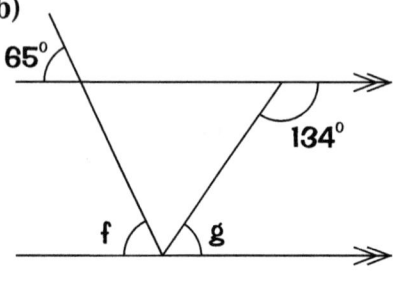

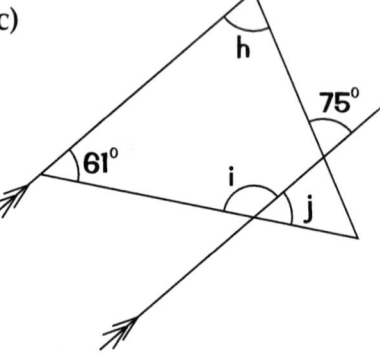

Q3 Find the sizes of the angles marked by letters in these diagrams.

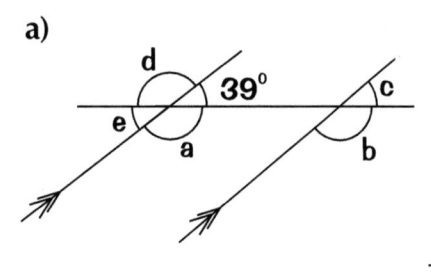

a) d, 39°, c, e, a, b
b) c, 47°, e, a, b, d
c) n, 40°, q, p, 46°, m, r

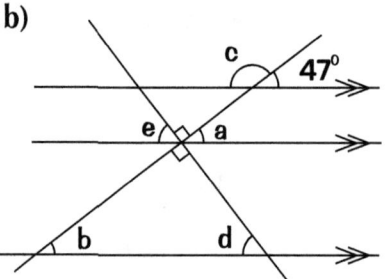

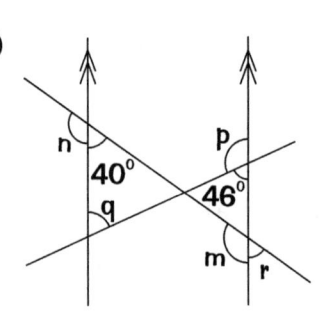

Q4 Find the value of x in each of the diagrams below.

a) $x + 60°$, $2x - 10°$
b) $x - 40°$, $2x$, $x + 20°$
c) $20x + 12°$, $4x$, $7x + 13°$

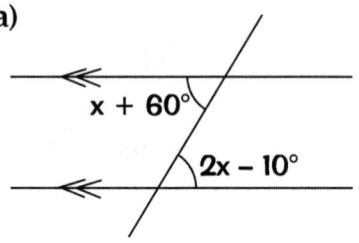

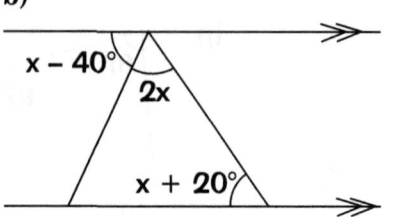

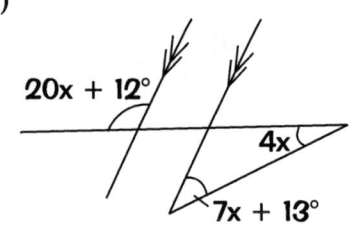

Polygons

Q1 What sort of triangles occur in every regular polygon (except a hexagon), when each vertex is joined to the centre by a straight line?

Q2 Sketch a regular hexagon and draw in all its lines of symmetry. State the order of rotational symmetry.

Q3 An irregular pentagon has interior angles of 100°, 104°, 120°. If the other two angles are equal, what is their size?

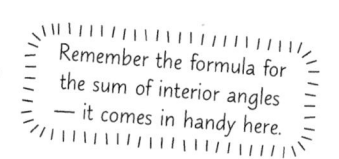

Remember the formula for the sum of interior angles — it comes in handy here.

Q4 A square and a regular hexagon are placed adjacent to each other.
  a) What is the size of ∠PQW?
  b) What is the size of ∠PRW?
  c) How many sides has the regular polygon that has ∠PQW as one of its angles?

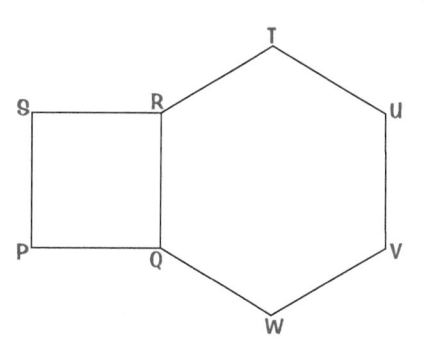

Q5 a) The sum of the interior angles of a regular 24-sided polygon is 3960°. Use this to calculate the size of one interior angle.
  b) From your answer to part a) calculate one exterior angle and show that the sum of the exterior angles equals 360°.

Q6 ABCDEFGH is a regular octagon.
  a) Copy the figure and mark on the axis of symmetry which maps H to A.
  b) Calculate the size of angle EFC.

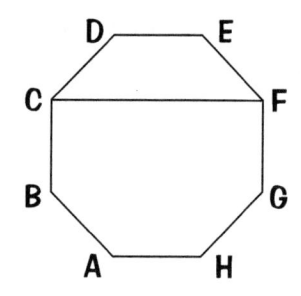

Q7 The sum of the interior angles of a regular polygon is 2520°. How many sides does this regular polygon have?

Q8 Look at the irregular polygon on the right. For any n-sided polygon, the sum of its interior angles is **(n – 2) × 180°**.

  a) Find the sum of the interior angles.

  b) Find the value of x.

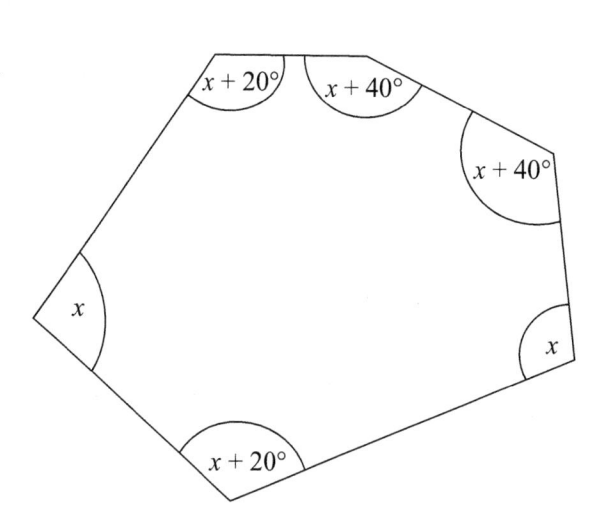

Section Five — Geometry and Measures

Triangles and Quadrilaterals

Make sure you know the names and properties of all the triangles and quadrilaterals. By 'properties', I mean things like the number of equal sides and angles, lines of symmetry, right angles, parallel sides etc. And by 'names' I mean 'rhombus', not 'Fred'.

Q1 Identify each of the triangles or quadrilaterals described below.

   a) A three-sided shape with one line of symmetry.

   b) A four-sided shape with two pairs of equal sides, one pair of equal angles and one line of symmetry.

   c) A three-sided shape with one right angle.

   Try sketching some of the shapes if you're getting a bit stuck.

   d) A four-sided shape with two pairs of parallel sides, two lines of symmetry and no 90° internal angles.

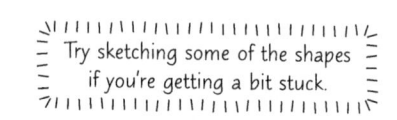

Q2 Stephen is measuring the angles inside a parallelogram for his maths homework. To save time, he measures just one and works out what the other angles must be from this. If the angle he measures is 52°, what are the other three?

Q3 a) A quadrilateral has angles measuring 150°, 30°, 150° and 30°. Write down the names of the three different shapes it could be.

   b) An isosceles triangle has an angle of 32°. What are the two different possibilities for the sizes of the other two angles in the triangle?

Q4 The shape on the right is made up of two identical squares and two identical kites. Find the sizes of the angles labelled u and v.

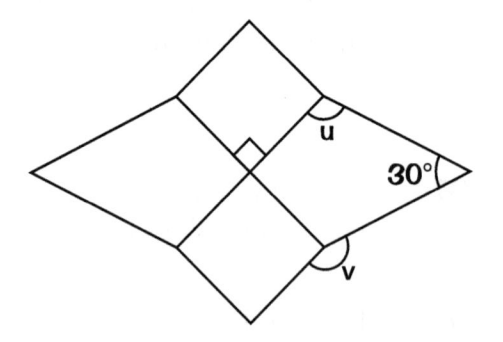

Q5 Find the value of y in each of the diagrams below.

   a) (triangle with angles y, $4y$, and isosceles marks)

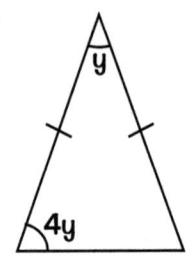

   b) (parallelogram with angles $3y$ and $2y$)

Section Five — Geometry and Measures

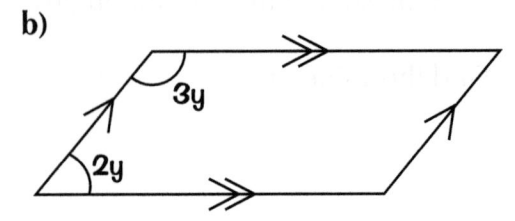

Circle Geometry

You'll need to know all the circle theorems to answer the questions on the next two pages — if you're not sure about them, brush up on them now.

Q1 ABCD is a cyclic quadrilateral with angle BCD = 100°.
EF is a tangent to the circle, touching it at A.
Angle DAF = 30°.
Write down the size of angle:
a) BAD
b) EAB.

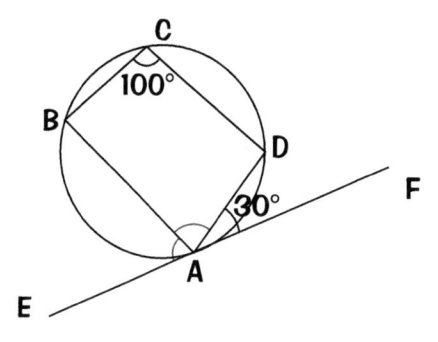

Q2 A, B and C are points on the circumference of a circle with centre O. BD and CD are tangents of the circle.
a) State the length BD.
b) Calculate the angle COD.
c) State the angle COB.
d) Find the angle CAB.

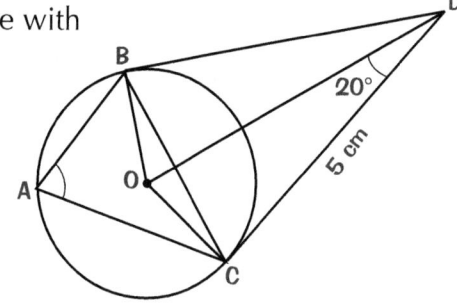

Q3 A, B, C, D and E are points on the circumference of a circle with centre O. Angle BDE = 53°. The line FG is a tangent to the circle, touching it at A. Angle EAF = 32°. Find:
a) angle BOE
b) angle ACE.

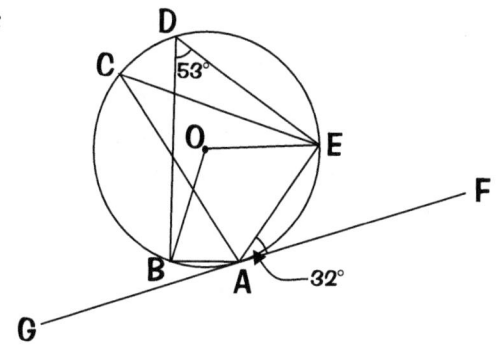

Q4 ABCD is a cyclic quadrilateral and the tangent to the circle at A makes an angle of 70° with the side AD. Angle BCA = 30°. Write down, giving a reason, the size of:
a) angle ACD
b) angle BAD.

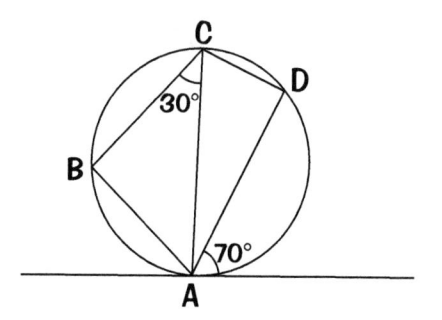

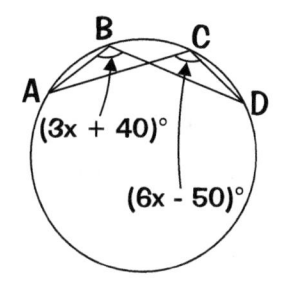

Q5 A, B, C and D are points on the circumference of a circle.
Angle ABD = $(3x + 40)°$ and angle ACD = $(6x - 50)°$.
a) Give a reason why angle ABD and angle ACD are the same.
b) Form an equation in x and, by solving it, find the size of angle ABD.

Section Five — Geometry and Measures

Circle Geometry

Q6 O is the centre of a circle, AB is a tangent to the circle and CE is a chord.
Find the size of:
a) angle CEO
b) angle EDO
c) angle COD.

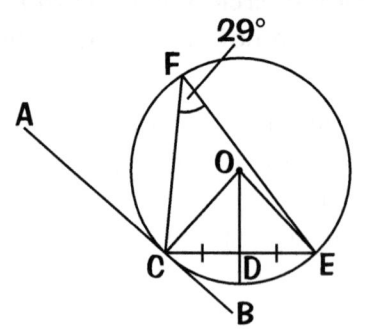

Q7 A, B, C and D are points on the circumference of a circle. O is the centre of the circle, AC is a diameter and angle AOD = 140°.
Write down:
a) angle ABD
b) angle ABC
c) angle DBC.

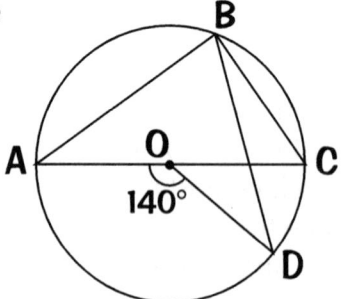

Q8 A tangent of a circle is drawn, touching it at A. C and B are two other points on the circumference and AOB is a diameter. O is the centre of the circle. Angle ABC is 23°.
a) Write down the size of angle ACB, giving a reason for your answer.
b) Find the size of the angle marked $x°$ in the diagram.

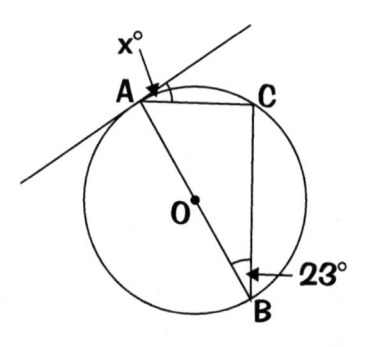

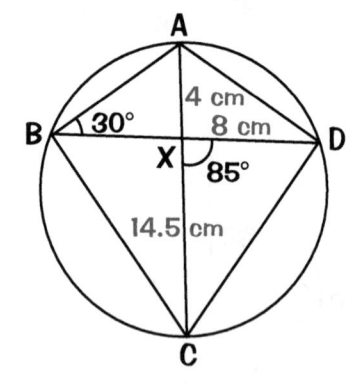

Q9 ABCD is a cyclic quadrilateral. The lines AC and BD intersect at X. Lengths AX = 4 cm, DX = 8 cm and XC = 14.5 cm. Angle DXC = 85° and ABD = 30°.
a) Show that triangles DXC and AXB are similar.
b) Find the length of XB.
c) Write down the size of angle BDC.

Q10 ABCD is a cyclic quadrilateral.
X is a point inside the circle.
Angle ADC = 92° and angle AXC = 178°.
Show that point X is NOT the centre of the circle.

Think about the properties of cyclic quadrilaterals and angles at the centre/circumference of a circle.

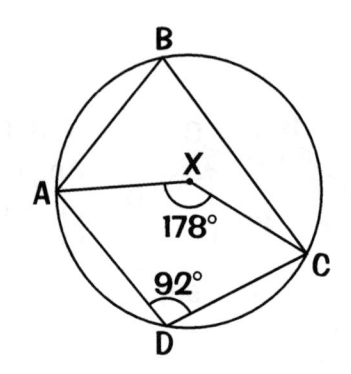

Congruent Shapes

**Remember the four conditions you need to prove that triangles are congruent —
SSS, AAS, SAS and RHS (you only need to show that one of these is true, not all four).**

Q1 Which two triangles are congruent? Explain why.

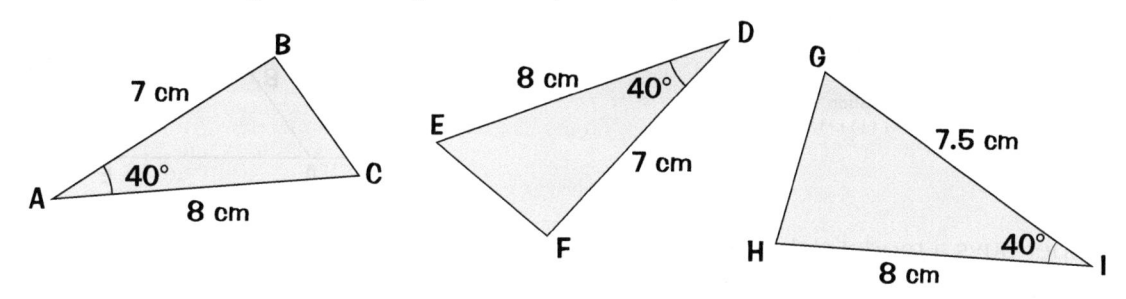

Q2 Another triangle, congruent to the triangle shown on the right, must be drawn with vertices at three of the dots. Show in how many different ways this can be done.

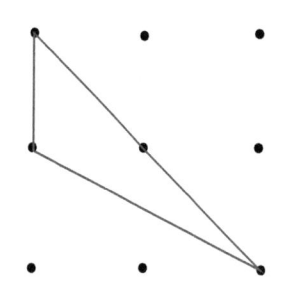

Q3 ABCD is a parallelogram. M is the point where the diagonals AC and BD intersect. Prove that the triangles ABM and CDM are congruent.

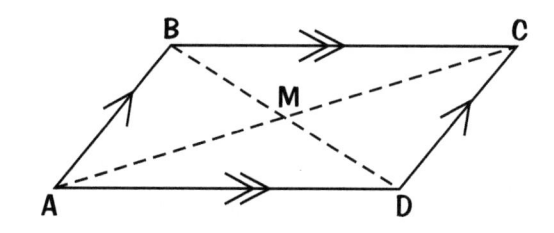

Q4 The circle on the right has centre O. AB is a chord. Prove that triangles AOC and BOC are congruent.

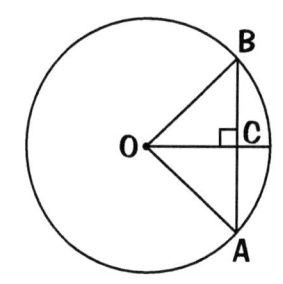

Q5 The lengths AB and BC of the triangle on the right are equal. By bisecting the angle ABC, use the congruence conditions to prove that the base angles in any isosceles triangle are equal.

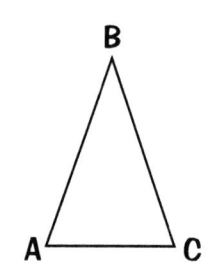

Q6 The lines AEC and DEB in the diagram on the right are straight lines. Prove that the triangles ABE and DEC are congruent.

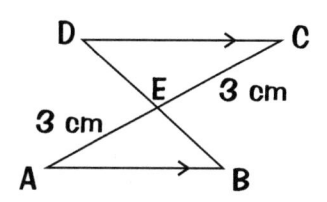

Section Five — Geometry and Measures

Similar Shapes

Similar shapes are exactly the same shape, but can be different sizes. Watch out for shapes being rotated or reflected — this doesn't stop them being similar.

Q1 Show that triangles ACE and BCD are similar.

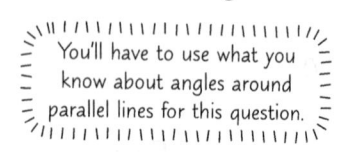

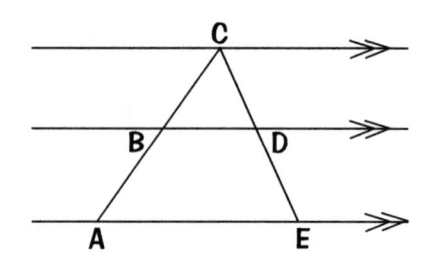

You'll have to use what you know about angles around parallel lines for this question.

Q2 Jasper buys a model statue of a man from a museum gift shop. The real statue is standing on a plinth. He places the model on a table in front of the real statue so the feet of the statues are the same height above the ground.

When Jasper is 1 m away from the model and looks at it with his eyes at the same level as the feet, the model appears to exactly cover the real statue, which is 5 m away. The model is 30 cm tall. How tall is the real statue?

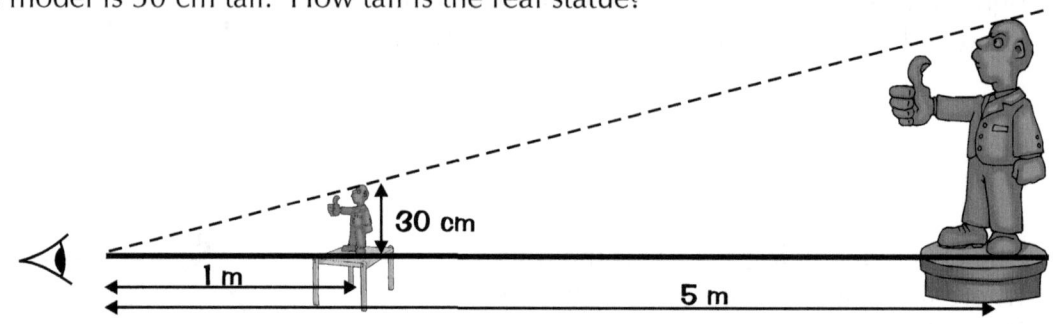

Q3 In the diagram below, BC is parallel to DE.
AB = 12 cm, BD = 8 cm, DE = 25 cm and CE = 10 cm.

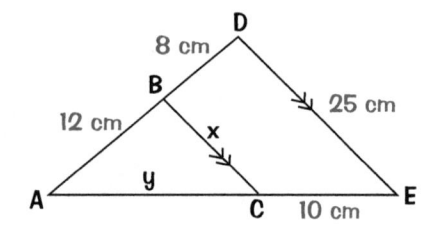

   a) Explain why triangles ABC and ADE are similar.
   b) Find the lengths of x and y in the diagram.

Q4 A boy made a symmetrical framework with metal rods as shown. Lengths AB = BC, ST = TC and AP = PQ. Angle BVC = 90° and length BV = 9 cm.
   a) Find two triangles which are similar to triangle ABC.
   b) Calculate the length of AP. Hence write down the length of PT.
   c) Calculate the area of triangle ABC.
   d) Find the area of triangle APQ. Give your answer correct to 3 significant figures.
   e) Hence write down the area of PQBST correct to 2 significant figures.

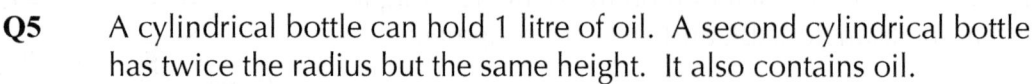

Q5 A cylindrical bottle can hold 1 litre of oil. A second cylindrical bottle has twice the radius but the same height. It also contains oil.
   a) Explain why these bottles are not similar.
   b) How much oil can the larger bottle hold?

Section Five — Geometry and Measures

The Four Transformations

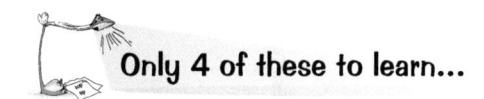

Only 4 of these to learn...

Q1 Copy the axes and mark on triangle A with corners (-1, 2), (0, 4) and (-2, 4). Use a scale of 1 cm to 1 unit.

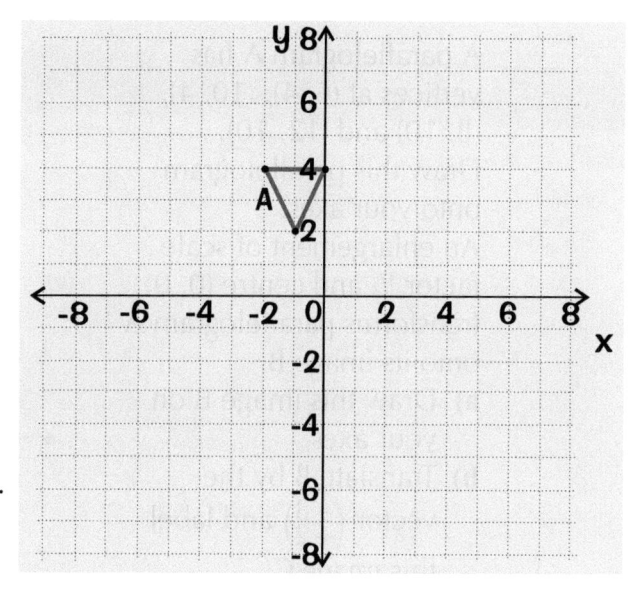

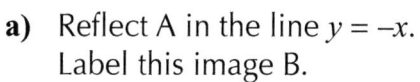

    a) Reflect A in the line $y = -x$. Label this image B.

    b) Reflect A in the line $x = 1$. Label the image C.

    c) Reflect A in the line $y = -1$. Label the image D.

    d) Translate triangle D with the vector $\binom{4}{2}$. Label this image E.

    e) Translate triangle C with the vector $\binom{3}{-3}$. Label this image F.

    f) Enlarge A by a scale factor of 3, centre (0, 4). Label this image G.

    g) Describe fully the rotation that sends C to E.

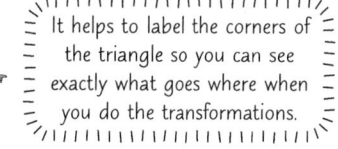

It helps to label the corners of the triangle so you can see exactly what goes where when you do the transformations.

Q2 Copy the axes using a scale of 1 cm to 1 unit. Mark on the axes a quadrilateral Q with corners (-2, 1), (-3, 1), (-3, 3) and (-2, 3).

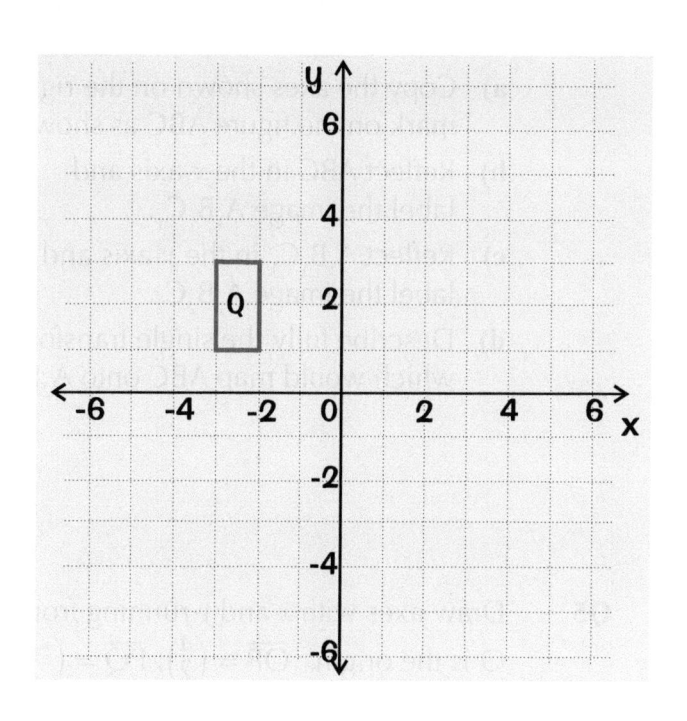

    a) Rotate Q clockwise through 90° about the point (-1, 2). Label the image R.

    b) Rotate R clockwise through 90° about the point (0, 1). Label the image S.

    c) Describe fully the rotation that maps Q to S.

    d) Rotate Q through 180° about the point (-½, -1). Label the image T.

    e) Rotate Q anticlockwise through 90° about the point (-1, -1). Label the image U.

    f) Enlarge Q by a scale factor of -2, centre (0, 0). Label this image V.

    g) Describe fully the rotation that sends U to T.

Section Five — Geometry and Measures

The Four Transformations

Move each point separately — then check your shape hasn't done anything unexpected while you weren't looking.

Q3 Copy the axes below using a scale of 1 cm to 1 unit.

A parallelogram A has vertices at (6, 4), (10, 4), (8, 10) and (12, 10). Draw this parallelogram onto your axes.
An enlargement of scale factor ½ and centre (0, 0) transforms parallelogram A onto its image B. 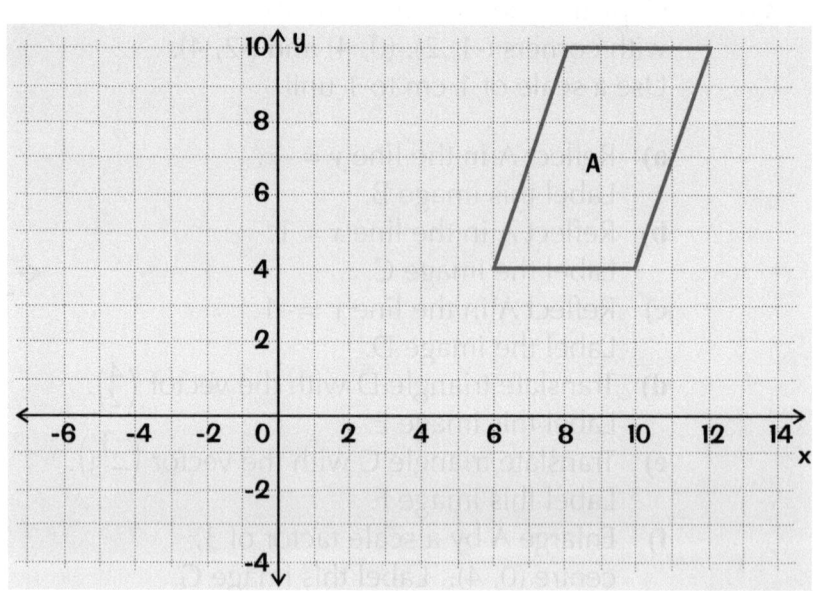
a) Draw this image B on your axes.
b) Translate B by the vector $\begin{pmatrix} -3 \\ -2 \end{pmatrix}$ and label this image C.
c) Calculate the ratio of the area of parallelogram C to the area of parallelogram A.

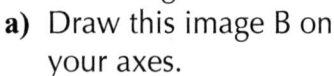

Q4 A is the point (4, 3), B is (4, 1) and C is (5, 1).
a) Copy the axes shown on the right, and mark on the figure ABC as shown.
b) Reflect ABC in the x-axis and label the image $A_1B_1C_1$.
c) Reflect $A_1B_1C_1$ in the y-axis and label the image $A_2B_2C_2$.
d) Describe fully the single transformation which would map ABC onto $A_2B_2C_2$.

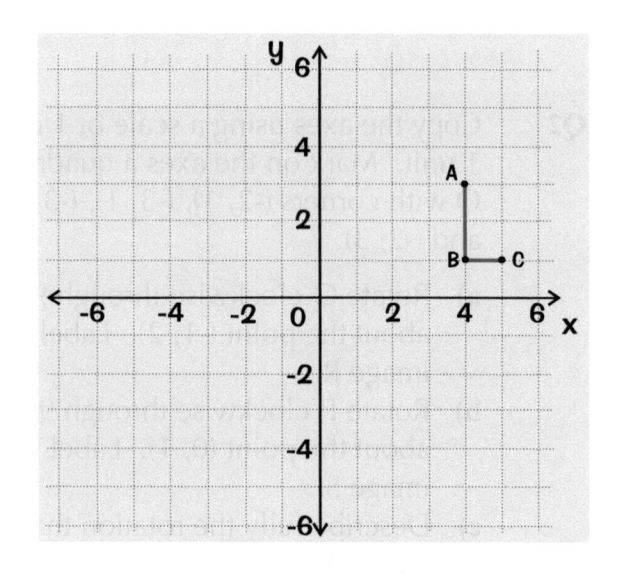

Q5 Draw axes with x and y running from 0 to 12 with a scale of 1 cm to 1 unit.
O is the origin. $\overrightarrow{OP} = \begin{pmatrix} 4 \\ 2 \end{pmatrix}$, $\overrightarrow{PQ} = \begin{pmatrix} -1 \\ 2 \end{pmatrix}$, and $\overrightarrow{QR} = 2\overrightarrow{OP}$.

a) Mark P, Q and R on your axes.
b) Translate R by $\overrightarrow{QO}$. Label the image T.
c) Verify that $\overrightarrow{PQ} + \overrightarrow{QR} + \overrightarrow{RT} + \overrightarrow{TP} = \begin{pmatrix} 0 \\ 0 \end{pmatrix}$.

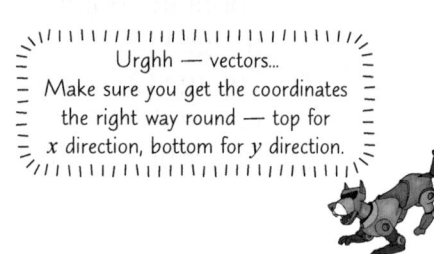

Urghh — vectors...
Make sure you get the coordinates the right way round — top for x direction, bottom for y direction.

Perimeter and Area

There are quite a few formulas you need to know for perimeter and area questions.
Most of them are dead easy though — but watch out for tricky contexts.

Q1 A rectangular dining room, with a width equal to half its length, needs carpet tiling.
   a) Calculate the area of the floor, if its width is 12 m.
   b) If carpet tiles are 50 cm by 50 cm squares, calculate how many tiles will be required.
   c) If carpet tiles cost £4.99 per m^2, calculate the cost of tiling the dining room.

Q2 Anandi is training for a marathon by jogging around the outside of a square field of area 9000 m^2. One evening, Anandi completed 11 laps of the field. How far did she run? Give your answer to the nearest 100 m.

Q3 A rectangular lawn with an area of 48 m^2 is being made.
If its width is 5 m, how long is it?
How many rolls of turf 50 cm wide and 11 m long should be ordered to grass this area?

Q4 This parallelogram has an area of 4773 mm^2.
How long is its base?

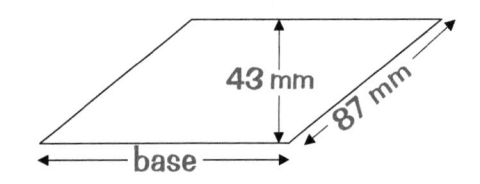

(43 mm, 87 mm, base)

Q5 Josh is making a cube bean bag out of material for his textiles coursework.
If each side of the cube is to have edges of length 60 cm,
how many square metres of material will Josh need?

Q6 A fighter aircraft's wing is shown on the right.
Calculate its area and its perimeter.

Two lots of Pythagoras are needed to find the length of the third side.

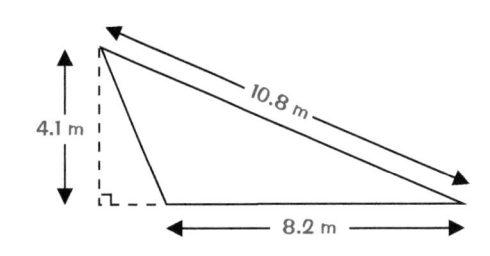

(4.1 m, 10.8 m, 8.2 m)

Q7 Jiro is making a metal bracket as part of his technology project.
The bracket is stamped out of sheet metal in a 2 phase process:
1st: The outer triangle, measuring 14.4 cm by 10 cm, is stamped out.
2nd: A smaller inner triangle measuring 5.76 cm by 4 cm is stamped out of the larger triangle.
The bracket should be made from no more than 50 cm^2 of sheet metal if the fixing is to support its weight.
Will the fixing take the weight of Jiro's bracket?

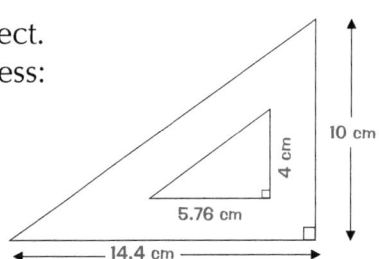

(10 cm, 4 cm, 5.76 cm, 14.4 cm)

Section Five — Geometry and Measures

Perimeter and Area

Q8 Calculate the area of a rhombus with diagonals 7 km and 11 km.

You'll need to split the rhombus into triangles for this question.

Q9 A modern glass sculpture is to be erected. It is made from glass in the shape of two mountain peaks. Calculate each <u>separate</u> area and hence find the <u>total</u> area of glass required.

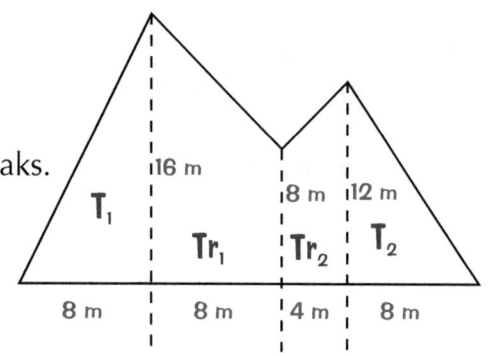

(Diagram labels: T_1, Tr_1, Tr_2, T_2; heights 16 m, 8 m, 12 m; bases 8 m, 8 m, 4 m, 8 m)

Q10 A simple tent is to be made in the shape of a triangular prism. The dimensions are shown in the diagram.
  a) The two end faces are isosceles triangles. Find their areas.
  b) The two sides and ground sheet are rectangles. Find their areas.
  c) How much material is required to make this tent?

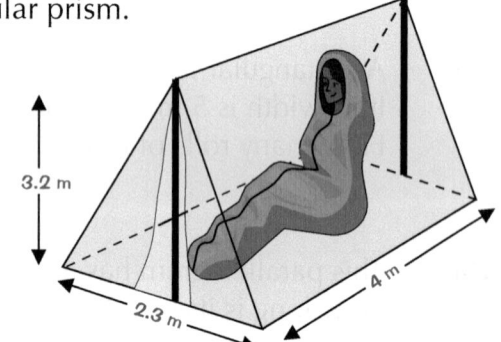

(Dimensions: 3.2 m, 2.3 m, 4 m)

Q11 A square with side length x cm is cut in half vertically, and the two pieces are joined together to make a rectangle (as shown in the diagram below).

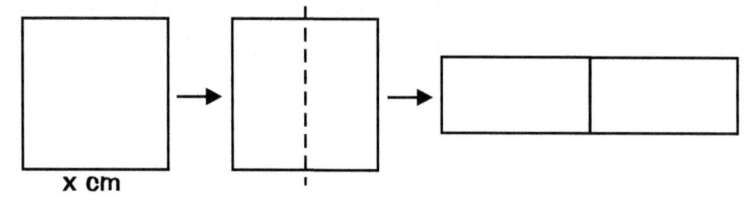

In terms of x, find an expression for:
  a) the perimeter of the rectangle,
  b) the area of the rectangle.

Q12 The diagram on the right shows the dimensions, given in cm, of an isosceles triangle. The diagram also shows a trapezium made up of three isosceles triangles, each identical to the one given. Find the perimeter of the trapezium.

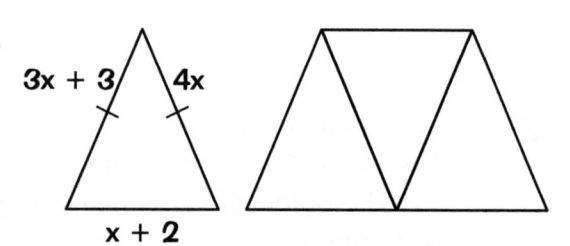

(Triangle sides: $3x + 3$, $4x$, base $x + 2$)

Q13 The square and the rectangle shown have the same area. The perimeter of the rectangle is 6 units bigger than the perimeter of the square. Find the values of x and y correct to 2 d.p.

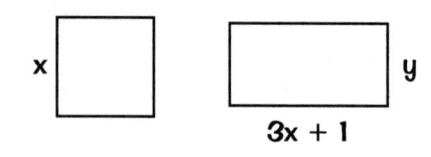

(Square side x; rectangle sides $3x + 1$ and y)

Section Five — Geometry and Measures

Area — Circles

Another page, another load of formulas you need to know. *Sigh*. As well as area and circumference, you also need to know how to find the area of a sector and length of an arc.

Q1 A <u>minor sector</u> is labelled A on the diagram. Name the features labelled B, C and D.

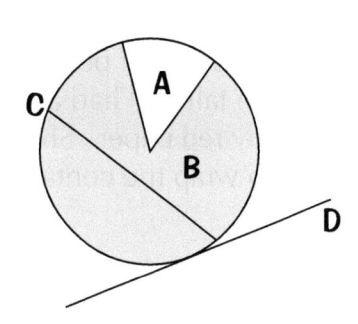

Q2 Find each of the following.
a) The area of a circle with radius = 6.12 m. Give your answer <u>to 2 d.p.</u>
b) The circumference of a circle with radius = 7.2 m. Give your answer <u>to 2 s.f.</u>
c) The circumference of a circle with diameter = 14.8 m. Give your answer <u>to 1 d.p.</u>
d) The area of a circle with diameter = 4.246 cm. Give your answer <u>to 3 s.f.</u>

Q3 Find the <u>area and the perimeter</u> of each of the shapes drawn here.

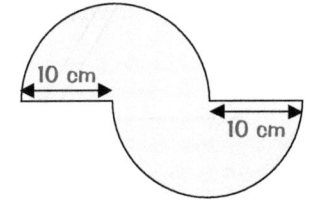

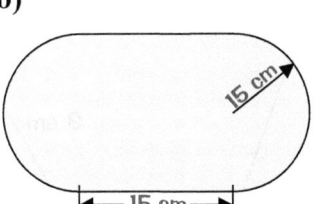

a) 10 cm, 10 cm

b) 15 cm, 15 cm

c) 5 m, Diameter 60 m

Q4 A plastic strip is made in the shape shown. The curves AC and BD are both arcs of circles with centre O. The larger circle has radius 30 mm and the smaller circle has radius 20 mm. The shaded ends of the shape are both semicircles.

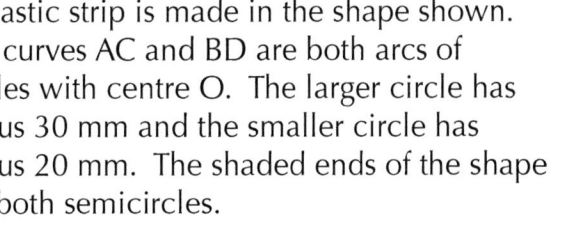

a) Find the area of the unshaded shape ABDC.
b) Find the area of the two semicircular ends. Hence write down the area of the complete shape.
c) Find the perimeter of the complete shape.

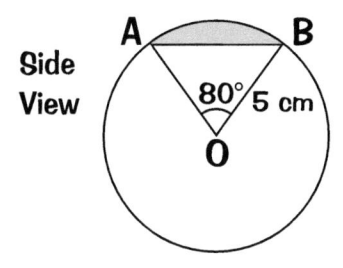

Q5 Side View

A washing powder ball looks from the side like a circle with the shaded area removed. The circle has radius 5 cm and the angle AOB = 80°.
a) Find the area of the sector OAB.
b) Find the area of triangle AOB and hence the shaded area.

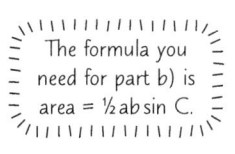

The formula you need for part b) is area = ½ ab sin C.

Section Five — Geometry and Measures

3D Shapes — Surface Area

If you're struggling with surface area, it might help to sketch the net of the shape — that's what you'd get if you unfolded a 3D shape and laid it out flat.
The area of the net is the same as the surface area.

Q1 Hannah bought a bottle of perfume as a present in a cylindrical container, which was 20 cm tall and had a radius of 4 cm. She wanted to wrap the container in shiny red paper. She has enough paper to cover an area of 600 cm². Is that enough to wrap the container?

Q2 Find the surface area of a sphere with a diameter of 6 cm.

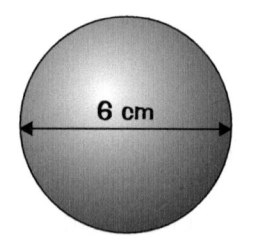

Q3 Which of these two shapes has the greater surface area? Show your working.

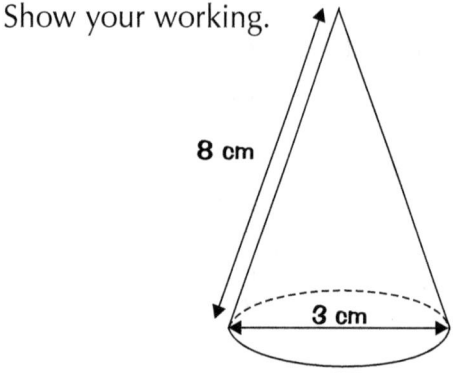

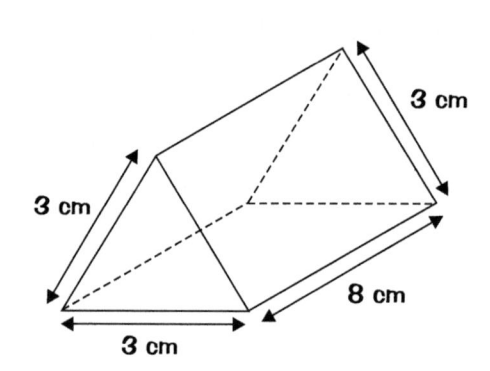

Q4 A hemisphere has a surface area of 75π cm². Find the radius, in cm, of the hemisphere.

Q5 Bill has a greenhouse with dimensions as shown. The roof is made up of eight panels of equal size.
A storm breaks all of the glass in the shaded area on the diagram.
Calculate the area of glass which Bill must buy to repair his greenhouse.

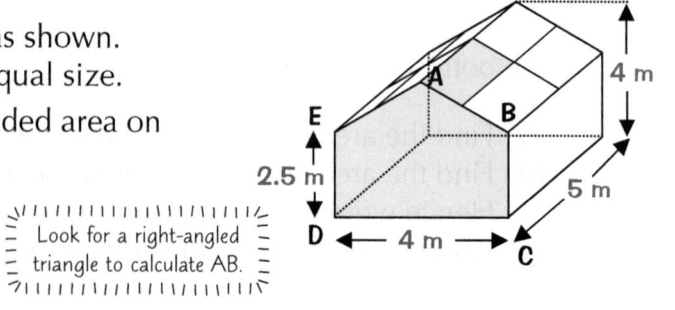

Look for a right-angled triangle to calculate AB.

Q6 Kaphiri is planning to build a square-based pyramid with dimensions as shown in the diagram.
  a) What will the surface area of the whole pyramid be?
  b) A 1 litre tin of paint will cover 15 m². Kaphiri wants to paint the four triangular faces of the pyramid. How many tins of paint will Kaphiri need?

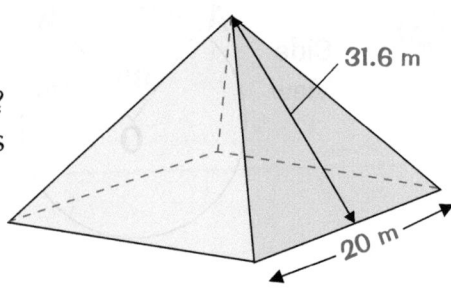

Section Five — Geometry and Measures

3D Shapes — Volume

Learn to love the volume formulas for cuboids, spheres, prisms, pyramids and cones.

> Volume of pyramid = $\frac{1}{3}$ × base area × vertical height
> Volume of cone = $\frac{1}{3}$ × πr^2 × vertical height
> Volume of sphere = $\frac{4}{3}$ × πr^3

Q1 Joe buys a polythene tunnel to protect his plants from frost. It has a semicircular cross-section with a diameter of 70 cm, and a length of 3 m.
  a) Find the cross-sectional area in m².
  b) Hence find the volume of the tunnel.

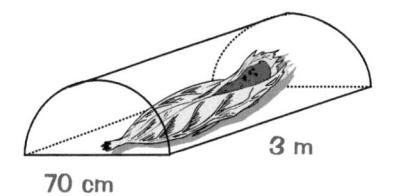

Q2 I am planning to build a circular pond in my garden surrounded by a ring-shaped paved area. The pond will be 50 cm deep and filled with water.
  a) Calculate the approximate cost of paving the area around the pond with slabs costing £16 per m². Give your answer to the nearest £10.
  b) I need to add 15 ml of liquid pond treatment for every m³ of water in the pond. Find the volume of treatment I will need to add to the pond. Give your answer to the nearest ml.

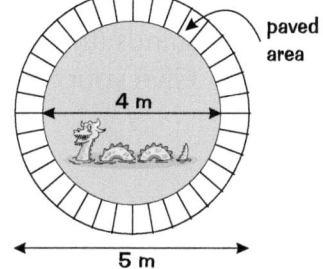

Q3 A solid metal cube, with sides of length 10 cm, is melted down and made into a solid cylinder 10 cm high.
  a) What is the radius of this cylinder?
  b) Find the surface area of the cylinder.

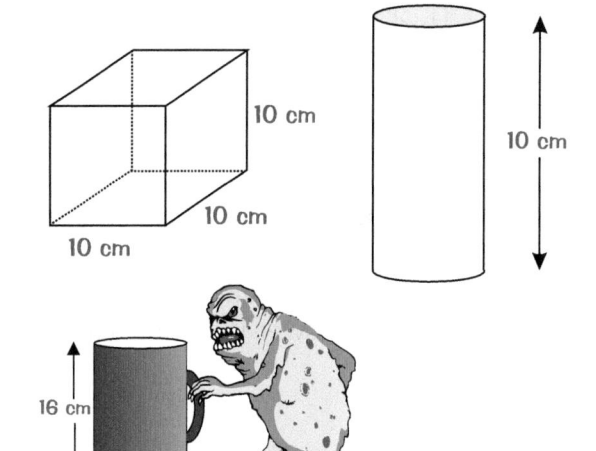

Q4 A tin mug has the dimensions shown.
  a) What is the greatest volume of milk the mug can hold?
  b) In fact, 600 cm³ of milk is poured in. How high will it go up the mug?

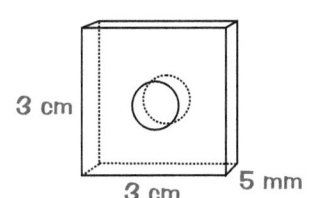

Q5 A nut has the cross-section illustrated. The circular hole has a diameter of 1.4 cm and the nut is 5 mm thick. Find the volume of the nut in cm³.

(Units...)

Q6 Ji-Su is pumping up a basketball. She knows the diameter of a fully-inflated basketball should be no more than 30 cm. Calculate the maximum volume of air that Ji-Su should use to inflate her basketball.

Section Five — Geometry and Measures

3D Shapes — Volume

Q7 The largest Egyptian pyramid has a square base with sides of length 230 m, and is 139 m high. What is the volume of this pyramid? Give your answer to the nearest m³.

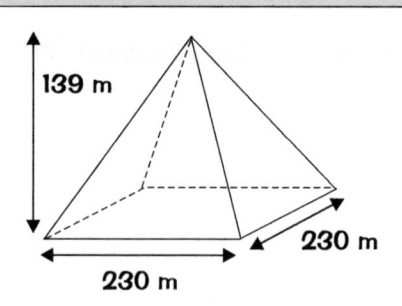

Q8 Steve has bought a pair of speaker stands. The base of each stand is a hollow prism with the dimensions shown. A hollow tube of diameter 4 cm and height 110 cm screws into the top of each base to form the stand.

Steve is filling the stands with sand to improve stability. Find the volume of sand Steve needs to use to fill both stands (the bases and the tubes).
Give your answer in litres to 2 d.p.

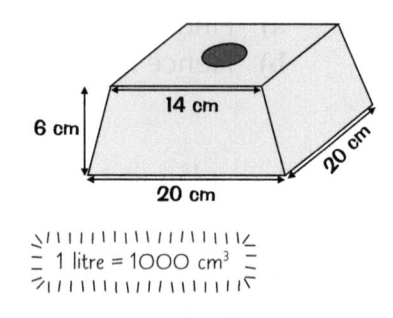

1 litre = 1000 cm³

Q9 Chun buys a bookshelf with the dimensions shown in the diagram.
 a) Find the cross-sectional area.
 b) Find the volume of the bookshelf in m³.

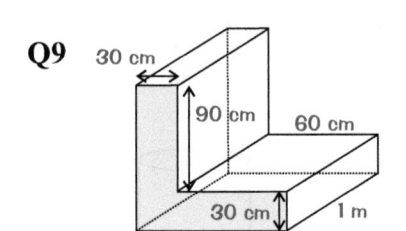

Q10 Giles is making Christmas baubles by filling plastic spheres of radius 3 cm with a glittery gel. He pours the gel into the plastic sphere at a rate of 5 ml per second. How long will it take him to fill 10 baubles?
Give your answer in minutes and seconds to the nearest second.

Q11 An egg timer is symmetrical and consists of hemispheres, cylinders and cones joined together as shown to the left.
 a) Calculate the volume of sand in the upper container.

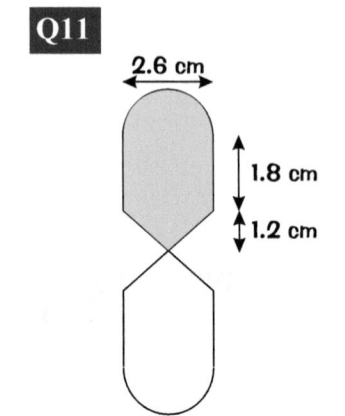

 You need to find three volumes and add them together.

Sand runs into the bottom container at a constant rate of 0.05 cm³ per second. At the end of a certain time period the sand has fallen through into the bottom container as shown to the right.

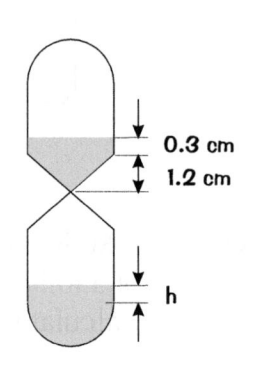

 b) How high (h) has it risen up the cylindrical part of the bottom container?
 c) How long has it taken the sand to fall through until it is at this height?

Section Five — Geometry and Measures

3D Shapes — Volume

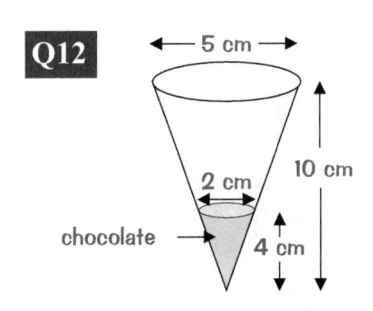

Q12 An ice-cream cone is 10 cm deep and has a base diameter of 5 cm. The bottom 4 cm of the cone is filled with solid chocolate as shown. The rest of the cone is filled with ice cream and a hemisphere of ice cream is mounted on top so that the base of the hemisphere coincides with the base of the cone.

(Diagram: cone 5 cm across top, 10 cm deep, chocolate portion 4 cm with 2 cm diameter)

a) Calculate the volume of ice cream required to make one ice cream.
b) Calculate the outer surface area of the cone.

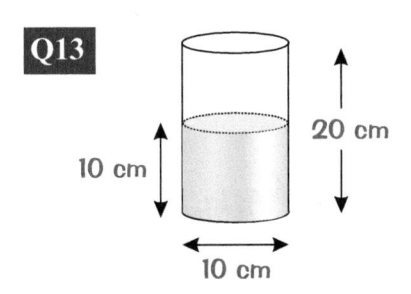

Q13 Aqil and Shelly are doing an experiment to find the radius of a marble. They fill a cylindrical container of diameter 10 cm and height 20 cm with water to a depth of 10 cm. 200 identical marbles are now submerged in the water. The depth increases to 14.5 cm. Calculate the radius of one marble.

The volume increase is a cylinder and you're told the height.

Q14 A cuboid has a height of x m, a width of $(3 - x)$ m and a length of $(5 - x)$ m.

a) Write down an expression for the volume of the cuboid.
b) Complete the table of values using your expression for the volume of the cuboid.
c) Draw a graph of V against x for $0 \leq x \leq 3$.
d) Use your graph to estimate the maximum volume of the cuboid.
e) Estimate the surface area of the cuboid when the volume is at its maximum.
f) A particular cuboid has a volume of 6 m³. By using your graph to find the two possible values of x, estimate the maximum total surface area of the cuboid for this volume.

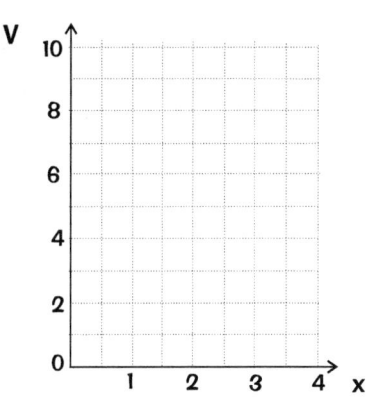

x	0	1	2	3
V			6	

Q15 A pipe has a hexagonal cross-section with dimensions as shown. Water comes halfway up the pipe and is 4 cm deep.

a) Find the cross-sectional area of water in the pipe.

The water is flowing at a rate of 500 cm³ per minute.

b) Find the speed of the water in cm/s to 3 s.f.

Convert the rate of flow into cm³/s, then find the speed by dividing the rate of flow by the cross-sectional area from part a).

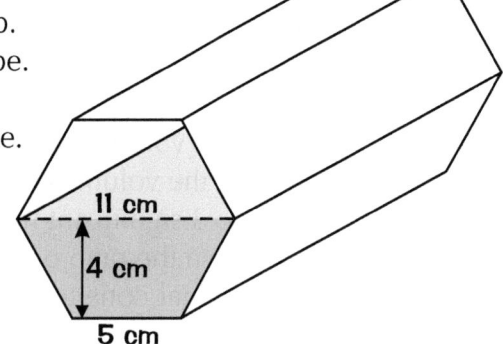

(Hexagonal prism with dimensions: 11 cm, 4 cm, 5 cm)

Section Five — Geometry and Measures

More Enlargements

Don't forget that when you're enlarging areas and volumes, there's a bigger scale factor — that one catches everyone out.

Q1 For a graphics project, Eliza makes a model of a chocolate box in the shape of a cuboid 5 cm long, 2 cm wide and 3 cm high. 
   a) Calculate the area of material needed to make the model (assuming no flaps are required for gluing).
   b) Eliza decides that the full size packaging will be similar to the model, but with lengths enlarged by a scale factor of 4. Calculate the area of material Eliza needs to make a full-size box.

Q2 Tomiko has a fish tank which is 42 cm wide and has a volume of 30 litres. She sees an enlarged version of this in the pet shop which is 63 cm wide. What is the volume of the larger fish tank to the nearest litre?

Q3 Soup comes in two different-sized tins — large and small. The tins are similar cylinders. The volume of the large tin is 1200 cm^3 and the volume of the small tin is 150 cm^3. The surface area of the large tin is 600 cm^2. Find the surface area of the small tin.

Q4 Cuboid A and cuboid B are similar. The surface area of cuboid A is 38 cm^2, and the surface area of cuboid B is 237.5 cm^2.
   a) The height of cuboid A is 4 cm. What is the height of cuboid B?
   b) What is the volume of cuboid A as a percentage of the volume of cuboid B?

Q5 On a holiday near the sea, children built a sandcastle in the shape of a cone. The radius of the base is 100 cm and the height is 100 cm.
   a) What is the volume of the sandcastle in m^3 correct to 3 significant figures?
   The children now remove the top portion to make a similar cone which is only 50 cm in height. 
   b) State the radius of the base of this smaller cone.
   c) State the ratio of the volume of the small cone to the volume of the original cone.
   d) Calculate the volume of the small cone in m^3 correct to 3 significant figures.
   e) Write down the ratio of the volume of the portion left of the original cone to the smaller cone in the form n:1.

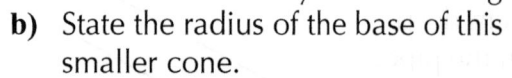

Section Five — Geometry and Measures

Projections

Projections are just different views of a 3D object. The front elevation is the view from the front, the side elevation is the view from the side and the plan is the view from the top.

Q1 The diagram shows an isometric projection of a triangular prism.

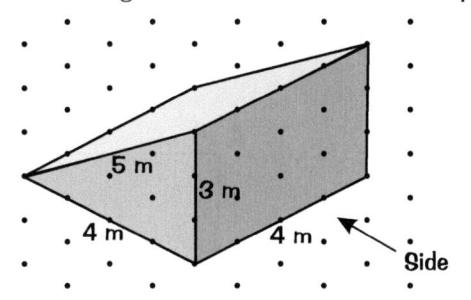

Draw:
a) the front elevation
b) the side elevation
c) the plan

Q2 Use the front, side and plan views of this object to sketch it in 3D.

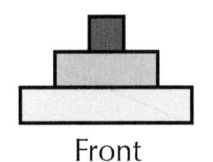

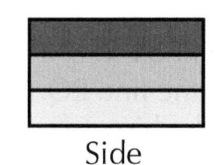

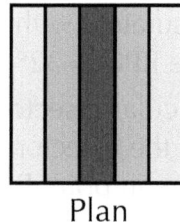

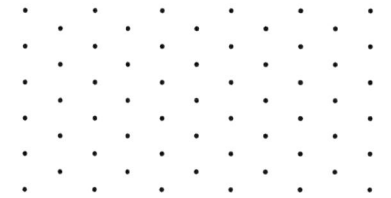

Front   Side   Plan

Q3 The diagrams below show the front elevation and plan view of a house. Use these to draw the side elevation. Use a scale of 1 cm = 1 m.

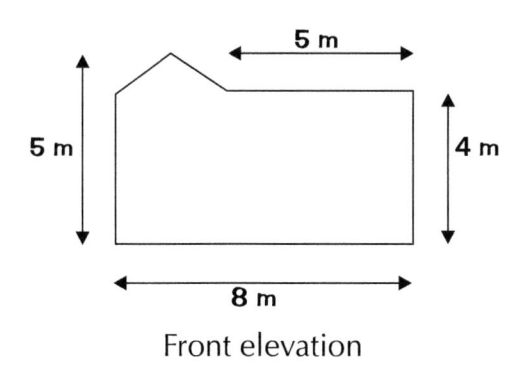

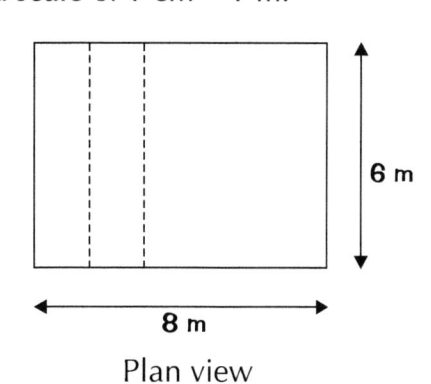

Front elevation

Plan view

Q4 Draw the front elevation, side elevation and plan view of the shape below.

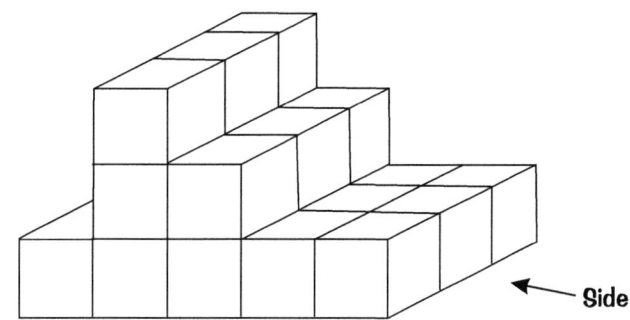

Loci and Construction

Don't let a silly word like <u>locus</u> put you off — there are <u>easy marks</u> to be had here, but you've got to do everything neatly, using a pencil, ruler and compasses.

Q1 Accurately construct an equilateral triangle with sides 4 cm.

Q2 a) Construct a rectangle, 6 cm by 4 cm, and label it as shown.
b) Inside the rectangle:
   i) draw the locus of points 5 cm from D
   ii) draw the locus of points equidistant from A and D
   iii) indicate with an X the point inside the rectangle which is 5 cm from D and equidistant from A and D.

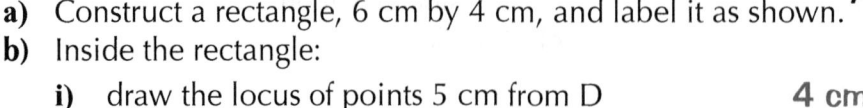

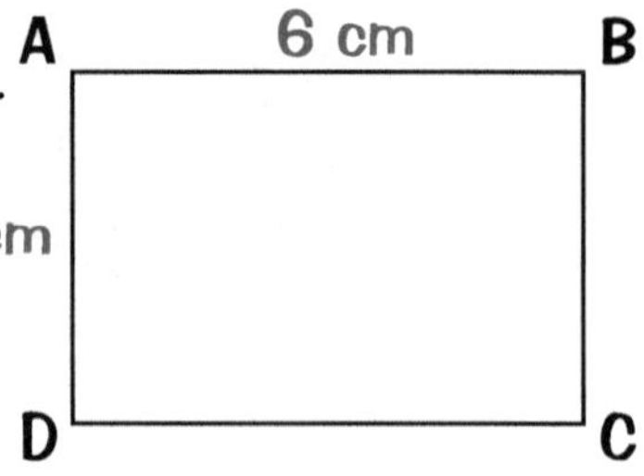

Q3 Construct triangle PQR accurately with length PQ = 10.5 cm, angle PQR = 95° and angle RPQ = 32°.
a) Construct the perpendicular bisector of the line PR. Draw in point A where the bisector crosses the line PQ.
b) Bisect angle PRQ. Draw in point B where the bisector crosses the line PQ. Measure the length BA.

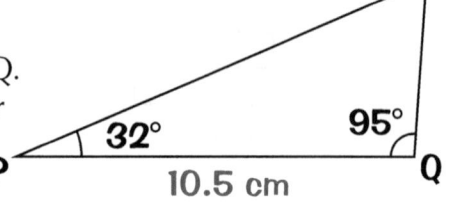

Q4 Omar is doing some garden landscaping. Because of gas and water pipes, he is not allowed to dig anywhere within 3 m of his house.

Using a scale of 1 cm to 1 m, draw a diagram for Omar showing the walls of his house and the area in which he cannot dig.

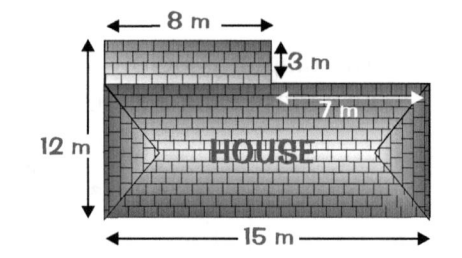

Q5 Construct triangle PQR with length PQ = QR = 11.5 cm and angle PQR = 38°.
a) Construct the bisectors of angles QPR and QRP. Mark the point O where the 2 bisectors cross.
b) With centre O draw the circle which just touches the sides PQ, PR and QR of the triangle. What is the radius of this circle?

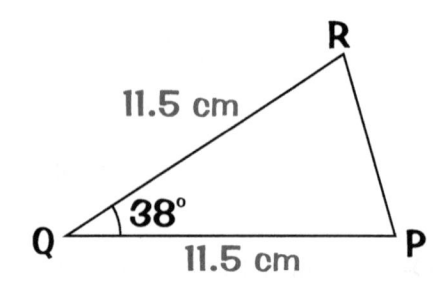

Q6 A and B are 2 points on a straight shore, 4 km apart with A due west of B.
a) Describe the locus of points P such that angle APB equals 90°.
b) Using a scale of 2 cm to 1 km draw an accurate scale diagram showing A, B, the shore line and the locus of P.

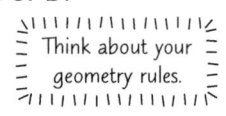

Think about your geometry rules.

An outcrop of rock is located on a bearing of 060° from A and 300° from B.
c) Indicate the rock on your diagram. Mark the spot with an X.
d) A ship steaming due east parallel to the shore avoids the rock by following the locus of P. How near does the ship come to the rock?

Section Five — Geometry and Measures

Loci and Construction

Q7 A running track is designed so that each point on the track is 32.5 m from a fixed line AB which is 100 m long.

•————————————— 100 m —————————————•
A   B

   a) Draw the locus of the line.
   b) Calculate the distance once round the running track.

Q8 Jim is landscaping his back garden, and has drawn the plan below. Two sides of the garden are bounded by fences and the other sides are bounded by the walls of the house and garage. The garden is in the shape of a rectangle.

   a) Using a scale of 1 cm to 1 m draw a plan of Jim's garden.
   b) Ben, the family dog, will be tethered to the garage at B by a lead of length 6 m. Construct accurately and shade the part of the garden where Ben can go.
   c) Jim wants to plant a tree in the garden. The tree must be planted more than 5 m away from the wall of the house and more than 4 m away from each fence. It must also be out of reach of Ben, and be more than 2 m away from the walls of the garage. On your plan of the garden, construct accurately and shade the region where Jim can plant his tree.

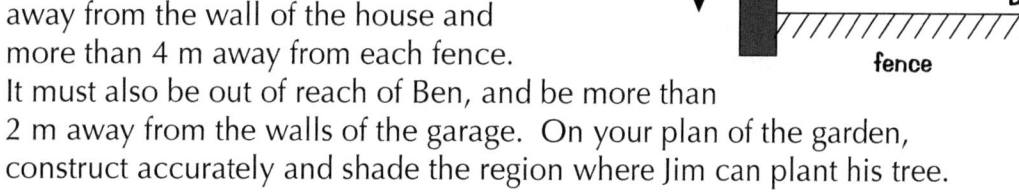

Q9 The positions of two islands A and B are found from the following information: A is 35 km from a jetty J on a bearing 065°, B is due south of A and on a bearing of 132° from J as shown below.

   a) Using a scale of 1 cm to 5 km, draw an accurate plan to show the positions of J, A and B.
   b) Find from your drawing the distance in km between the islands A and B.
   c) A boat leaves the jetty at 09.00 and reaches A at 11.30. What is its average speed in km/h?
   d) A lightship L is 20 km from J, equidistant from A and B and on the same side of J as A and B. Mark L on the drawing.
   e) Find the bearing of L from J.

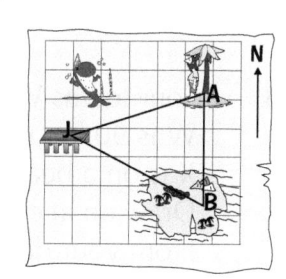

Q10 The triangle ABC on the right is first rotated 90° clockwise about vertex A, then 180° clockwise about vertex C. Draw the locus of vertex B.

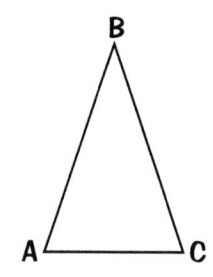

Section Five — Geometry and Measures

Bearings

Q1 Calculate the bearings required in these diagrams.

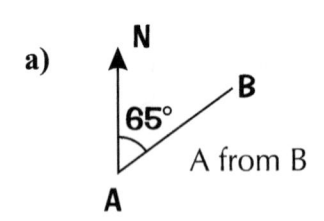

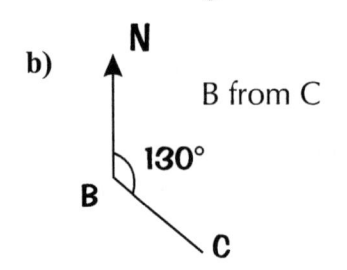

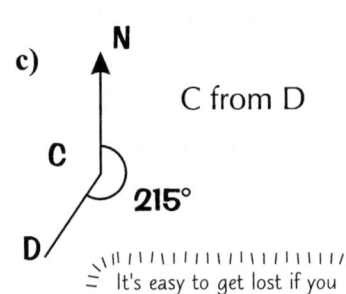

a) A from B (65° shown from north at A to B)

b) B from C (130° shown from north at B to C)

c) C from D (215° shown from north at C to D)

d) D from E (49° shown from north at E to D)

e) E from F, G from F, F from G (117° shown at F to E, 152° shown at F below to G)

It's easy to get lost if you don't follow the easy rule: always measure bearings from the north line.

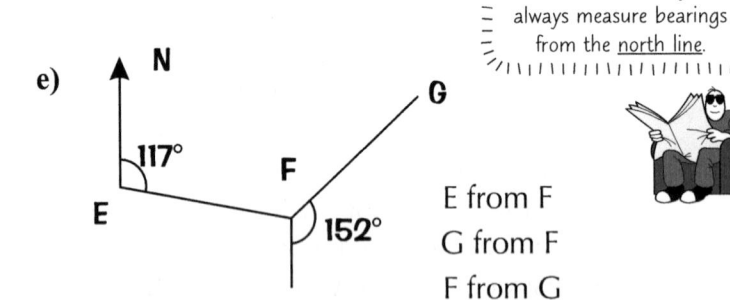

Q2 A coastguard spots a boat on a bearing of 040° and at a distance of 350 m. He can also see a tree due east of him. The tree is due south of the boat.
   a) Draw a scale diagram and measure accurately the distances from the:
      i) boat to the tree
      ii) coastguard to the tree
   b) Check by Pythagoras to see if your answers are reasonable.

Top tip: The word "from" is the most important word in a bearings question, so look out for it — it tells you where to start from.

Q3 Four towns W, X, Y and Z are situated as follows:
W is 90 km north of X, Y is on a bearing of 175° and 165 km from X,
X is on a bearing of 129° and 123 km from Z.
Draw an accurate scale diagram to represent the situation.
From your drawing measure the distances:
   a) WZ   b) WY   c) ZY.
Measure the bearings:
   d) Y from Z   e) W from Z   f) Y from W.

Q4 A walker travels 1200 m on a bearing of 165° and then another 1500 m on a bearing of 210°. By accurate measurement, find how far she is now from her starting point. What bearing must she walk on to return to base?

Section Five — Geometry and Measures

Section Five — Mixed Questions

Mixed Questions

You've covered all the topics in section five — great job. But before your thinking starts going off at a tangent, try these mixed questions to see how you're shaping up...

Q1 Find the sizes of the angles marked by letters. AB and CD are straight lines.

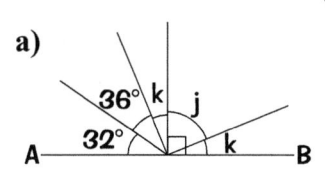

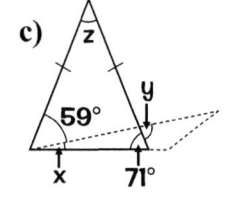

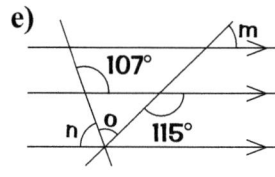

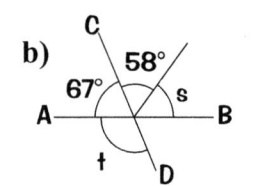

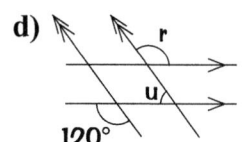

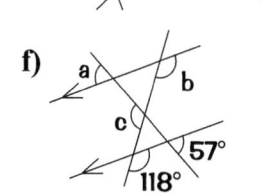

a) [diagram with 36°, 32°, angles j, k, k on line AB with right angle]

b) [diagram with 67°, 58°, angles s, t at intersection of AB and CD]

c) [triangle with 59°, 71°, angles x, y, z]

d) [parallel lines with 120°, angles r, u]

e) [parallel lines with 107°, 115°, angles n, o, m]

f) [intersecting lines with 57°, 118°, angles a, b, c]

Q2 Shapes ABCDH and DEFGH are regular pentagons.
 a) Work out the size of:
   i) Angle DEF   iii) Angle HGA
   ii) Angle AHG
 b) Write down the order of rotational symmetry of
   i) Shape ABCDH   ii) Shape AHG

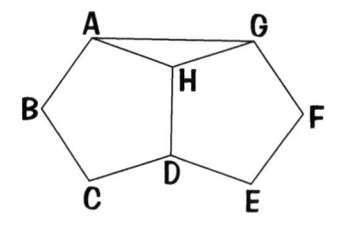

Q3 Identify each of the triangles or quadrilaterals described below.
 a) A three-sided shape that has rotational symmetry of order three.
 b) A four-sided shape with four equal angles and rotational symmetry of order two.
 c) A shape with four equal sides and two lines of symmetry.
 d) A three-sided shape with three different sized angles and no right angles.

Q4 A, B, C and D are points on the circumference of a circle. O is the centre of the circle and AC is a chord. Find the size of:
 a) angle AOC   b) angle ABC   c) angle ADC.

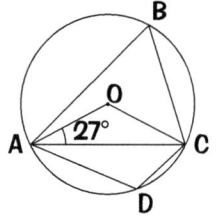

[circle diagram with 27° at O]

Q5 Ellie has a piece of paper shaped like a parallelogram. She cuts it exactly in half from corner to corner, making two scalene triangles. Prove that these triangles are congruent.

Q6 The two isosceles triangles on the right are similar.
 a) What is the value of a?   b) What is the value of b?

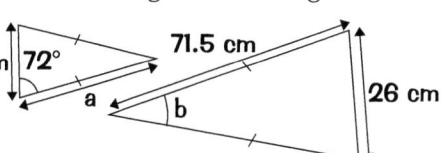

[two similar triangles: 4 cm, 72°, a; 71.5 cm, 26 cm, b]

Q7 Copy the axes using a scale of 1 cm to 1 unit. Mark on the axes a quadrilateral A with corners (3, 2), (4, 3), (4, 5) and (3, 4).
 a) Rotate A anticlockwise 90° about point (1, 2). Label the image B.
 b) Reflect A in the line $y = 1$. Label the image C.
 c) Enlarge A by a scale factor 3 about point (6, 6). Label the image D.
 d) Translate A with the vector $\binom{-7}{-1}$. Label this image E.
 e) Describe fully the rotation that sends E to B.

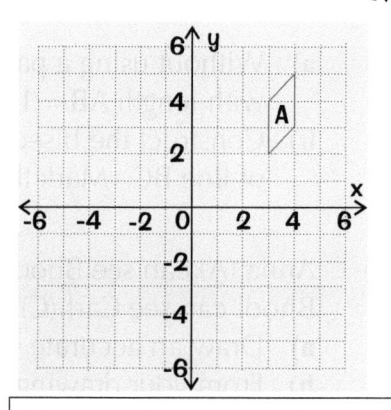

More mixed practice on the next page...

Mixed Questions

Q8 Katya made this design to sew onto a bag for her textiles project.
It uses two identical felt trapeziums and eight identical fleece parallelograms.
  a) How much fleece material will Katya need?
  b) How much felt material will Katya need?
  c) What is the total perimeter of the felt area of her design?

Q9 Find each of the following, giving each answer to 2 s.f.
  a) The area of a circle with radius = 2.5 cm.
  b) The circumference of a circle with radius = 9.1 m.
  c) The area of a sector with angle 57° of a circle with radius = 12 cm.
  d) The arc length of a sector with angle 195° of a circle with diameter = 18.2 m.

Q10 Which of the shapes below has a surface area closest to that of a cube with side length 26 cm?

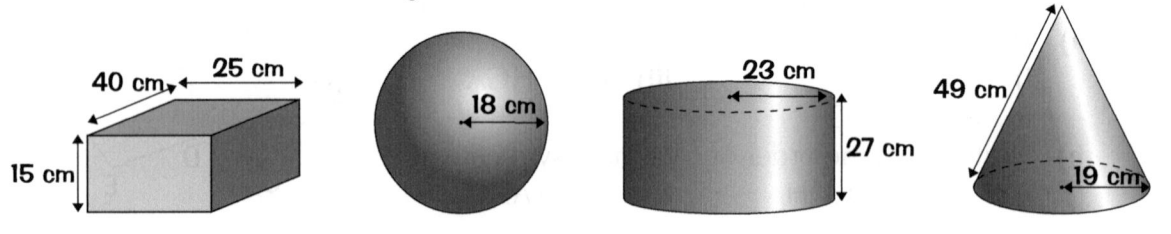

Q11 A cylindrical paddling pool with a radius of 65 cm and a depth of 45 cm is being filled with water at a rate of 540 litres an hour.
How long, to the nearest minute, will it take to fill 70% of the pool?

Q12 On the right are two cones — A and B. They are similar shapes.
The surface area of cone B is $10\,584\pi$ cm².
  a) What is the surface area of cone A in terms of π?
  b) What is the radius of cone B?
  c) What is the volume of cone B in terms of π?

Q13 Josh built the shape below out of 12 identical cubes.
Draw:
  a) the front elevation
  b) the side elevation
  c) the plan

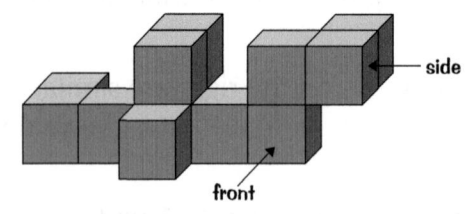

Q14 a) Without using a pair of compasses, accurately construct triangle ABC with length AB = 12 cm, angle CAB = 30° and angle ABC = 90°.
  b) Construct the bisector of angle ACB and the perpendicular bisector of line BC. Mark the point X where the two bisectors cross.

Q15 Anna (A) can see Bhodi (B) on a bearing of 295° and at a distance of 100 m.
Bhodi can see Carl (C) on a bearing of 211° and at a distance of 76 m.
  a) Draw an accurate scale diagram to represent the situation.
  b) From your drawing, work out:
    i) the distance from Carl to Anna.
    ii) the bearing from Carl to Anna.

Section Six — Pythagoras and Trigonometry

Pythagoras' Theorem

Don't try and do it all in your head — you've got to label the sides or you're bound to mess it up. Go on, get your pen out...

Q1 Find the length of the hypotenuse in each of the following triangles.

a) 10 cm, 4 cm, h
b) 3.5 m, 5 m, h
c) 3 cm, 4 cm, h
d) 15.2 mm, 22.3 mm, h
e) 6 m, 6 m, h
f) 5 m, 6.1 m, h
g) 2.4 cm, 9.3 cm, h
h) 4.5 cm, 2.1 cm, h
i) 4.5 cm, 5.1 cm, h
j) 4 cm, 7.5 cm, h

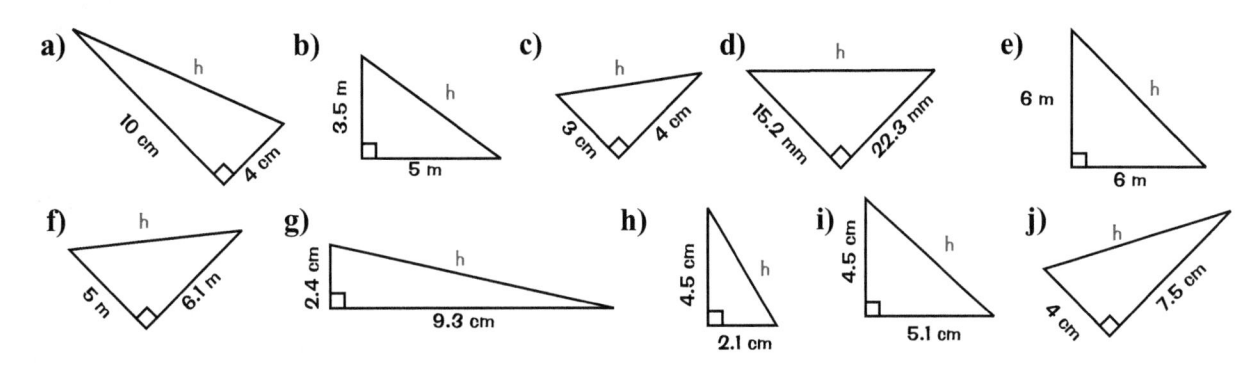

Q2 Find the unknown length in each of the following triangles.

a) 6 cm, 5 cm
b) 10 cm, 8 cm
c) 8.4 m, 5.6 m
d) 7 mm, 4.2 mm
e) 10.3 mm, 12.5 mm
f) 10.5 m, 6 m
g) 9.8 m, 7.4 m
h) 27 mm, 19 mm
i) 13.4 m, 9.3 m
j) 53 mm, 21 mm

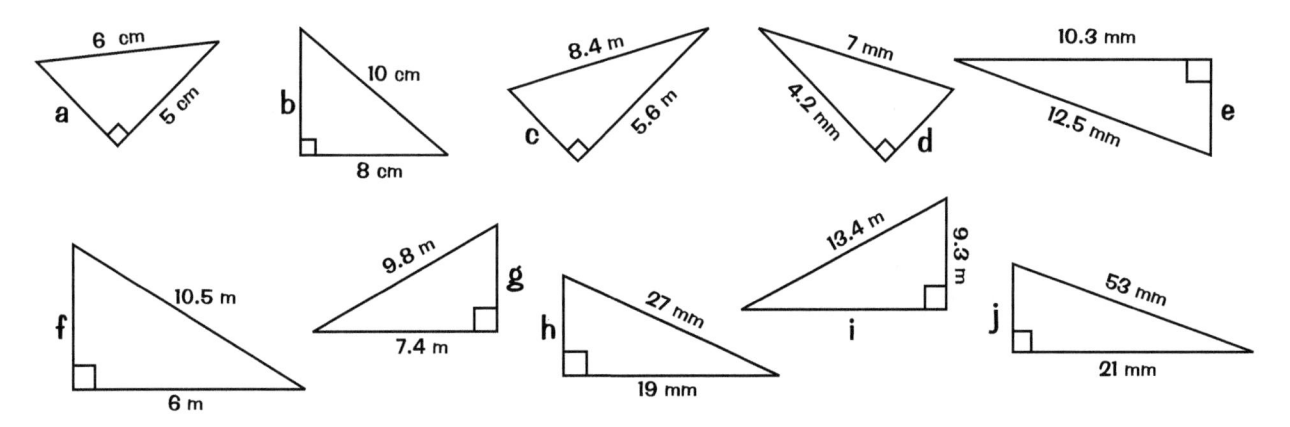

Q3 Find the unknown length in each of the following triangles.

k) 3.4 cm, 5.6 cm
l) 4.3 m, 6.5 m
m) 10.5 m, 12.1 m
n) 7.8 cm, 9.6 cm
p) 5.7 cm, 2.3 cm
q) 8.6 cm, 4.9 cm
r) 5.3 m, 5.3 m
s) 11.3 mm, 6.2 mm
t) 8.4 cm, 7.2 cm
u) 10 m, 7 m

Section Six — Pythagoras and Trigonometry

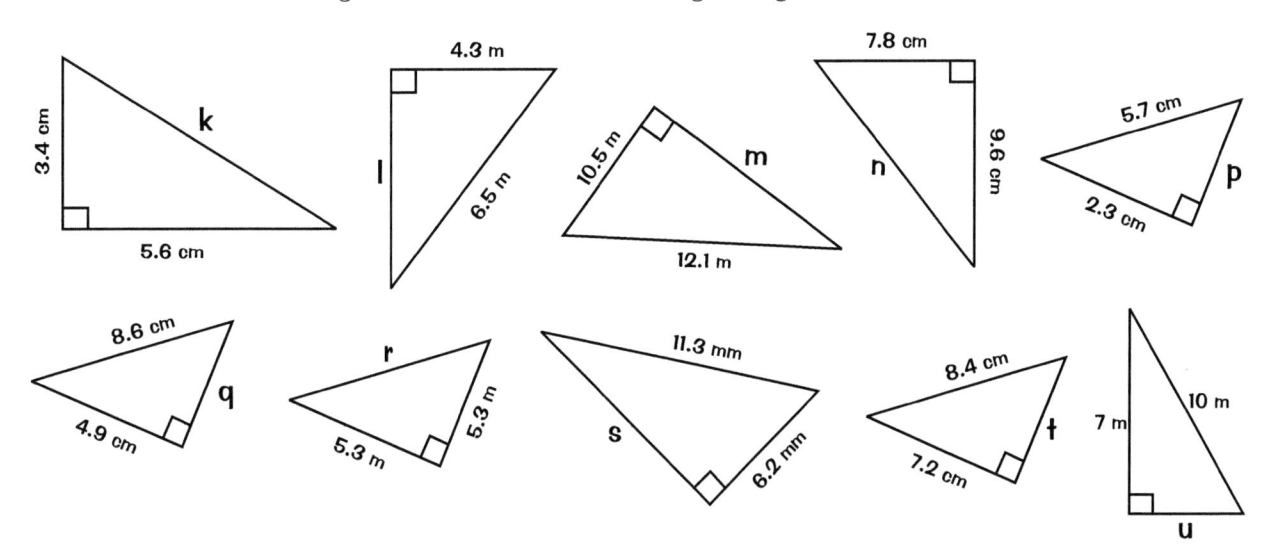

Pythagoras' Theorem

Q4 A window cleaner wants to clean the upstairs windows of an office. To meet safety regulations, her 10 m long ladder needs to be angled so that the bottom of the ladder is at least 2.6 m away from the wall. What is the maximum height that the top of the ladder can reach when used safely? Give your answer to 1 decimal place.

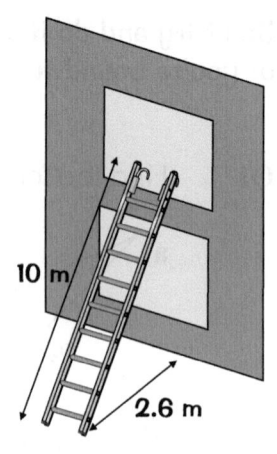

Q5

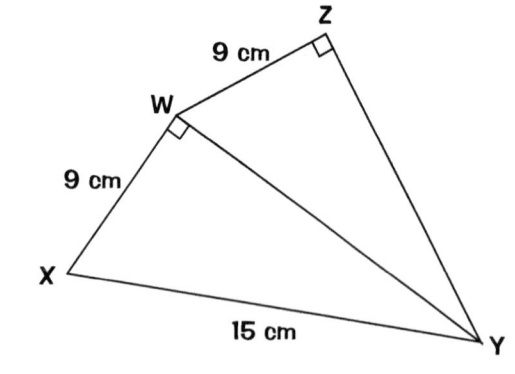

a) Calculate the lengths WY and ZY.
b) What is the perimeter of quadrilateral WXYZ?
c) What is the area of quadrilateral WXYZ?

Q6 A rectangular field is 250 m by 190 m. How far is it across diagonally?

Q7 A square tablecloth has a diagonal measurement of 130 cm. What is the length of one side?

Q8 A builder is replacing a roof beam and wants to work out how long it needs to be. It has to be the same width as the house. The measurements he already knows are shown on the diagram. How long should the beam be?

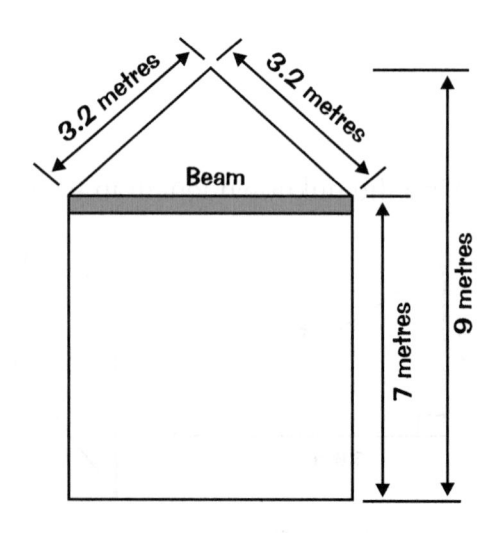

Q9 A flagpole 10 m high is supported by metal wires each 11 m long. How far from the foot of the pole must the wires be fastened to the ground if the other end is attached to the top of the pole?

Pythagoras' Theorem

Q10 Find the length of each of the lines on this graph.

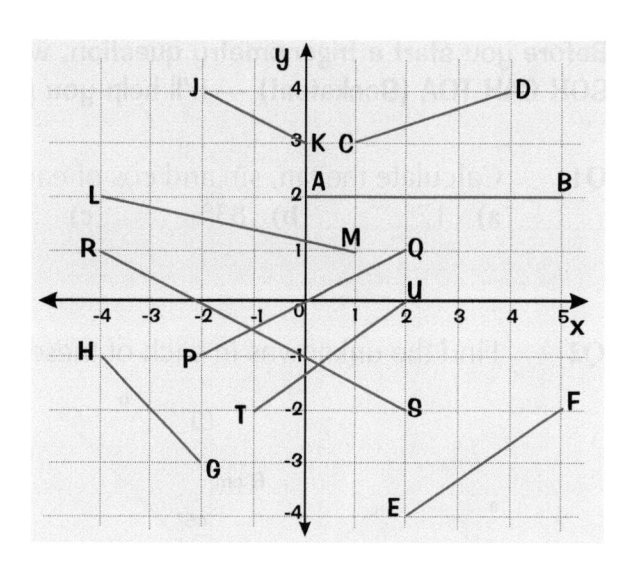

Q11 The coordinates of four points are A(2, 1), B(6, 4), C(7, 0) and D(3, –3).
    a) Calculate the distances:
        i) AB   **ii)** BC   **iii)** CD   **iv)** BD   **v)** AC
    b) What shape is ABCD?

Q12 Find the length of line MN, where M and N have coordinates:
    a) M(6, 3) N(2, 8)   **d)** M(9, 5) N(4, 8)
    b) M(1, 5) N(8, 12)   **e)** M(10, 4) N(10, 0)
    c) M(0, 1) N(7, 3)   **f)** M(12, 6) N(13, 0)

Q13 Find the length of line PQ, where P and Q have coordinates:
    a) P(2, –3) Q(3, 0)   **d)** P(–6, –1) Q(7, –9)
    b) P(1, –8) Q(4, 3)   **e)** P(12, –3) Q(–5, 5)
    c) P(0, –1) Q(2, –3)   **f)** P(–10, –2) Q(–2, –8)

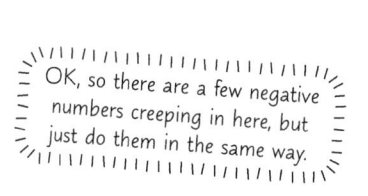

OK, so there are a few negative numbers creeping in here, but just do them in the same way.

Q14 A plane flies due east for 153 km then flies due north for 116 km. How far is it now from where it started?

Q15 A fishing boat travels at 12 km/h for an hour due north. It then turns due west and travels at 7 km/h for an hour. How far is it from its starting point now?

Q16 The grid on the right is made up of square units. The hypotenuse of a right-angled triangle is $\sqrt{13}$ units long. Given that the lengths of the other two sides are integers, find each of these side lengths and draw the triangle on the grid.

Section Six — Pythagoras and Trigonometry

Trigonometry — Sin, Cos, Tan

Before you start a trigonometry question, write down the formulas using
SOH CAH TOA (Sockatoa!) — it'll help you pick the right one.

Q1 Calculate the tan, sin and cos of each of these angles:
 a) 17°   b) 83°   c) 5°   d) 28°   e) 45°

Q2 Find the unknowns in each of these triangles:

(Triangle with a, 3 cm, 25°)
(Triangle with b, 6 cm, 45°)
(Triangle with 7.5 cm, 4 cm, θ)
(Triangle with 4.3 cm, 39°, c)
(Triangle with 9.7 cm, 42°, d)

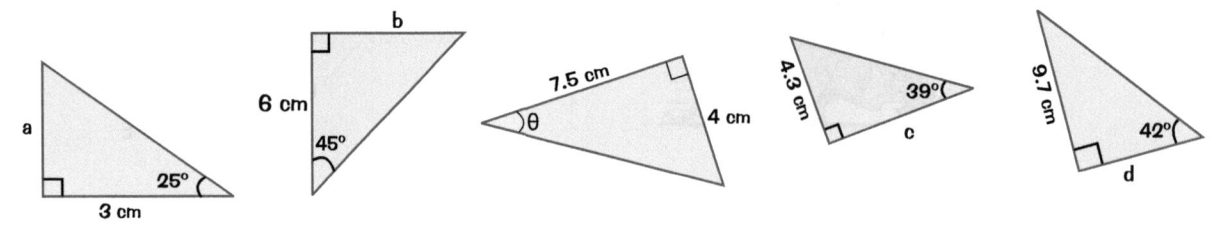

Q3 Find the value of each unknown in these triangles:

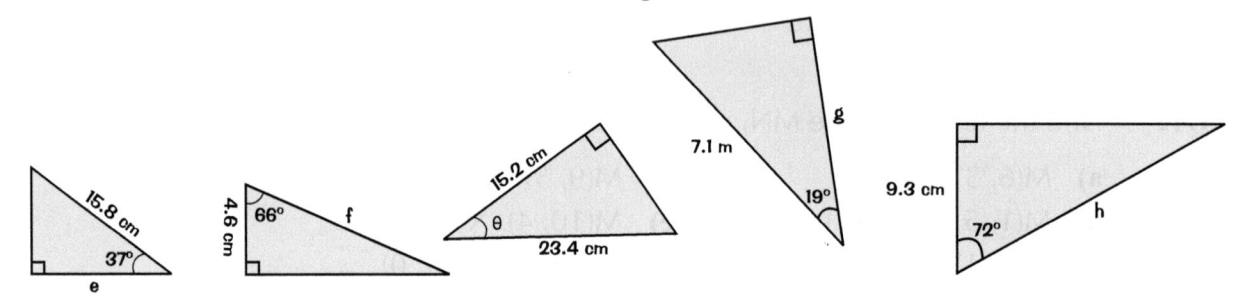

(Triangle with 15.8 cm, 37°, e)
(Triangle with 4.6 cm, 66°, f)
(Triangle with 15.2 cm, 23.4 cm, θ)
(Triangle with 7.1 m, 19°, g)
(Triangle with 9.3 cm, 72°, h)

Q4 Calculate the unknowns in the following:

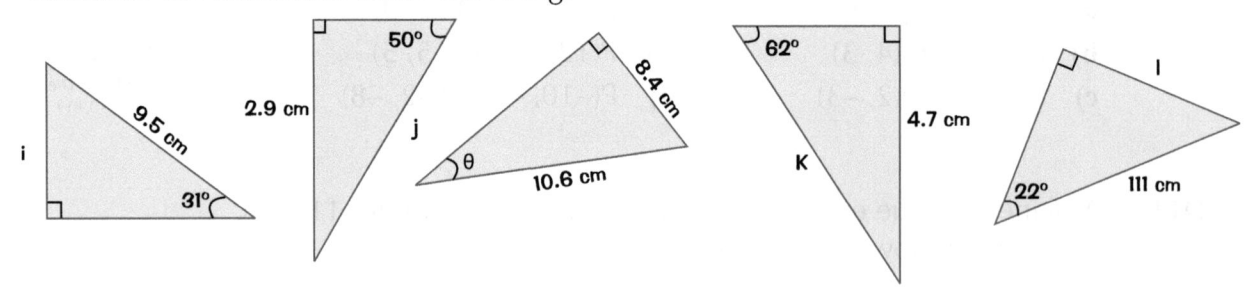

(Triangle with 9.5 cm, 31°, i)
(Triangle with 2.9 cm, 50°, j)
(Triangle with 8.4 cm, 10.6 cm, θ)
(Triangle with 62°, 4.7 cm, k)
(Triangle with 22°, 111 cm, l)

Q5 Without using a calculator, find the exact value of the letters in each of these triangles:

(Triangle with m, n, 15 cm, 30°)
(Triangle with q, p, 23 cm, 60°)
(Triangle with s, r, 9.5 cm, 45°)
(Triangle with 58 cm, u, t, 60°)
(Triangle with 16.5 cm, w, v, 45°)

Section Six — Pythagoras and Trigonometry

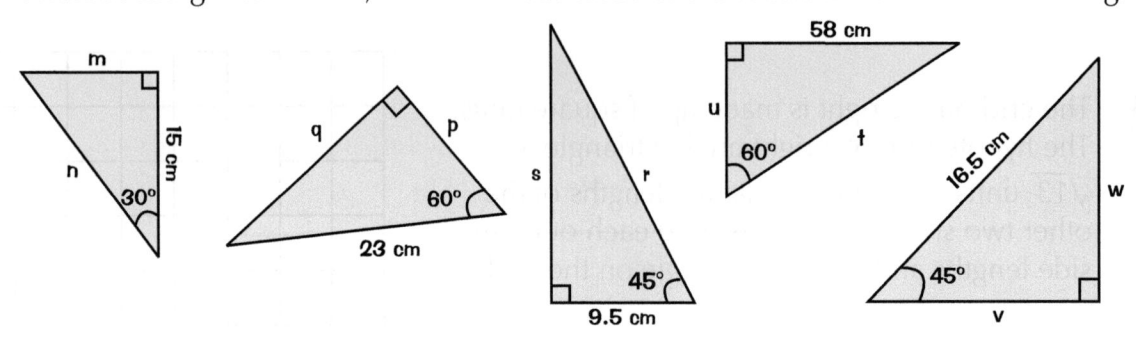

Trigonometry — Sin, Cos, Tan

Q6 A right-angled triangle has sides measuring 30 m, 40 m and 50 m.
    a) Draw a rough sketch of the triangle, clearly labelling the hypotenuse.
    b) Calculate the size of the smallest angle.

Make sure you've got the hang of the inverse SIN, COS and TAN functions on your calc... and check it's in DEG mode or you'll get nowhere fast.

Q7 The points P(1, 2), Q(4, 2) and R(4, -3) when joined together form a right-angled triangle.
    a) Draw a rough sketch of the triangle, labelling the length of each side.
    b) <u>Without measuring</u>, calculate the angle RPQ.
    c) Deduce angle PRQ.

Q8 The points A(1, -2), B(4, -1) and C(1, 3) are the vertices of the triangle ABC.
    a) On graph paper, plot the points A, B and C.
    b) By adding a suitable horizontal line, or otherwise, calculate the angle CAB.
    c) Similarly calculate the angle ACB.
    d) By using the fact that the interior angles of a triangle add up to 180°, work out the angle ABC.

Q9 Mary was lying on the floor looking up at the star on top of her Christmas tree. She looked up through an angle of 55° when she was 1.5 m from the base of the tree. How high was the star?

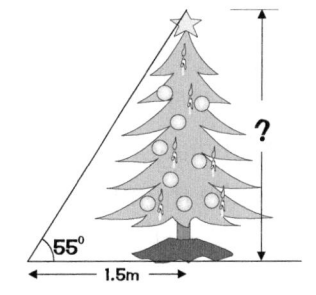

Q10 Jun is tiling her bathroom. She needs to cut off the right-angled triangle shown so that the tiles will fit nicely on her wall. Calculate the angle, θ, she needs to cut the tile at. Give your answer to the nearest degree.

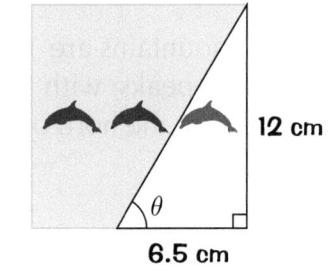

Q11 Mr Brown took his dog for a walk in the park. The dog's lead was 2 m long. The dog ran 0.7 m from the path Mr Brown was walking on, and Mr Brown dropped its lead.

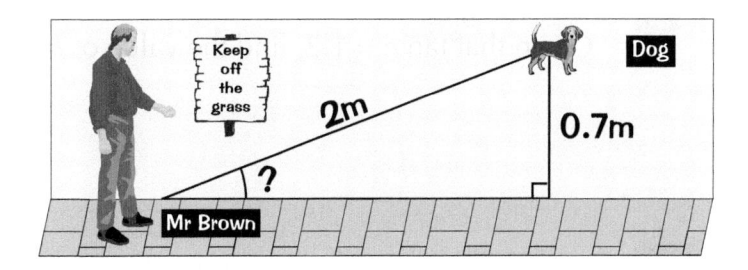

What angle did the lead make with the path?

Q12 A boat travels 9 km due south and then 7 km due east.
What bearing must it travel on to return directly to base?

Section Six — Pythagoras and Trigonometry

Trigonometry — Sin, Cos, Tan

Q13 This isosceles triangle has a base of 28 cm and a top angle of 54°. Calculate:
a) the length of sides AC and BC
b) the perpendicular height to C
c) the area of the triangle.

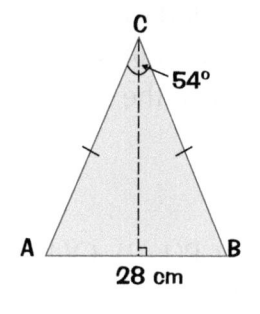

Q14 An isosceles triangle has two equal sides of 7 cm and an angle between them of 65°. Calculate the area of the triangle.

Q15 In this parallelogram the diagonal CB is at right angles to AC. AB is 10 cm and ∠CAB is 60°.
Without using a calculator, find:
a) CB   b) BD   c) the area of the parallelogram.

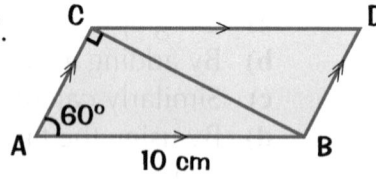

Q16 This rhombus WXYZ has sides of length 15 cm and diagonal WY of 28 cm. Calculate the:
a) length of diagonal XZ
b) area of the rhombus
c) angle WY makes with WX.

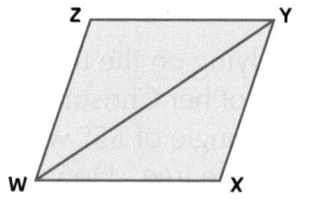

Q17 Two mountains are 1020 m and 1235 m high. A cable car connects the two peaks, with the cable at an angle of 16° to the horizontal. Calculate the horizontal distance between the two mountain peaks.

Q18 The triangles shown on the right are similar. Given that tan a = 1.2, find the value of b.

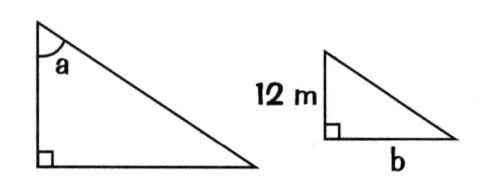

Q19 Without using a calculator, show that $\sin 60° + \cos 45° = \dfrac{\sqrt{3} + \sqrt{2}}{2}$

Q20 A ship sails on a bearing of 300° for 100 km. The captain can then see a lighthouse due south of her that she knows is due west of her starting point. Calculate how far west the lighthouse is from the ship's starting point.

Section Six — Pythagoras and Trigonometry

The Sine and Cosine Rules

Make sure you know the Sine Rule and both forms of the Cosine Rule. The one to use depends on which angles and sides you're given.

Q1 Calculate the lengths required to 3 s.f.

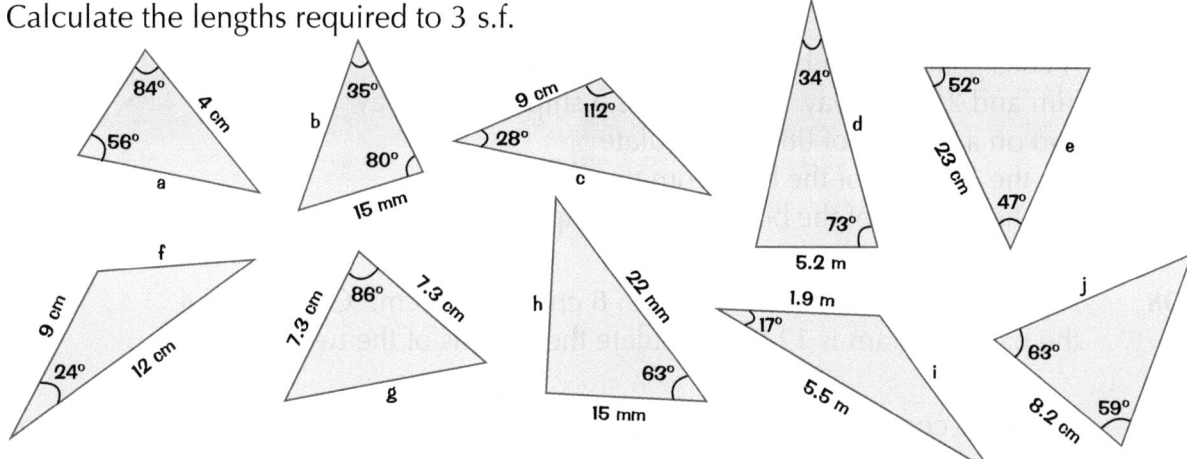

(Triangles showing:)
- Triangle with angles 84°, 56°, side 4 cm, find a
- Triangle with angles 35°, 80°, side 15 mm, find b
- Triangle with angles 112°, 28°, side 9 cm, find c
- Triangle with angles 34°, 73°, side 5.2 m, find d
- Triangle with angles 52°, 47°, side 23 cm, find e
- Triangle with sides 9 cm, 12 cm, angle 24°, find f
- Triangle with sides 7.3 cm, 7.3 cm, angle 86°, find g
- Triangle with sides 22 mm, 15 mm, angle 63°, find h
- Triangle with sides 1.9 m, 5.5 m, angle 17°, find i
- Triangle with side 8.2 cm, angles 63°, 59°, find j

Q2 Calculate the angles required, to the nearest degree.

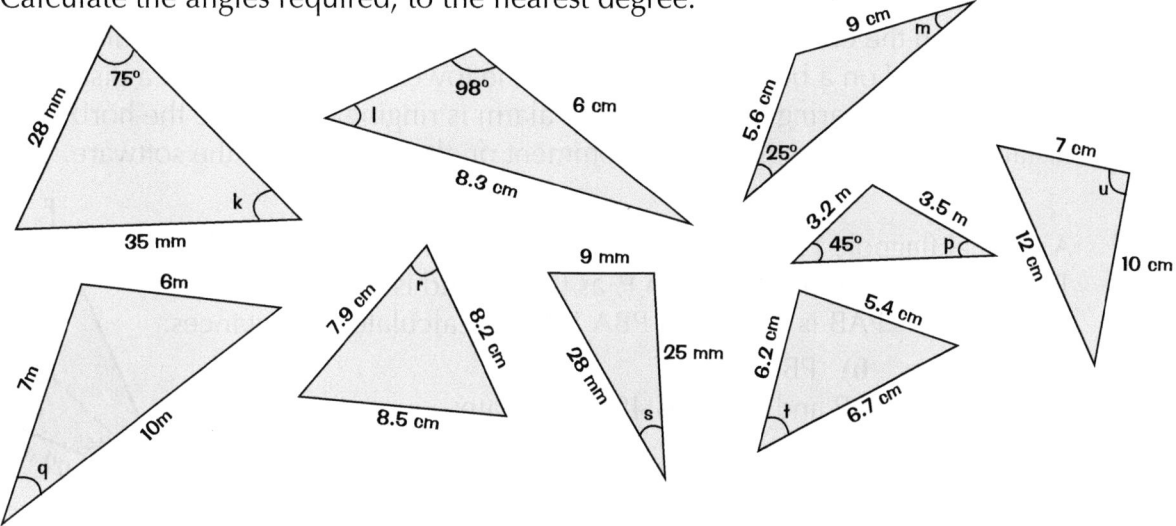

(Triangles showing:)
- Triangle with sides 28 mm, 35 mm, angle 75°, find k
- Triangle with sides 6 cm, 8.3 cm, angle 98°, find l
- Triangle with sides 9 cm, 5.6 cm, angle 25°, find m
- Triangle with sides 3.2 m, 3.5 m, angle 45°, find p
- Triangle with sides 7 cm, 12 cm, 10 cm, find u
- Triangle with sides 6 m, 7 m, 10 m, find q
- Triangle with sides 7.9 cm, 8.2 cm, 8.5 cm, find r
- Triangle with sides 9 mm, 25 mm, 28 mm, find s
- Triangle with sides 6.2 cm, 5.4 cm, 6.7 cm, find t

Q3 Find the values of the labelled angles, to the nearest degree.

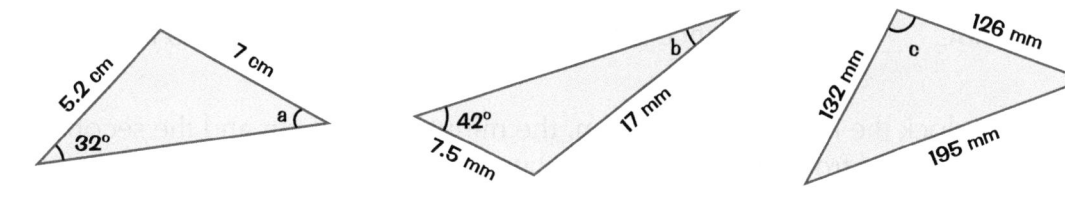

(Triangles showing:)
- Triangle with sides 5.2 cm, 7 cm, angle 32°, find a
- Triangle with sides 7.5 mm, 17 mm, angle 42°, find b
- Triangle with sides 132 mm, 126 mm, 195 mm, find c

Q4 Calculate the lettered sides and angles.

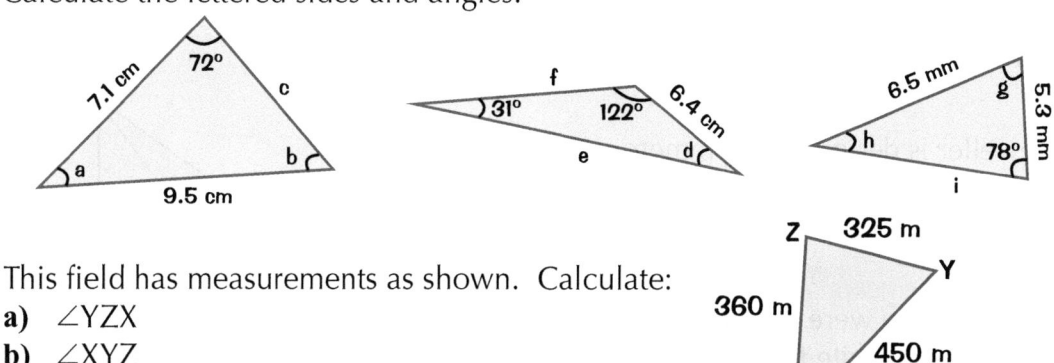

(Triangles showing:)
- Triangle with sides 7.1 cm, 9.5 cm, angle 72°, find a, b, c
- Triangle with side 6.4 cm, angles 31°, 122°, find d, e, f
- Triangle with sides 6.5 mm, 5.3 mm, angle 78°, find g, h, i

Q5 This field has measurements as shown. Calculate:
a) ∠YZX
b) ∠XYZ
c) ∠ZXY.

(Triangle XYZ with ZY = 325 m, XZ = 360 m, XY = 450 m)

Section Six — Pythagoras and Trigonometry

The Sine and Cosine Rules

Q6 Sushil is standing on a bridge over a river. He can see a tree on each bank, one 33 m away and the other 35 m away. If he looks through an angle of 20° going from one tree to the other, how far apart are the two trees?

Q7 A coastguard sees a boat on a bearing of 038° from him and 25 km away. He also sees a ship 42 km away and on a bearing of 080°. Calculate:
  a) the distance of the boat from the ship
  b) the bearing of the boat from the ship.

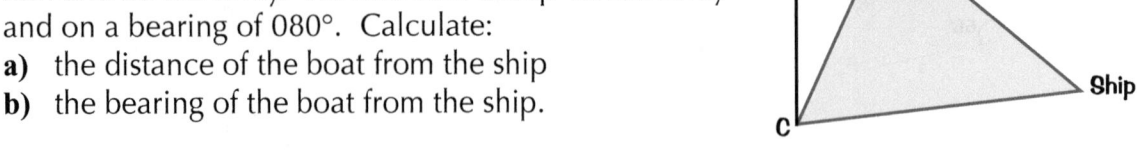

Q8 A parallelogram has sides of length 8 cm and 4.5 cm. One angle of the parallelogram is 124°. Calculate the lengths of the two diagonals.

Q9 Air traffic control are testing the reliability of their computer software by monitoring two aeroplanes and checking the computer's calculations with their own. If the horizontal distance between the planes drops to 3 miles or less, an alarm should be triggered on the computer. One of the test planes is at a distance of 5 miles from the tower, and on a bearing of 020° from the tower. The second is at a distance of 4.6 miles on a bearing of 034° and the alarm is ringing. Calculate the horizontal distance between the planes and comment on the reliability of the software.

Q10 A vertical flagpole FP has two stay wires to the ground at A and B. They cannot be equidistant from P, as the ground is uneven. AB is 22 m, ∠PAB is 34° and ∠PBA is 50°. Calculate the distances:
  a) PA   b) PB.
If A is level with P and ∠FAP is 49°, calculate:
  c) FA   d) PF.

Q11 An aircraft leaves A and flies 257 km to B on a bearing of 257°. It then flies on to C, 215 km away on a bearing of 163° from B. Calculate:
  a) ∠ABC   b) distance CA   c) the bearing needed to fly from A direct to C.

Q12 On my clock the hour hand is 5.5 cm, the minute hand 8 cm and the second hand 7 cm, measured from the centre. Calculate the distance between the tips of the:
  a) hour and minute hands at 10 o'clock
  b) minute and second hands 15 seconds before 20 past the hour
  c) hour and minute hands at 1020.

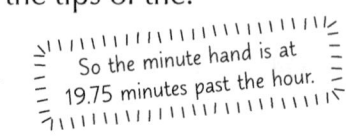

So the minute hand is at 19.75 minutes past the hour.

Q13 A jeweller is designing a symmetrical silver pendant with the dimensions shown in the diagram. Find the height of the pendant to the nearest millimetre.

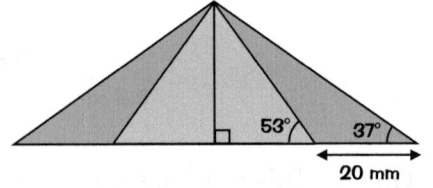

Q14 Mary and Jane were standing one behind the other, 2.3 m apart, each holding one of the two strings of a kite flying directly in front of them. The angles each girl's string made with the horizontal were 65° and 48° respectively. Assuming the ends of both strings are held at the same height above the ground, calculate the length of each string.

The Sine and Cosine Rules

Q15 Find the areas of the following triangles. Give your answers to 1 decimal place.

a) 5 cm, 37°, 12 cm

b) 9 m, 13°, 8.4 m

c) 18 cm, 52°, 28 cm

d) 18.1 m, 12°, 15.7 m

e) 16.9 cm, 149°, 22°, 12.3 cm

f) 71°, 88°, 8.2 mm, 8.7 mm

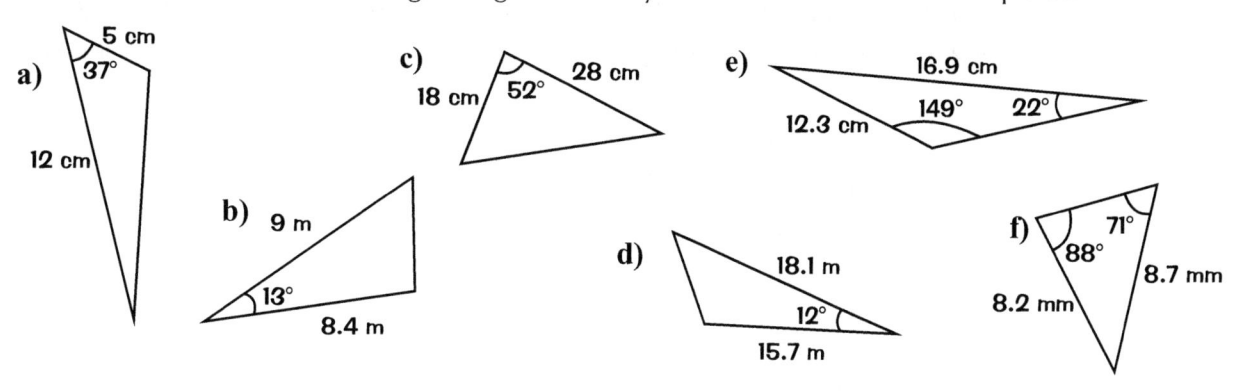

Q16 Calculate the areas of each of the triangles below, giving your answers to 1 decimal place.

You need an angle enclosed by two sides to work out the area. Hmm... looks like you'll have to use either the sine or cosine rule first for this question.

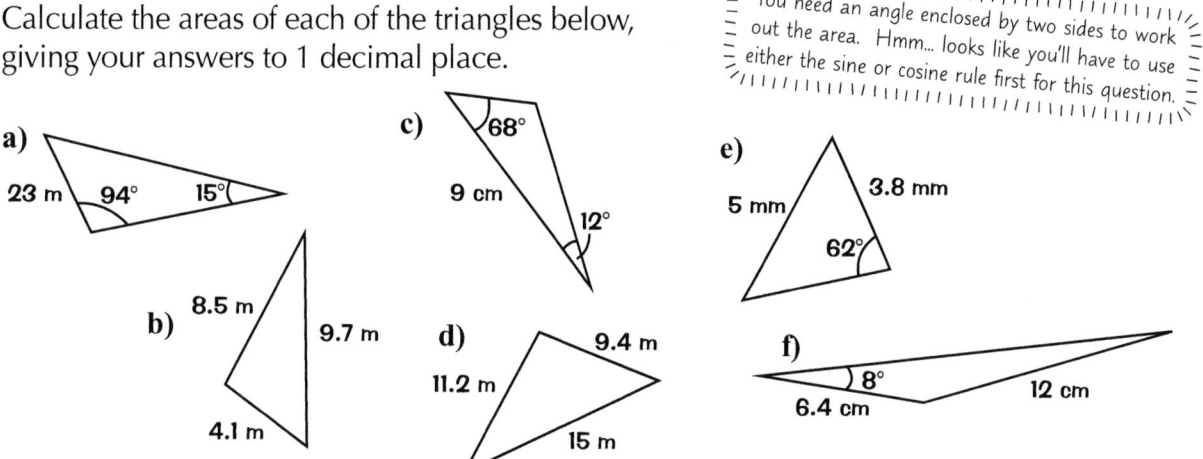

a) 23 m, 94°, 15°

b) 8.5 m, 9.7 m, 4.1 m

c) 68°, 9 cm, 12°

d) 11.2 m, 9.4 m, 15 m

e) 5 mm, 3.8 mm, 62°

f) 6.4 cm, 8°, 12 cm

Q17 Owen's garden is split into a patio area and a grass area. On the diagram, triangle ABC represents the patio and the triangle ACD represents the grass. AB is 11 m, BC is 21 m, ∠ABC is 95° and ∠ACD is 70°. The total area ABCD of his garden is 280 m².

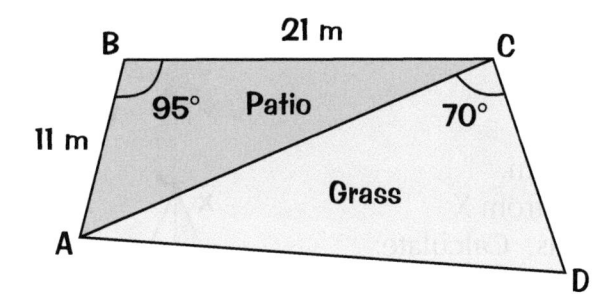

a) What is the area of the grass to 1 decimal place?

b) Owen wants to build a wall along the edge CD of his garden. How long will the wall be, correct to 1 decimal place?

Q18 Tom is painting a mural of a boat. The sails of the boat are made up of two triangles. Some of the lengths and angles of the sails are shown in the diagram.

a) What is the area of the left sail to 2 decimal places?

b) The total area of the two sails is 1.7 m². Using your answer from a), calculate the value of x to 1 decimal place.

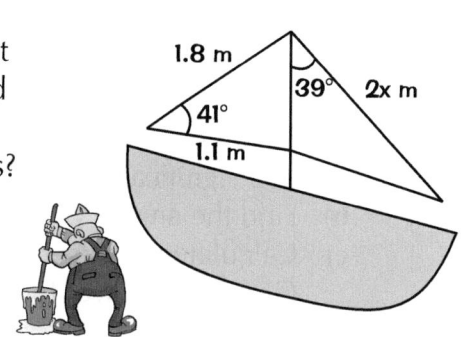

Section Six — Pythagoras and Trigonometry

3D Pythagoras and Trigonometry

Remember — the longest diagonal of a cuboid is found using $a^2 + b^2 + c^2 = d^2$. Always draw any triangles that you need and then label them with what you already know — that way everything's clear, so you're less likely to make mistakes.

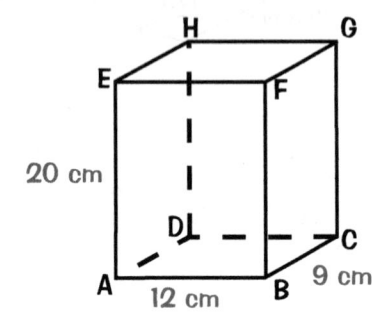

Q1 This rectangular box is 20 cm by 12 cm by 9 cm. Calculate:
a) angle ABE
b) length AF
c) length DF
d) angle EBH.

Q2 This pyramid is on a square base with sides of length 56 cm. Its vertical height is 32 cm. Calculate the length of:
a) the line from E to the midpoint of BC
b) the sloping edge BE.

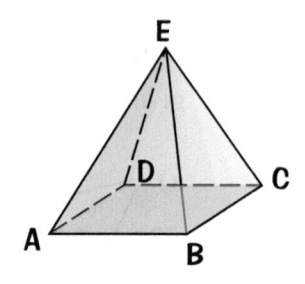

Q3 A rectangular box measures 20 cm by 30 cm by 8 cm. Calculate the lengths of:
a) the diagonal of each rectangular face
b) the diagonal through the centre of the box.

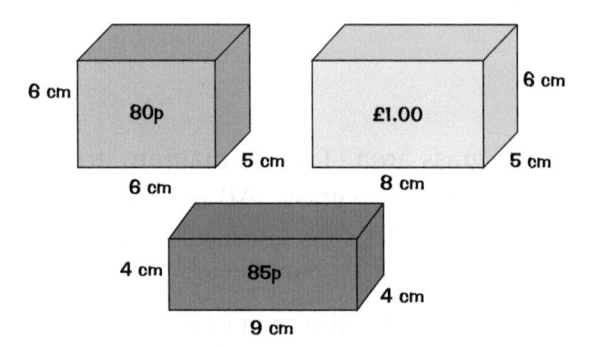

Q4 A shop sells the three different gift boxes shown on the left. Katie wants to buy the cheapest box that will fit a pen that is 10 cm long. Which box should she buy?

(Box 1: 6 cm × 6 cm × 5 cm, 80p)
(Box 2: 6 cm × 8 cm × 5 cm, £1.00)
(Box 3: 4 cm × 9 cm × 4 cm, 85p)

Q5 This cone has a perpendicular height of 9 cm. The centre of the base is O. The slant line from X makes an angle of 23° with the central axis. Calculate:
a) the radius of the base
b) the area of the base
c) the volume of the cone.

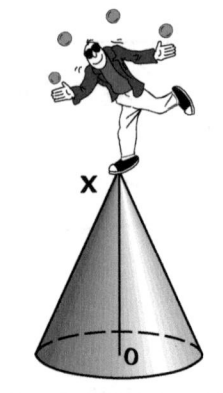

Q6 The cuboid shown is 12 cm by 5 cm by 8 cm.
a) Find the perimeter of the triangle YTW to 3 significant figures.
b) Find the angle TWY to 1 decimal place.
c) Calculate the area of the triangle YTW. Give your answer to 3 significant figures.

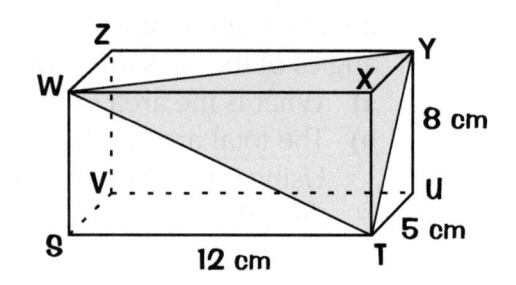

Section Six — Pythagoras and Trigonometry

Vectors

Vectors are used to describe a direction with a given size. Don't forget — a negative number means the vector is going in the opposite direction.

Q1 ABCDE is a pentagon.

$$\vec{AB} = \begin{pmatrix} 3 \\ 3 \end{pmatrix} \quad \vec{AC} = \begin{pmatrix} 2 \\ 6 \end{pmatrix} \quad \vec{AD} = \begin{pmatrix} -2 \\ 6 \end{pmatrix} \quad \vec{AE} = \begin{pmatrix} -3 \\ 2 \end{pmatrix}$$

a) Draw this pentagon accurately.
b) Write down the vectors:
   i) $\vec{DE}$ ii) $\vec{DC}$ iii) $\vec{EC}$
c) What sort of triangle is ACD?

Q2 $p = \begin{pmatrix} 2 \\ 3 \end{pmatrix}, \; q = \begin{pmatrix} 0 \\ -2 \end{pmatrix}, \; r = \begin{pmatrix} 3 \\ -1 \end{pmatrix}, \; s = \begin{pmatrix} -1 \\ -2 \end{pmatrix}$

Calculate then draw:

a) $p + q$ c) $2r$ e) $2p - 2s$ g) $2r - q$ i) $p + 2s$

b) $p - q$ d) $s + p$ f) $3q + s$ h) $\frac{1}{2}q + 2r$ j) $q - 2r$

Q3 ABCD is a parallelogram. M, N, P and Q are the midpoints of the sides, as shown. $\vec{MQ} = x$ and $\vec{AM} = y$.

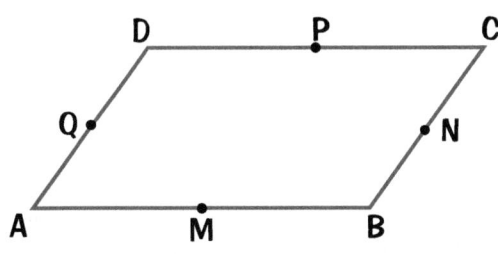

Express in terms of x and y:

a) $\vec{AB}$ c) $\vec{NB}$ e) $\vec{AC}$
b) $\vec{AQ}$ d) $\vec{BC}$ f) $\vec{BD}$

Don't try and do this in your head — mark the vectors on the diagram and follow your arrows. Otherwise you'll get lost.

Q4 The grid below is made up of dots which are equally spaced horizontally and vertically. Express the vectors l, m and n in terms of j and k.

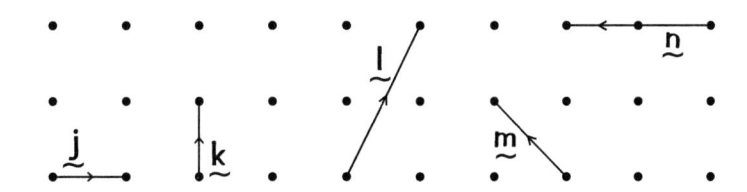

Q5 A wall is made up of identical bricks, with each successive layer shifted to the right by the width of exactly half a brick. The vectors a and b are shown on an individual brick.

Express:
a) $\vec{XY}$ in terms of a and b
b) $\vec{XZ}$ in terms of a and b.

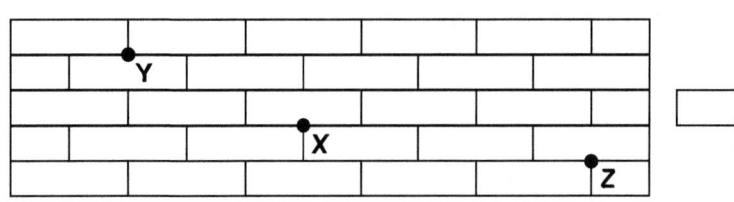

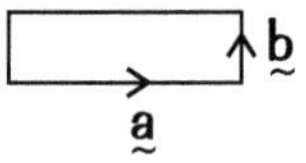

Section Six — Pythagoras and Trigonometry

Vectors

Q6 In the diagram on the right, EB and AC are perpendicular. ABCE is a parallelogram. ∠EDC is a right angle.

    a) Name a vector equal to: *(Equal vectors will have same size and direction.)*

        i) $\vec{FC}$ v) $2\vec{CD}$
        ii) $\vec{FB}$ vi) $\vec{AE} + \vec{EC}$
        iii) $\vec{BC}$ vii) $\vec{EF} - \vec{CF}$
        iv) $\vec{CE}$ viii) $\vec{ED} + \vec{DC} + \vec{CB}$

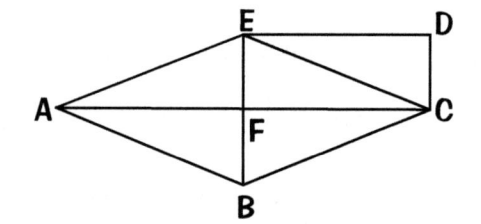

    b) If AC = 16 cm and EB = 6 cm:
        i) what is the area of ABCE?
        ii) what is the area of ABCDE?

Q7 The diagram of the quadrilateral ABCD shows that $\vec{AD} = 3\underline{a}$, $\vec{AC} = 2\underline{a} - 2\underline{b}$ and $\vec{BC} = 4\underline{a} + 2\underline{b}$.
Prove that $\vec{AB}$ and $\vec{DC}$ are parallel.

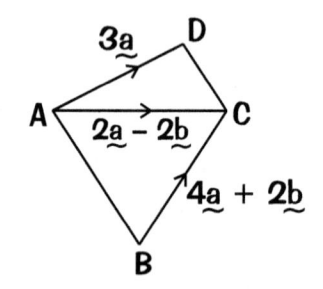

Q8 The point F lies on the straight line EG so that EF : FG = 1 : 2. $\vec{EF} = \underline{x} + 2\underline{y}$. Find the vector $\vec{FG}$ in terms of $\underline{x}$ and $\underline{y}$.

Q9 $\vec{LM}$ and $\vec{NP}$ are identical vectors. Q lies on the line LM so that LQ : QM = 1 : 2. R lies on the line NP so that NR : RP = 3 : 1. The vector $\vec{LQ} = 3\underline{a} + 4\underline{b}$. Find the vector $\vec{NR}$ in terms of $\underline{a}$ and $\underline{b}$.

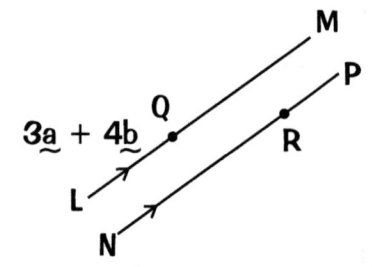

Q10 In the diagram to the right, HGF is a straight line where HG : GF = 3 : 2. Find vector $\vec{EG}$ in terms of $\underline{a}$ and $\underline{b}$.

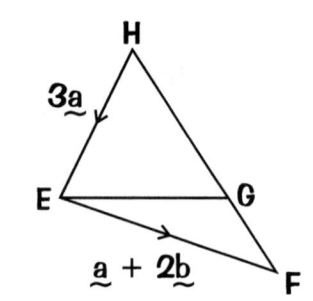

Q11 ABC is a triangle. P is the point on BA such that BA = 2PA. Q is the point on BC such that BC = 2BQ. $\vec{BQ} = \underline{a}$ and $\vec{PA} = \underline{b}$.

    a) Express in terms of $\underline{a}$ and $\underline{b}$:
        i) $\vec{BC}$
        ii) $\vec{CP}$
        iii) $\vec{PQ}$

    b) Prove that $\vec{PQ}$ is parallel to $\vec{AC}$.

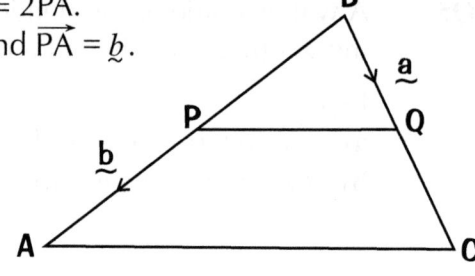

Section Six — Pythagoras and Trigonometry

Section Six — Mixed Questions

Mixed Questions

What do you call a three-sided shape that'll give anything a go? A try-angle...
Anyway — try these mixed questions to test out your skills with Pythagoras and Trigonometry.

Q1 Find the unknown length in each of the following triangles.

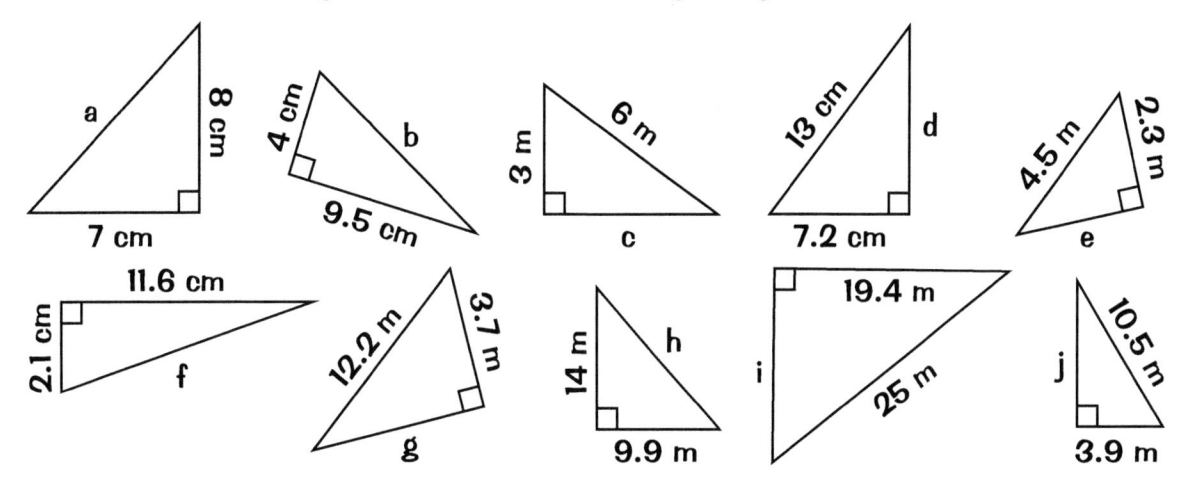

[Triangles with the following measurements:
- Triangle with sides 7 cm, 8 cm, hypotenuse a
- Right-angled triangle with sides 4 cm, hypotenuse 9.5 cm, unknown b
- Triangle with sides 3 m, 6 m, unknown c
- Triangle with sides 13 cm, 7.2 cm, unknown d
- Triangle with sides 4.5 m, 2.3 m, unknown e
- Triangle with sides 2.1 cm, 11.6 cm, unknown f
- Triangle with sides 12.2 m, 3.7 m, unknown g
- Triangle with sides 14 m, 9.9 m, unknown h
- Triangle with sides 19.4 m, 25 m, unknown i
- Triangle with sides 10.5 m, 3.9 m, unknown j]

Q2 A sail is cut out of fabric in the shape of a right-angled triangle. It has a hypotenuse of 5.9 m and a height of 5.4 m. What is the area of the sail, to 2 decimal places?

Q3 Find the length of the line AB where A and B have coordinates:

a) A(2, 3) B(0, 7)
b) A(–6, 5) B(3, –1)
c) A(–8, 7) B(–6, 2)
d) A(–1, 10) B(–5, 8)
e) A(7, –4) B(–7, –1)
f) A(2, 1) B(–10, 8)

Q4 Find the unknown length or angle in each of the following triangles.

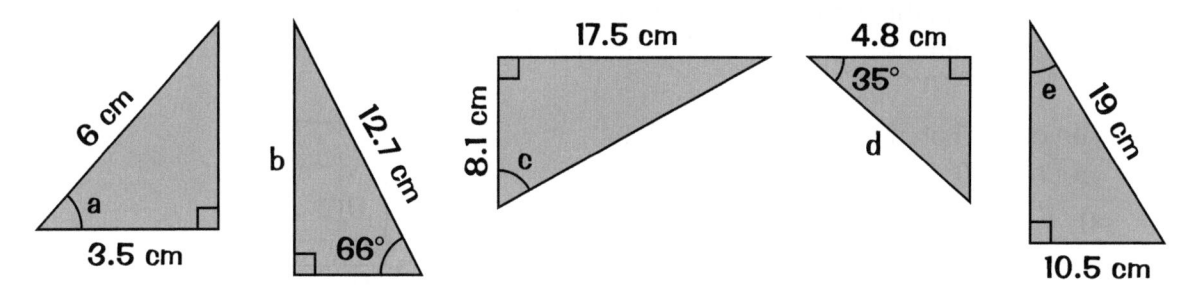

[Triangles with:
- 6 cm hypotenuse, 3.5 cm base, angle a
- 12.7 cm side, 66° angle, unknown b
- 17.5 cm and 8.1 cm, unknown c
- 4.8 cm, 35° angle, unknown d
- 19 cm hypotenuse, 10.5 cm base, unknown e]

Q5 A guy rope is tied to a point on a tent 80 cm above the horizontal ground, and stretched out until taut. The other end of the guy rope is tied to a peg in the ground and makes an angle of 30° with the horizontal. Without using a calculator, work out the length of the guy rope between the tent and the peg.

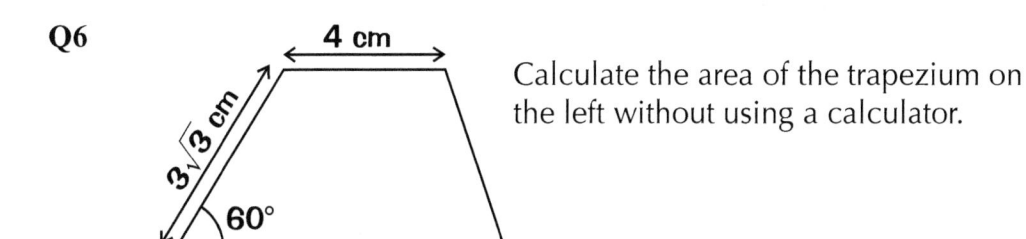

Q6 [Trapezium with parallel sides 4 cm (top) and 8 cm (bottom), slant side $3\sqrt{3}$ cm, and 60° angle at bottom left]

Calculate the area of the trapezium on the left without using a calculator.

More mixed practice on the next page...

Mixed Questions

Q7 Calculate each of the labelled values to 1 decimal place.

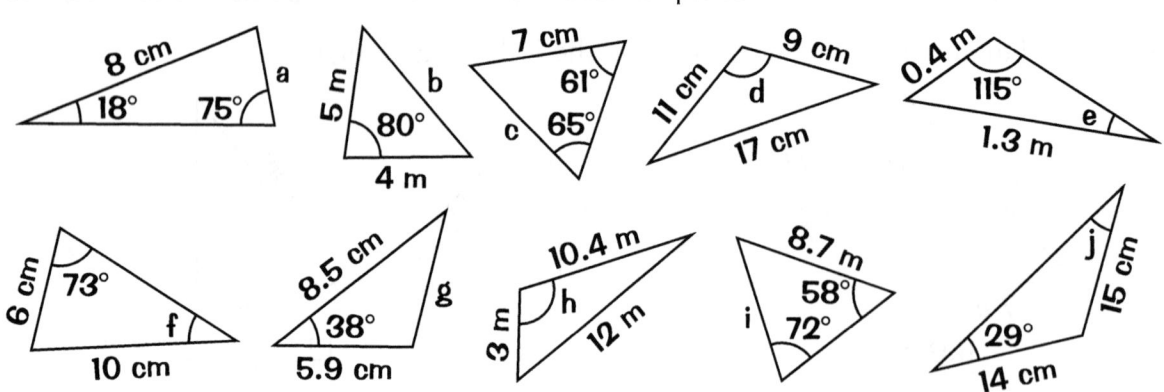

[Triangles with labels:
- Triangle: 8 cm, 18°, 75°, side a
- Triangle: 5 m, 80°, 4 m, side b
- Triangle: 7 cm, 61°, 65°, side c
- Triangle: 9 cm, 17 cm, 11 cm, angle d
- Triangle: 0.4 m, 115°, 1.3 m, side e
- Triangle: 6 cm, 73°, 10 cm, angle f
- Triangle: 8.5 cm, 38°, 5.9 cm, side g
- Triangle: 10.4 m, 12 m, 3 m, angle h
- Triangle: 8.7 m, 58°, 72°, side i
- Triangle: 29°, 14 cm, 15 cm, angle j]

Q8 Work out the areas of the triangles with the measurements given below.

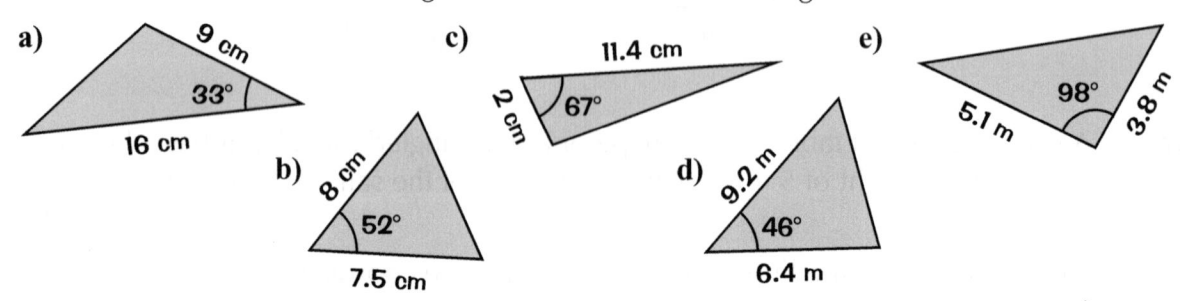

a) 9 cm, 33°, 16 cm
b) 8 cm, 52°, 7.5 cm
c) 11.4 cm, 67°, 2 cm
d) 9.2 m, 46°, 6.4 m
e) 5.1 m, 98°, 3.8 m

Q9 Jean is painting a triangle on a playing field. He starts at point A and paints a straight line 15 m long along a bearing of 017°. He then returns to point A and paints a 20 m long straight line along a bearing of 348°. He then draws a third line joining the two lines together, as shown.
  a) Calculate the length of the third side of the triangle.
  b) Calculate the area covered by the triangle.

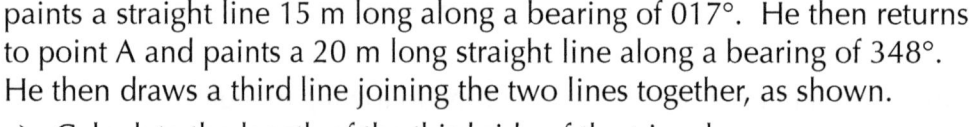

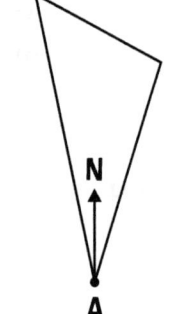

Q10 The cuboid on the left has dimensions 15 cm by 8 cm by 6 cm.
  a) Calculate the length of diagonal AG.
  b) Calculate the size of angle CAG.

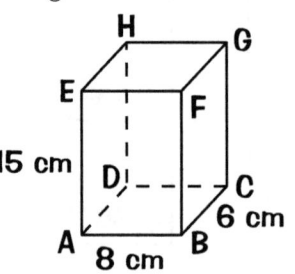

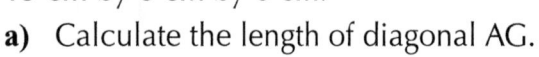

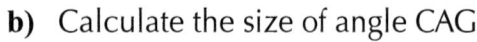

Q11 The vectors $r = \begin{pmatrix} -5 \\ 2 \end{pmatrix}$, $s = \begin{pmatrix} 2 \\ 4 \end{pmatrix}$ and $t = \begin{pmatrix} -1 \\ 5 \end{pmatrix}$. Calculate and draw the following vectors.
  a) $r + s$
  b) $2s + t$
  c) $r - s + 2t$
  d) $t - r - s$

Q12 Shape ABCDEF is a regular hexagon. M is the midpoint of the line FB and N is the midpoint of the line FD.
The vectors $\vec{BA} = x$, $\vec{AF} = y$ and $\vec{FE} = z$.
Express the following vectors in terms of x, y and z.
  a) $\vec{CE}$
  b) $\vec{MF}$
  c) $\vec{AM}$
  d) $\vec{DN}$
  e) $\vec{BN}$
  f) $\vec{MN}$

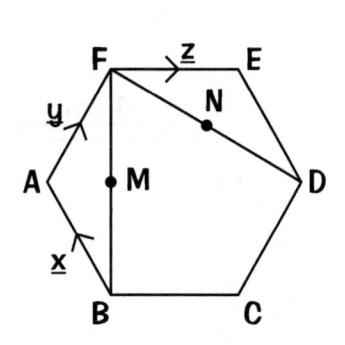

Section Six — Mixed Questions

Section Seven — Probability and Statistics

Probability Basics

> Remember... you can express probabilities as a fraction, decimal or percentage.
> 1) A probability of ZERO means that it definitely will not happen.
> 2) A probability of ONE means it definitely will happen.

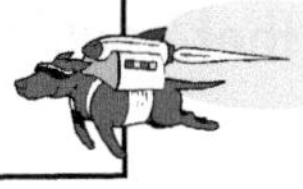

Q1 This number line is a probability scale. Place the letters a-d on the scale to show the probabilities of the following events.

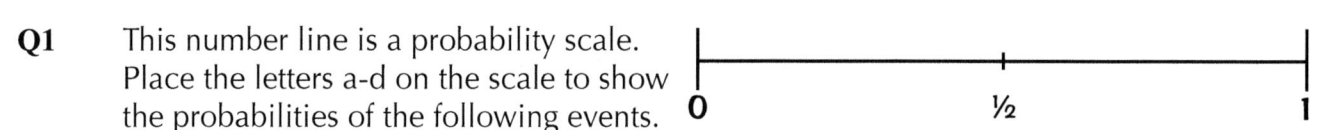

0 — ½ — 1

a) The probability of getting a head on a toss of a 10p coin.
b) The probability of choosing a red ball from a bag containing 2 red balls and 1 green ball.
c) The probability of rolling a five on an ordinary dice.
d) The probability of choosing a Guatemalan stamp from a bag containing 60 British stamps and 40 French stamps.

Q2 After 49 tosses of an unbiased coin, 24 have been heads and 25 have been tails. What is P(50th toss will be a head)?

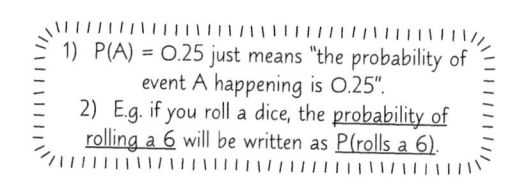

> 1) P(A) = 0.25 just means "the probability of event A happening is 0.25".
> 2) E.g. if you roll a dice, the probability of rolling a 6 will be written as P(rolls a 6).

Q3 A bag contains 3 red balls, 4 blue balls and 5 green balls. A ball is chosen at random from the bag. What is the probability that:
a) it is green
b) it is blue
c) it is red
d) it is not red?

Q4 If the probability of picking a banana from a fruit bowl is 0.27, what is the probability of not picking a banana?

Q5 Students at a school conduct a survey of the colours of parents' cars, where every parent owns one car. The table shows the results.

Red	Blue	Yellow	White	Green	Other
40	29	13	20	16	14

a) What is the probability of a randomly chosen parent owning a red car?
b) What is the probability of a randomly chosen parent owning a car that's not blue or green?

Q6 Debbie's employer organises a weekly prize draw, where the winning employee is selected at random. Debbie only joins in if her chance of winning is at least 0.1. If there are 8 other people playing this week, will Debbie choose to join in?

Q7 Simon has an unfair coin. He knows the probability of it landing on heads is $5 - 4y$. Find the probability of it landing on tails.

Q8 Tamara has a bag containing n balls, each of which is either purple, white or black. The probabilities of a randomly selected ball being each colour are shown in the table.

Colour	Purple	White	Black
Probability	$11x$	$15x$	$24x$

a) Find the value of x.
b) Find the probability that a randomly selected ball is black.

Counting Outcomes

Counting outcomes often involves listing (in as sensible a way as possible) everything that could happen. Tables often turn out to be really useful.

Q1 There are 2 spinners: one with 3 sides numbered 1-3, and the other with 7 sides numbered 1-7.

a) If both are spun together, list all the possible outcomes.

b) Complete the following table showing the sum of the 2 numbers for each outcome.

In part a), show each combination of scores by writing them in brackets. E.g. (3, 7) means 3 on the 3-sided spinner and 7 on the 7-sided spinner.

	1	2	3	4	5	6	7
1							
2							
3							

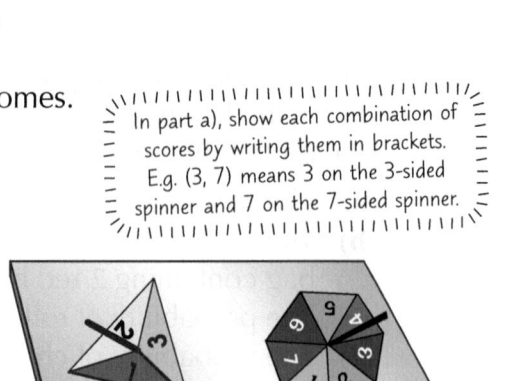

c) What is the probability that the sum is 6?

d) What is the probability that the sum is even?

e) What is the probability that the sum is greater than or equal to 8?

f) What is the probability that the sum is less than 8?

Q2 Draw a sample space diagram showing all the possible combinations of scores after throwing a standard dice and spinning this spinner. Use your diagram to answer the following.

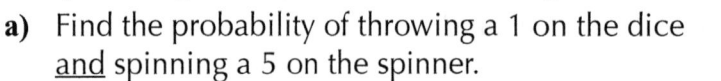

E.g. 6, 1 means a 6 on the dice and a 1 on the spinner.

a) Find the probability of throwing a 1 on the dice <u>and</u> spinning a 5 on the spinner.

b) Find the probability of getting a total score of 10.

c) Find the probability of getting a total score of at least 9.

Q3 A fair ten-sided dice has faces numbered 1-10. The dice is rolled five times.

a) On each roll, how many ways are there to roll a multiple of 3?

b) How many different ways are there to roll a multiple of 3 on all five rolls?

c) What is the probability of rolling a multiple of 3 on all five rolls?

Q4 A car wash offers different levels of cleaning for different parts of a car:
- 3 different levels of cleaning for the outside of a car
- 5 different levels of cleaning for the inside of a car
- 2 different levels of cleaning for the underneath of a car.

a) A customer wants the outside, inside and underneath of her car washed. How many options in total are there for her to choose from?

b) Another customer only wants two of the three parts of her car washed. Show that she can choose from 31 possible options in total.

Probability Experiments

Q1 Charlton is making a bet with his friend before the local cricket team play a match. He thinks the match will end in a draw. A local newspaper prints the team's results over their last 20 matches, as shown.

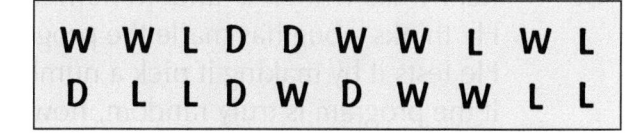

| W | W | L | D | D | W | W | L | W | L |
| D | L | L | D | W | D | W | W | L | L |

Outcome	Frequency
W	
D	
L	

a) Complete the frequency table.
b) Charlton reasons that since there are 3 possible results for any match, the probability that the next match will be a draw (D) is $\frac{1}{3}$. Explain why Charlton is wrong.
c) Suggest a value for the probability of a draw based on the team's past results.
d) Based on their past results, are the team most likely to win, lose, or draw?
e) Based on these results, estimate how many of the next 40 matches you'd expect the team to lose.

Q2 The notepad below shows orders for 4 different sorts of rice at a certain Indian restaurant. Use the data to answer the following questions.

boiled	20
pilau	24
spicy mushroom	10
special fried	6

a) Estimate the probability that the next order of rice is for pilau rice.
b) Estimate the probability that the next order of rice is for spicy mushroom or special fried rice.
c) Estimate the probability that the next order of rice is not for boiled rice.
d) The restaurant hosts a birthday party for 30 people. If all 30 people order rice, estimate how many you would expect to order pilau rice.

Q3
a) A biased dice is rolled 40 times. A six came up 14 times. Calculate the relative frequency that a six was rolled.
b) The same dice is rolled another 60 times. From this, a six came up 24 times. Calculate the relative frequency that a six was rolled on these 60 rolls.
c) Use the data from **a)** and **b)** to make the best estimate you can of the probability of rolling a six with the dice.

Q4
a) A 20-sided dice is rolled 150 times. A one came up 13 times. Calculate the relative frequency of rolling a one.
b) A 12-sided dice is rolled 80 times. A five came up 4 times. Calculate the relative frequency of rolling a five.
c) Two 10-sided dice were rolled together 250 times. One dice was green and the other was red.
- Three came up on the green dice 23 times.
- Ten came up on the red dice 38 times.

One of these dice is biased.
i) Explain which one you think it is and why.
ii) What could you do to be more sure of your conclusion?

Probability Experiments

Q5 Kenny has written a random number generating computer program, Numbertron 5000. He thinks a bug has made the program biased towards odd numbers.
He tests it by making it pick a number from 1 to 10. He does this 80 times.
If the program is truly random, how many times in 80 trials would you expect it to pick:
 a) 4?
 b) an odd number?

Here are the results of Kenny's experiment:

Number	1	2	3	4	5	6	7	8	9	10
No. of times picked	7	7	9	8	10	7	9	6	8	9

 c) What is the relative frequency of Numbertron 5000 picking an odd number?
 d) If the program is truly random, what would you expect to happen to the relative frequency of each number if Kenny repeated the experiment with 100 000 trials?

Q6 150 learner drivers recently took their driving test. Two-thirds of these people had taken 30 or more hours of driving lessons before their test. Among the 99 drivers that passed the test, the ratio of those who had taken 30 or more hours of lessons to those who hadn't was 10:1.

 a) Use the information above to complete this frequency tree.

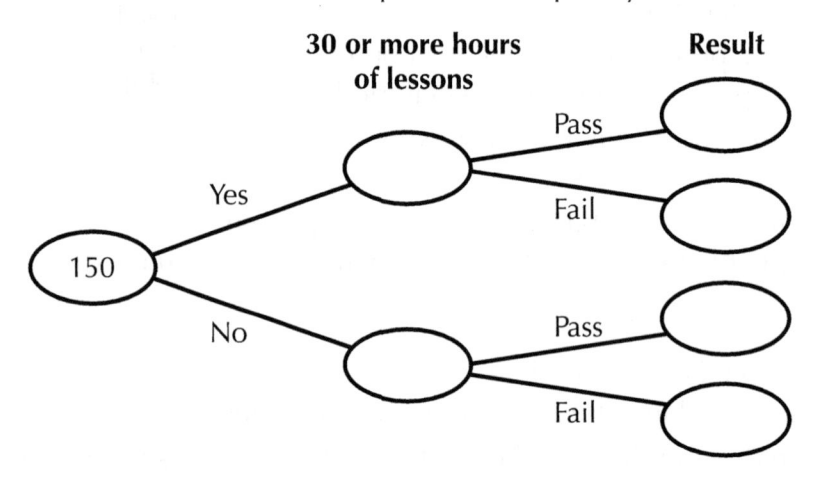

 b) Given that a learner driver has had fewer than 30 hours of lessons, use the frequency tree to estimate the probability that they will pass their driving test.
 c) If another 60 people who have had fewer than 30 hours of driving lessons were to take their driving test, estimate how many will pass.

Q7 Kristina and Ed each dropped a slice of buttered toast a number of times to see if it was more likely to land buttered side down. Their results are shown in the table below.

	Number of slices dropped	Number of times slice landed buttered side down
Kristina	8	6
Ed	62	28

 a) Whose results are likely to give the best estimate of the probability of a slice of buttered toast landing buttered side down? Explain why.
 b) Another 2 slices of buttered toast are dropped. Estimate the probability they both land buttered side down.

The AND / OR Rules

Q1 A spinner has segments that are coloured either red or blue. The probability that the spinner lands on a red segment is 0.25. The spinner is spun twice.

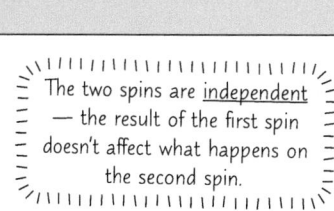

The two spins are independent — the result of the first spin doesn't affect what happens on the second spin.

    a) Find the probability that the spinner lands on red twice.
    b) Find the probability that the first spin lands on red and the second spin lands on blue.

Q2 A fair 20-sided dice with faces numbered 1-20 is thrown.

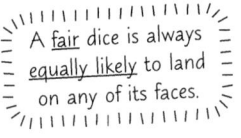

A fair dice is always equally likely to land on any of its faces.

    a) Find the probability that it lands on an odd number.
    b) Find the probability that it lands on a multiple of 5.
    c) **i)** Explain why the probability of the dice landing on either an odd number or a multiple of 5 does not equal the sum of your answers to a) and b).
        ii) Find the probability that the dice lands on <u>either</u> an odd number <u>or</u> a multiple of 5.
    d) Find the probability that the dice lands on <u>either</u> a multiple of 3 <u>or</u> an even number.

Q3 How many times must you roll an ordinary 6-sided dice for the probability of getting <u>no sixes</u> to be less than 0.5?

Q4 For the spinner shown, the probability that it lands on each of the numbers is listed in the table below.

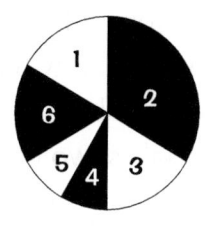

Number	1	2	3	4	5	6
Probability	$\frac{1}{6}$	$\frac{1}{3}$	$\frac{1}{6}$	$\frac{1}{12}$	$\frac{1}{12}$	$\frac{1}{6}$

    a) Find the probability of landing on an even number.
    b) What is the probability of landing on white?
    c) Why is the probability of landing on white or 3 not $\frac{5}{12} + \frac{1}{6}$?

Q5 Janine has an ordinary pack of playing cards.
    a) Janine selects one card at random. What is the probability that Janine selects either a black Ace or black King?
    b) Janine selects a card at random and returns it to the pack. She then randomly selects another card.
        i) What is the probability that Janine selects a red card followed by the Ace of spades?
        ii) What is the probability that Janine selects the Ace of spades followed by a red card?
        iii) What is the probability that Janine selects the Ace of spades and a red card in either order?

Q6 Fatima has 16 cards, numbered 1-16. n of these cards are green, and the rest are blue. She picks out two cards, without replacing her first card.
    a) Find the probability that Fatima picks out a green card, followed by a blue card.
    b) Explain why the events 'getting a green card with the first pick' and 'getting a blue card with the second pick' are dependent events.
    c) The probability of Fatima selecting one card of each colour in either order is 0.4. If Fatima knows that more than half the cards are green, find n.

Section Seven — Probability and Statistics

Tree Diagrams

When you're faced with a question where more than one thing's happening, a tree diagram is amazingly useful. Practise your skills with these.

Q1 How many times must you roll an ordinary 6-sided dice for the probability of getting <u>at least one</u> multiple of 3 to be more than 0.7?

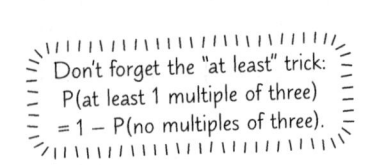

Don't forget the "at least" trick: P(at least 1 multiple of three) = 1 − P(no multiples of three).

Q2 An unbiased dice in the shape of a tetrahedron has faces numbered 1, 2, 3, 4. To win a game with this dice, you must throw a 4. In each game you have a maximum of 3 attempts.
   a) Using a tree diagram, calculate the probability of winning a game on the second throw.
   b) What is the probability of winning a game?

Q3 Fabrizio is practising taking penalties.
   - The probability that he misses the goal completely is $\frac{1}{8}$.
   - The probability that the goalkeeper saves the penalty is $\frac{3}{8}$.
   - The probability that he scores is $\frac{1}{2}$.

   Fabrizio takes two penalties.
   a) Calculate the probability that Fabrizio fails to score with his two penalties.
   b) Calculate the probability that he scores only one goal.
   c) Calculate the probability that Fabrizio scores on neither or both of his 2 attempts.

Q4 Sam is keeping a running total of his scores on an ordinary dice using the following rules:
   - If he rolls an odd number, he adds the score to the running total.
   - If he rolls an even number, he divides the score by 2 and adds the result to the running total.

   a) By multiplying along the thicker branches of this tree diagram, find the probability that Sam's running total after two rolls is equal to 2.

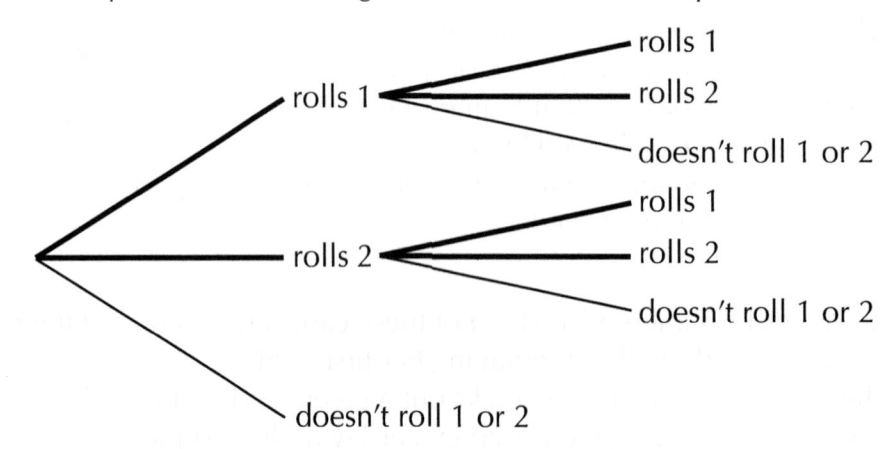

   ```
              ┌── rolls 1
       rolls 1┼── rolls 2
       │      └── doesn't roll 1 or 2
       │      ┌── rolls 1
       ├rolls 2┼── rolls 2
       │      └── doesn't roll 1 or 2
       └── doesn't roll 1 or 2
   ```

   b) Use a tree diagram to find the probability that Sam's running total after <u>either</u> one <u>or</u> two rolls is equal to 3.

   Think what Sam could get on those two rolls to give a running total of 3.

Conditional Probability

Q1 3 balls are drawn at random, without replacement, from a bag containing 4 green balls and 3 red balls.

a) Complete the tree diagram below showing all the possible outcomes and their probabilities.

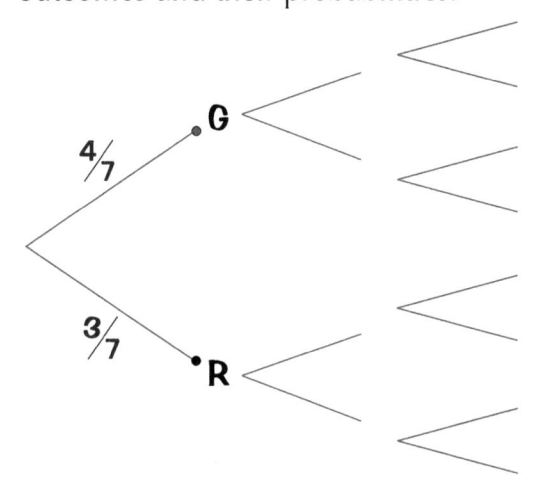

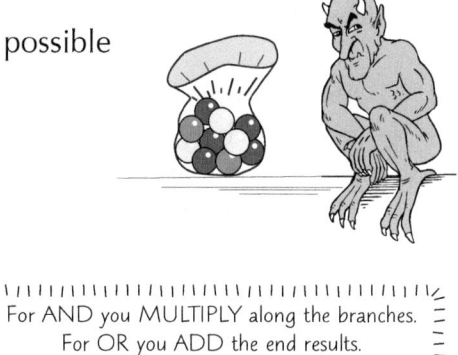

[Tree diagram: first branches 4/7 to G and 3/7 to R, each leading to further branches]

For AND you MULTIPLY along the branches.
For OR you ADD the end results.

b) What is the probability that exactly 2 green balls are drawn?
c) What is the probability that the last ball drawn is the same colour as the first?

Q2 Jo runs every day. Jo has discovered that if she sleeps well, the probability that she will run well the next day is 0.8. However, if Jo sleeps badly, the probability that she will run well falls to 0.1.

Jo is always twice as likely to sleep well as sleep badly (and whether Jo sleeps well on any particular night is independent of what happened the night before).

What is the probability that Jo sleeps well tonight and runs well tomorrow?

Q3 3 coins are drawn at random, without replacement, from a piggy bank containing 7 pound coins and 4 twenty-pence pieces.
a) Draw a tree diagram showing all possible outcomes and their probabilities.
b) Find the probability that the first coin selected is different in value from the third.
c) Find the probability that less than £1.50 is drawn altogether.

Q4 A box contains 6 tabby cats, 3 black cats and 4 Siamese cats. There is a hole in the box which is only big enough for one cat to walk through at a time. The cats never walk back into the box. Use a tree diagram to work out the probability that:
a) the first two cats to leave the box are both Siamese
b) if three cats leave the box at least one of them will be black
c) the first three cats to leave the box will all be of different types
d) the first three cats will be a Siamese, a tabby and a black cat in that order.

Section Seven — Probability and Statistics

Sets and Venn Diagrams

Don't be put off by the weird symbols that go with the sets — once you've figured them out you'll find that Venn diagrams are a pretty handy tool. Remember, the squiggly symbol ξ means the 'universal set' — this contains all the elements you need to consider in a particular question.

Q1 The Venn diagram on the right shows which numbers between 1 and 10 belong to each of the sets P and Q.
Use the Venn diagram to find:
a) the number of elements in set P.
b) the elements that aren't in set Q.
c) the total number of elements that are either in set P, or set Q, or both.
d) the elements in both P and Q.

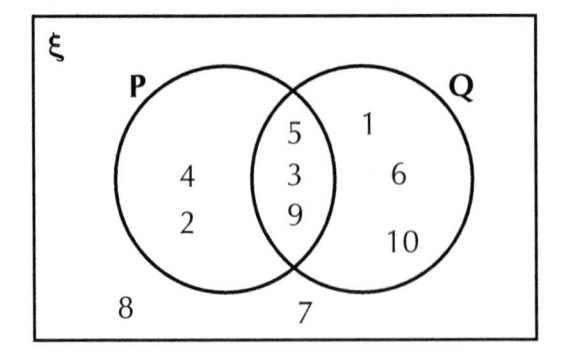

Q2 Draw a Venn diagram to show the following sets.
- ξ = {1, 2, 3, 4, 5, 6, 7, 8, 9, 10, 11, 12, 13, 14, 15}
- M = {1, 2, 3, 5, 6, 15}
- N = {1, 2, 4, 5, 8, 10}
- P = {1, 2, 4, 7, 14}

Q3 A survey asked people if they like bananas and pies.
- 12 people said they only like bananas
- 11 people said they only like pies
- 7 people said they like both
- 3 people said they like neither

a) Draw a Venn diagram to show this data.
b) A person from the survey is chosen at random. What is the probability that the chosen person:
   i) likes bananas?
   ii) doesn't like pies?

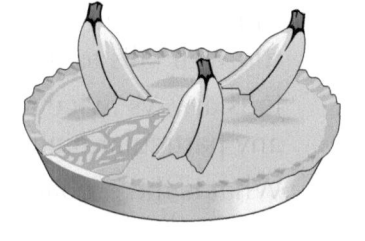

Q4 ξ = {integers from 1-16 inclusive}, A = {odd numbers} and B = {multiples of 3}.
a) List the elements that are in both set A and set B.
b) Draw a Venn diagram, showing the number of elements in each part of the diagram.
c) If a card from a set of cards numbered 1-16 is chosen at random, what is the probability that:
   i) the number on the card is odd?
   ii) the number on the card is both odd and a multiple of 3?
   iii) the number on the card is not a multiple of 3?

Q5 All 100 students in a year group sat a test in English and a test in Science. Everyone passed at least one of the tests.
82 of the students passed the English test and 57 passed the Science test.
a) Show this information on a Venn diagram.
b) One student is chosen at random from the year group. Given that this student had passed the Science test, find the probability that she had also passed the English test.

Section Seven — Probability and Statistics

Sets and Venn Diagrams

Q6 A bank does a survey of 1000 people to find out how many have an account open with them. Respondents are put into sets according to the types of account they have:
- C = {people with current accounts}
- E = {people with easy-access accounts}
- F = {people with fixed-rate accounts}

The number of people in each set is shown in this Venn diagram. (The overlaps show the number of people with more than one type of account open.)

a) Work out the number of people that have:
  i) No accounts with the bank.
  ii) A current account and a fixed-rate account, but not an easy access account.
  iii) Exactly one account with the bank.
  iv) Either an easy-access or fixed-rate account, but not both.

b) What is the probability of a randomly selected respondent having either an easy-access or a fixed-rate account (or both) with the bank, but not a current account?

c) Given that a randomly selected respondent has a current account with the bank, what is the probability that they also have at least one other account with the bank?

Q7 One year, 121 films were shown at a film club.
The films were divided into three overlapping categories:
- comedies (C)
- films based on books (B)
- films that received good reviews when they were originally released (G)

The number of films in each of the categories is shown in the Venn diagram below.

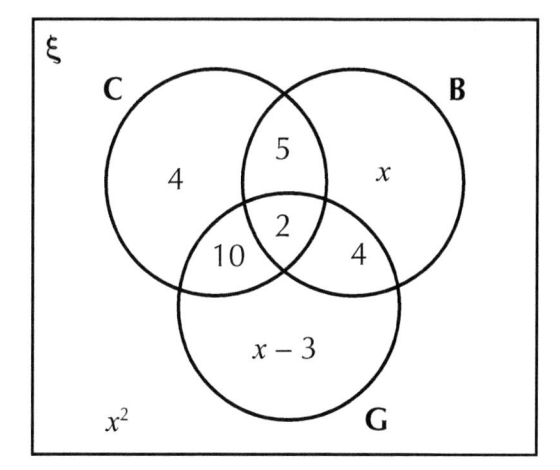

a) Find the value of x.
b) A film is selected at random. Find the probability that it received good reviews.
c) Given that a randomly chosen film is a comedy and is based on a book, find the probability that it received good reviews when it was originally released.

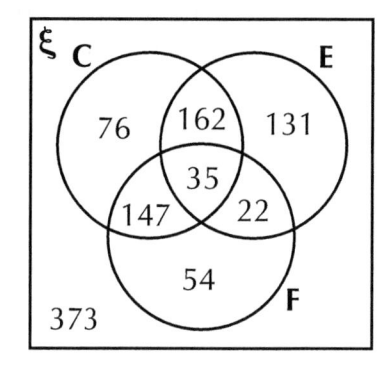

Section Seven — Probability and Statistics

Sampling and Bias

Q1 Say what the population is for each of these surveys:
   a) The health effects of smoking on 20- to 30-year-old women.
   b) The average number of trees in public parks in London.
   c) The average number of hours British squirrels spend juggling nuts.
   d) The pay of football players in the Premier League.

Q2 Professor Xavier Entric is doing a research project on the lifespan of moorland dung beetles in the UK.
   a) What population would Professor Entric use for his research?
   b) Give one reason why Professor Entric would use a sample, rather than surveying the whole population.

Q3 Katie wants to know the average weekly wage earned by teenagers in her town. She calculates the mean from the weekly wages of three of her classmates at school.

Give two reasons why this sample may not give her a true estimate of the average wage for teenagers in the town.

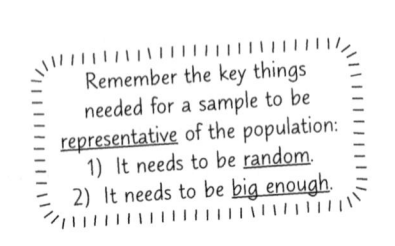

Remember the key things needed for a sample to be representative of the population:
1) It needs to be random.
2) It needs to be big enough.

Q4 Give a reason why the following methods of sampling are poor.
   a) A survey carried out inside a newsagent's concluded that 80% of the population buy a daily newspaper.
   b) A phone poll conducted at 11 am on a Sunday morning revealed that less than 2% of the population regularly go to church.

Q5 A bakery makes 50 Battenberg cakes every day.
The quality controller tests the cakes every Friday for weight and tastiness.
She can only use a sample of 5 cakes because the cakes get eaten in the tastiness test.
   a) Each week the quality controller chooses the first 5 cakes off the production line for her sample. What is wrong with this method?
   b) On one Friday, all the cakes are weighed, giving the following results:

201 g	203 g	206 g	194 g	203 g	194 g	208 g	194 g	203 g	184 g
206 g	197 g	196 g	206 g	189 g	198 g	204 g	196 g	199 g	204 g
205 g	201 g	211 g	222 g	204 g	194 g	203 g	198 g	199 g	194 g
212 g	195 g	206 g	202 g	198 g	206 g	201 g	205 g	201 g	194 g
198 g	197 g	204 g	203 g	201 g	205 g	202 g	199 g	195 g	198 g

Describe how you would choose a simple random sample of 5 cake weights.

Q6 Spencer wants to know how many people in his school watch Come Lancing, a televised celebrity jousting competition. He asks 18 randomly selected students from his school whether they watch the programme, and 6 of them say they do.
   a) If there are 945 students in the school, estimate how many watch the programme.
   b) Spencer carries out a similar survey of 18 students at a different school. He says he'll be able to estimate more accurately the number of people in each school who watch the programme, since he effectively now has a sample size of 36. Explain one possible problem for Spencer if he combines the results from his two surveys in this way.

Collecting Data

There are different types of data. There are also different ways to collect and organise data.
If you collect your data sensibly, it makes analysing it so much easier.

Q1 Ziru collects some data about his school. The data items are listed below.
Say whether each data item is qualitative or quantitative.

a) The colours of pants worn by the teachers.
b) The number of students late to school from each form on the first day of term.
c) The distance travelled to school by each student.
d) The star sign of each student.

Q2 Ayra collects some data at her school sports day. The data items are listed below.
Say whether each data item is discrete or continuous.

a) The number of competitors in each event.
b) The finishing times of each competitor in the 100-metre sprint.
c) The total number of points scored by each form at the end of the day.
d) The distances jumped by each competitor in the long jump.

Q3 Fumio asked each of his 30 classmates how long (in minutes) it took them to eat their dinner. Here are the results he recorded:

42 13 6 31 15 20 19 5 50 14
8 25 16 27 4 45 32 31 31 10
32 17 16 19 29 42 43 30 29 18

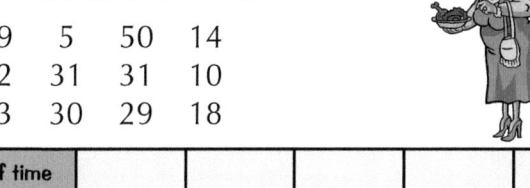

Group the data appropriately and fill in the table.

Length of time (mins)					
Number of people					

Q4 Stacey is researching the use of the school canteen.
She asks this question to a sample of students at the school:

> *How often do you use the canteen? Tick one of the boxes.*
>
> *Very often* ☐ *Quite often* ☐
>
> *Not very often* ☐ *Never* ☐

a) Give one criticism of Stacey's question.
b) Write a question that Stacey could use to find out how often students at her school use the canteen.

Q4 A drinks company is trying to profile their customers. They want to find out which age groups to target their marketing at. They use this question as part of a questionnaire:

> *How old are you?*
> ☐ Under 18 ☐ 18 to 30 ☐ 30 to 40 ☐ 40 to 60 ☐ over 60

a) Give one criticism of this question.
b) How would you improve this question?

Section Seven — Probability and Statistics

Mean, Median, Mode and Range

When finding the <u>mode</u> and <u>median</u>, put the data in order of size — it's much easier to find the most frequent and middle values.
The <u>mean</u> involves a bit more calculation, but hey, you're doing maths...

Q1 The local rugby team scored the following number of tries in their first 10 matches of the season:

3	5	4	2	0	1	3	0	3	4

Find their modal number of tries.

Q2 Find the mean, median, mode and range of these numbers:

1	2	−2	0	1	8	3	−3	2	4	−2	2

Q3 An ordinary dice is rolled 6 times, landing on a different number each time.
   a) What is the mean score?
   b) What is the median score?
   c) What is the range of scores?

Q4 Molly is writing a letter of complaint to the bus company because she thinks her bus to school is regularly late. Over 3 weeks, Molly kept a record of how many minutes her bus was either early or late, and put this in her letter. (She used + for late and − for early.)

+2	−1	0	+5	−4
−7	0	−8	0	+4
−4	−3	+14	+2	0

   a) Calculate the mean lateness/earliness of the bus.
   b) Calculate the median.
   c) What is the mode?
   d) The bus company use the answers to **a)**, **b)** and **c)** to claim they are always on time. Is this true?

Q5 The range for a certain list of numbers is 26. One of the numbers in the list is 48.
   a) What is the lowest possible value a number in the list could be?
   b) What is the highest possible value a number in the list could be?

Q6 The mean weight of the 11 players in a football team was 72.5 kg. The mean weight of the 5 reserve players was 75.6 kg. What was the mean weight of the whole squad? (Give your answer to 3 s.f.)

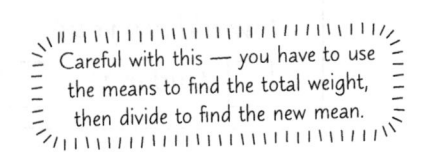

Careful with this — you have to use the means to find the total weight, then divide to find the new mean.

Mean, Median, Mode and Range

Q7 The mean daily weight of potatoes sold in a greengrocer's from Monday to Friday was 14 kg. The mean daily weight of potatoes sold from Monday to Saturday was 15 kg. How many kg of potatoes were sold on Saturday?

Q8 Colin's mean mark over three exams was 83%.
His mean mark for the first two exams was 76%.
What was Colin's score in the final exam?

Q9 The dual bar chart shows the amount of time Jim and Bob spend watching TV during the week.

   a) Find the mean amount of time per day each spends watching TV.

   b) Find the range of times for each of them.

   c) Using your answers from a) and b), comment on what you notice about the way they watch TV.

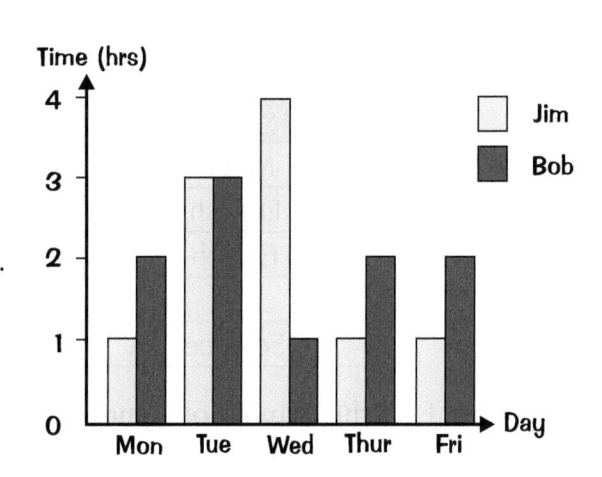

Q10 Mr Jones posted 88 Christmas cards first class on Monday.
His friends received them over the week:
   - 40 on Tuesday
   - 28 on Wednesday
   - 9 on Thursday
   - 6 on Friday
   - the remainder on Saturday

   To find the median, imagine writing a list of when all the letters arrived — e.g. Tuesday, Tuesday, Tuesday (40 times), Wednesday, Wednesday (28 times), and so on. What day would be in the middle of your list?

   a) Find the modal number of days it took for the cards to arrive.

   b) Find the median number of days it took for the cards to arrive.

   c) *"The majority of first class post arrives within 2 days."*
   Use the data above to say whether this statement is true or false.

Q11 Seven whole numbers have a mode of 8 and a median of 9.
Find the smallest possible range of the seven numbers.

Q12 A set of five positive whole numbers has a mean of 5, a mode of 2 and a range of 6.
Find the median of the numbers.

Section Seven — Probability and Statistics

Frequency Tables — Finding Averages

You've got to be able to do these questions no matter whether your table's got its headings in the top row or the left-hand column. There's no real difference — the rules are still the same.

Q1 A student has classes in Mathematics (M), English (E), French (F), Art (A) and Science (S). Her timetable is shown opposite.

Monday	S S E E A
Tuesday	E M M A A
Wednesday	S M E F F
Thursday	F E E A S
Friday	M M E S S

a) Complete the frequency table below showing a week's lessons.

Subject	Frequency
Maths	
English	
French	
Art	
Science	

b) Find the number of French lessons that the student will attend during a 12-week term.

c) What is the modal lesson?

Q2 To monitor their annual performance, a travel company logs all calls to their complaints department. The number of calls received per day over a given year are shown in this table.

a) Find the median number of calls.
b) Find the modal number of calls.

Number of calls	Number of days
10	110
11	70
12	120
13	27
14	18
15	12
16 and over	8

Q3 20 pupils are asked to estimate the length (to the nearest m) of their gardens. The results are shown in the box below.

```
10  8  6  4  10  8  0  14  12  8
10  6  1  6  10  8  6   6   8  8
```

Copy and complete this frequency table:
a) Find the mode of the data.
b) Find the median of the data.
c) State the range of the data.

Length (m)	Frequency
4 and under	
6	
8	
10	
12	
14 and over	

Section Seven — Probability and Statistics

Frequency Tables — Finding Averages

Q4 130 students were weighed to the nearest kg.
  a) Find the median weight.
  b) Find the modal weight.
  c) Find the range of the weights.
  d) Calculate the mean weight, by first completing the table.

Weight (kg)	Frequency	Weight × Frequency
51	40	
52	30	
53	45	
54	10	
55	5	

Q5 A football magazine rates teams according to how many goals they're likely to score in a match, based on their last 20 matches. The table below shows the number of goals scored by Spark Bridge Wanderers over this period.

No. of goals	0	1	2	3	4	5	6
Frequency	0	1	1	7	6	3	2

Find the mean, mode and median of the data.

Q6 A tornado has struck the hamlet of Moose-on-the-Wold. Many houses have had windows broken. The frequency table below shows the devastating effects.

Number of windows broken per house	Frequency
0	5
1	3
2	4
3	11
4	13
5	7
6	2

  a) Find the modal number of broken windows.
  b) Find the median number of broken windows.
  c) Calculate the mean number of broken windows.

Q7 Using the computerised till in a shoe shop, the manager can predict what stock to order based on the previous week's sales. This table shows the data for last week's sales. Decide whether each of the following statements is true or false.

  a) The mode for this data is 70.
  b) The mean is greater than the median for this data.
  c) The mean, median and mode are all equal for this data.

Shoe size	Frequency
5	9
6	28
7	56
8	70
9	56
10	28
11	9

Section Seven — Probability and Statistics

Grouped Frequency Tables

Remember... if you're given a grouped frequency table instead of the actual data values, then you have no way of knowing what the actual values were. Try not to worry too much about it... you can still do some useful maths.

Q1 The weights (in kg) of 20 newly felled trees are noted below:
272.7 333.2 251.0 246.5 328.0 310.7 259.6 200.2 312.8 344.3
226.8 362.0 329.1 348.3 256.1 232.9 309.7 398.0 284.5 327.4

a) Copy and complete this frequency table.

Weight (w, in kg)	Tally	Frequency
$200 \leq w < 250$		
$250 \leq w < 300$		
$300 \leq w < 350$		
$350 \leq w < 400$		

Use the 'Tally' column to help you count the weights.

b) What is the modal group?

c) Which class contains the median?

Q2 The speeds of 32 skiers at a certain corner of a downhill course are shown in this table.

Speed (s, in km/h)	$40 \leq s < 45$	$45 \leq s < 50$	$50 \leq s < 55$	$55 \leq s < 60$	$60 \leq s < 65$
Frequency	4	8	10	7	3
Mid-Interval					
Frequency × Mid-Interval					

a) By completing the frequency table, estimate the mean speed.

b) How many skiers were travelling at less than 55 km/h?

c) What percentage of skiers were travelling at 50 km/h or faster?

Q3 The times (n, in seconds) taken for 48 students to react to a sound in an experiment are summarised in the table below.

Time (n, in seconds)	Frequency (f)	Mid-interval value (x)	fx
$0 \leq n < 0.2$	12		
$0.2 \leq n < 0.4$	6		
$0.4 \leq n < 0.6$	12		
$0.6 \leq n < 0.8$	10		
$0.8 \leq n < 1$	8		

a) Write down the modal class(es).

b) Which group contains the median?

c) Estimate the mean value.

d) Comment on the claim that 40% of the times are less than 0.4 s.

Section Seven — Probability and Statistics

Box Plots

Remember to put the data in **ascending** order before you work out where the quartiles come in a list.

Q1 Use the box plot below to answer the following questions.

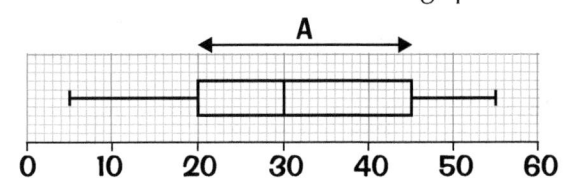

[Box plot showing minimum at about 5, Q1 at 20, median at 30, Q3 at 45, maximum at 55, with distance A marked from 20 to 45]

a) What percentage of the values are greater than 20?
b) What is the range of the data represented in the box plot?
c) What's shown by the distance A? Why is this sometimes used instead of the range as a measure of how spread out the data is?

Q2 The following table shows the number of cars parked in a multi-storey car park at midday on each day in December:

690	720	580	590	210	650	640	710
700	750	790	220	790	840	830	820
900	880	480	1000	990	1020	1010	1000
80	240	370	510	460	600	580	

a) What is the range?
b) What is the lower quartile, Q_1?
c) What is the median?
d) What is the upper quartile, Q_3?
e) Use your results to draw a box plot for the data.

Remember... quartiles divide the data into 4 equal groups.

Q3 The masses (in g) of 27 eggs are:

| 60 | 72 | 58 | 60 | 68 | 69 | 59 | 72 | 54 | 56 | 65 | 68 | 63 | 70 |
| 67 | 64 | 63 | 69 | 62 | 63 | 67 | 59 | 72 | 61 | 66 | 65 | 67 | |

a) Find the median mass.
b) Find the upper and lower quartiles for the data.
c) Use your results to draw a box plot for the data.

Q4 The latest census results from the country of Polygonia showed the following:
- Exactly half the population is over 42 years of age.
- 25% of the population is over 67 years of age.
- The range of people's ages is 97 years.
- The interquartile range of people's ages is 33 years.

a) Represent the above facts on a box plot.
b) Can you use the above facts to find out the size of the population of Polygonia? Explain your answer.

Section Seven — Probability and Statistics

Box Plots

Q5 The box plots below represent the number of people per day going on four different rides at a children's theme park one summer.

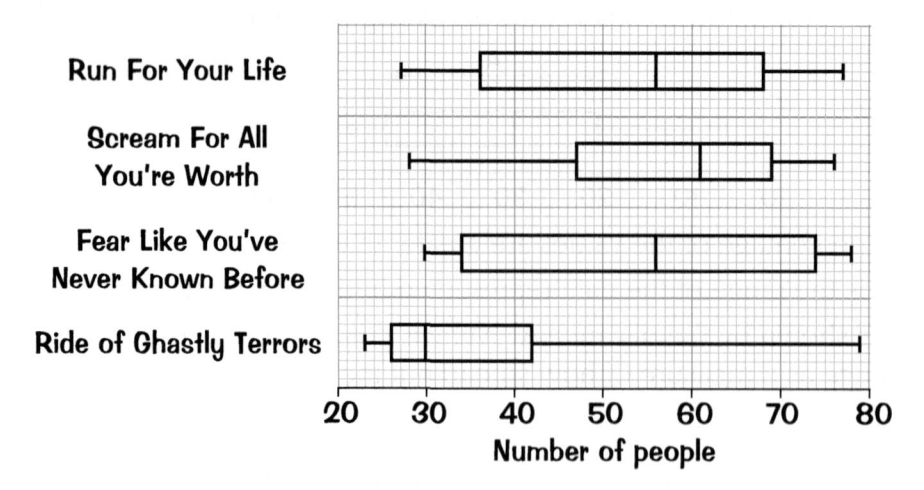

- Run For Your Life
- Scream For All You're Worth
- Fear Like You've Never Known Before
- Ride of Ghastly Terrors

Number of people

a) Which two rides had, on average, the same number of people riding on them each day?

b) Describe one difference and one similarity between the distributions for *Scream For All You're Worth* and *Fear Like You've Never Known Before*.

c) Which was the least popular ride? Explain your answer.

d) Which was the most popular ride? Explain your answer.

Don't be fooled by outliers — look for a consistently high or low number of people for c) and d).

Q6 15 students awarded marks to the following two acts in a talent contest:
- a singer
- an impressionist

The marks are shown on this scatter graph.

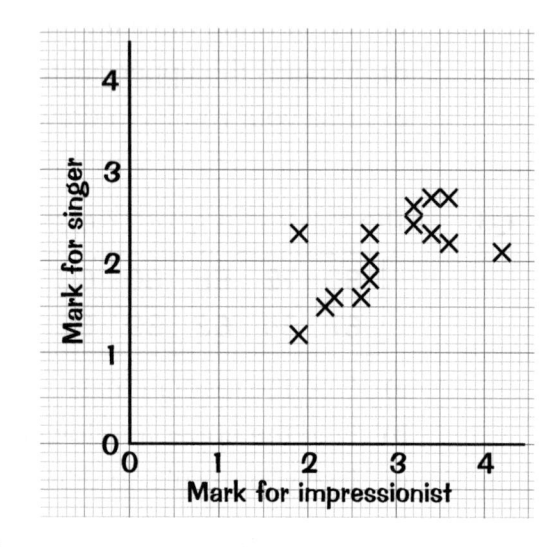

a) For the singer's marks, find:
- the minimum and maximum marks
- the median mark
- the lower and upper quartiles of the marks

b) Use your results to represent the singer's marks on a box plot.

c) This box plot shows the marks awarded to the impressionist. What can you say about the marks awarded to the two acts?

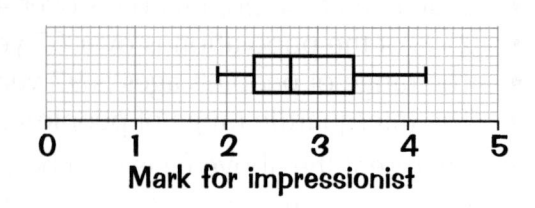

Mark for impressionist

Section Seven — Probability and Statistics

Cumulative Frequency

Q1 Using the cumulative frequency graph, read off the:
a) median
b) lower quartile
c) upper quartile
d) interquartile range.

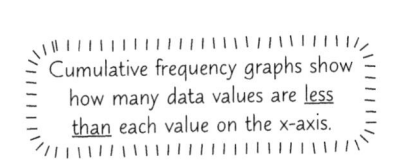

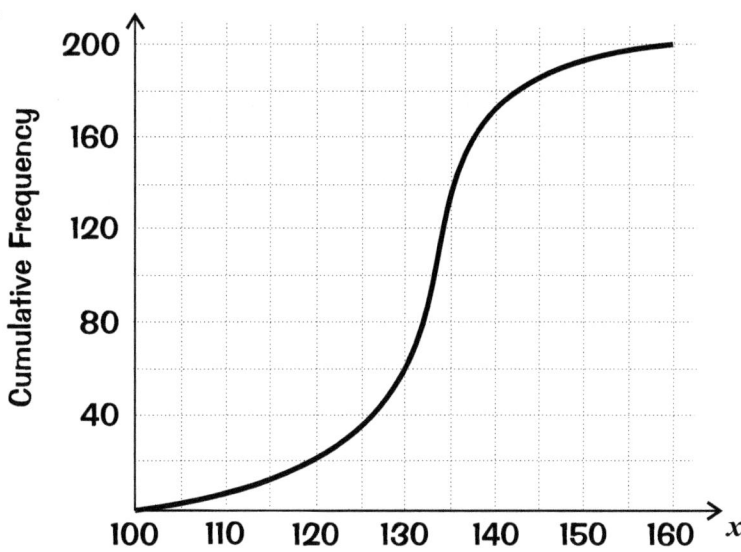

Cumulative frequency graphs show how many data values are less than each value on the x-axis.

Q2 The number of passengers using a bus service each day has been recorded over a 4-week period. The data is presented in the table below:

Number of passengers, n	0 ≤ n < 50	50 ≤ n < 100	100 ≤ n < 150	150 ≤ n < 200	200 ≤ n < 250	250 ≤ n < 300
Frequency	2	7	10	5	3	1
Cumulative Frequency						
Mid-Interval						
Frequency × Mid-Interval						

a) By completing the table, estimate the mean number of passengers.
b) By plotting a cumulative frequency graph, determine the median value.
c) What is the modal group?

With cumulative frequency you always plot the highest value from each class.

A mean passenger

Q3 40 pupils have taken an exam and their marks are recorded in a frequency table.

Mark (m%)	0 ≤ m < 20	20 ≤ m < 40	40 ≤ m < 60	60 ≤ m < 80	80 ≤ m < 100
Frequency	2	12	18	5	3
Cumulative Frequency					

a) Complete the table and plot the cumulative frequency graph.
b) What is the value of the lower quartile?
c) What is the interquartile range?
d) What is the median mark?
e) If pupils achieve a certain mark they get a prize. The number of pupils who got a prize to those who didn't is in the ratio 3 : 7. Estimate the mark required to get a prize.

Section Seven — Probability and Statistics

Cumulative Frequency

Q4 A crossword tournament has been held. The times (t, in minutes) taken by one hundred people to complete a crossword are presented in the table below.

Time (t, mins)	Frequency	Cumulative frequency
$31 \leq t < 41$	4	
$41 \leq t < 51$	12	
$51 \leq t < 61$	21	
$61 \leq t < 71$	32	
$71 \leq t < 81$	19	
$81 \leq t < 91$	8	
$91 \leq t < 101$	4	

a) What is the modal group?
b) Which group contains the median time?
c) By plotting the cumulative frequency graph, estimate the actual value of the median time.
d) Anyone taking more than 75 minutes to complete the crossword is awarded a consolation prize. Estimate how many consolation prizes were awarded.
e) Why might your answer for d) not match exactly the number of consolation prizes actually awarded?

Q5 A company that manufactures electric light bulbs records the lifetimes of a sample of 120 bulbs in a grouped frequency table with classes of width 200 hours. The following cumulative frequency graph shows the data that was recorded.

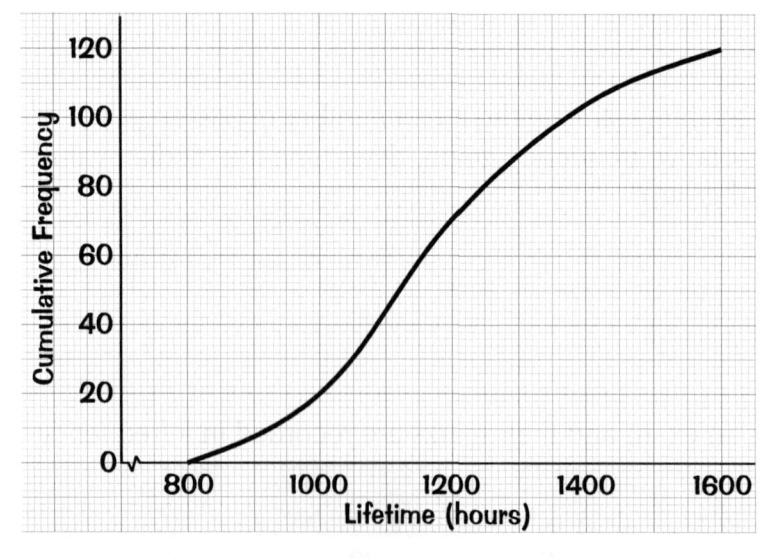

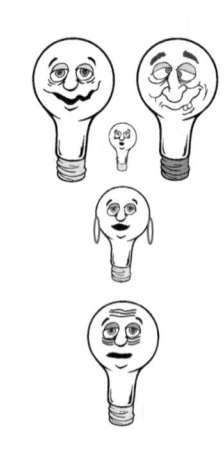

a) Estimate the number of bulbs in the sample that had a lifetime of more than 1300 hours.
b) The company's policy is to say that any bulb with a lifetime of 900 hours or less has failed quality control. Estimate the percentage of bulbs in the sample that failed quality control.
c) The company's managing director claims that 90% of the company's bulbs have a lifetime of more than 1100 hours. Does the data from this sample back up that claim? Explain your answer.

Section Seven — Probability and Statistics

Histograms and Frequency Density

It's the size that counts... You've got to look at the area of the bars to find the frequency. That means looking at the width as well as the height.

Q1 The Bog Snorkelling Appreciation Society conducts a survey on the ages of all their members. The histogram below shows the age distribution of the people surveyed. The Society organises a 'Seniors' bog snorkelling event for members aged 60 or older. Use the graph to estimate the maximum number of people that might take part.

Use the key to work out the frequencies.

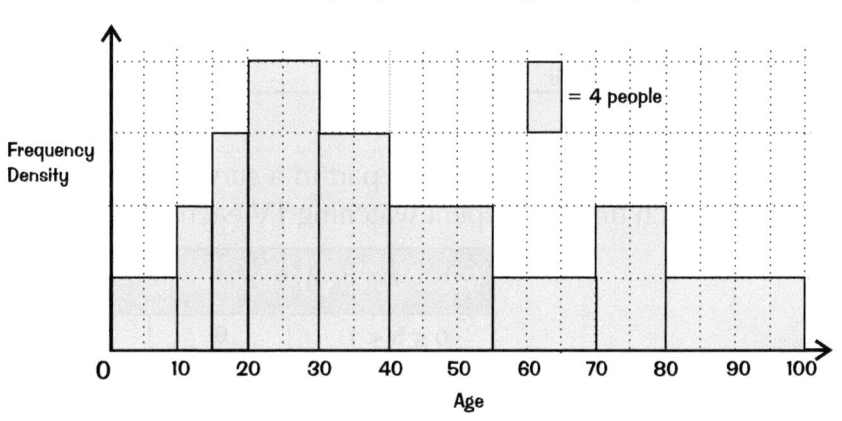

□ = 4 people

Q2 The table below shows the results of a maths test for some Year 11 students. Draw a histogram to represent this information.

Score (x%)	0 < x ≤ 40	40 < x ≤ 60	60 < x ≤ 70	70 < x ≤ 80	80 < x ≤ 100
Frequency	8	14	36	32	10

Q3 A farmer measures the heights of the sunflowers growing in his field. His results are shown in the table and the histogram below.
  a) Use the information in the table and the histogram to number the vertical axis.
  b) Use the histogram to complete the table.
  c) Use the table to add the missing bar to the histogram.

Height (x, in cm)	Frequency
0 < x ≤ 100	50
100 < x ≤ 150	150
150 < x ≤ 200	
200 < x ≤ 220	160
220 < x ≤ 250	90

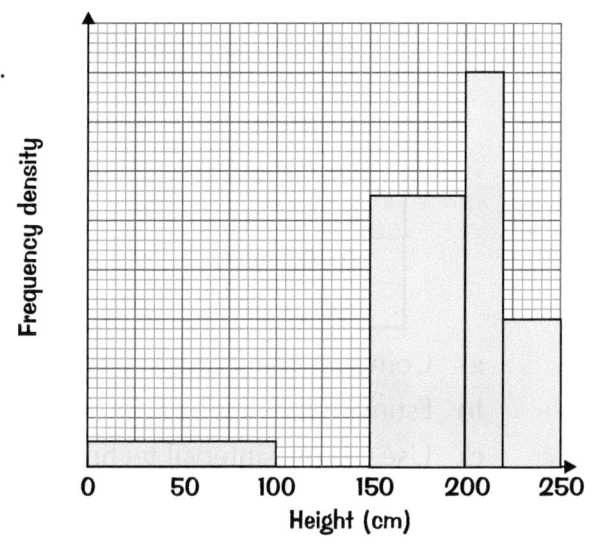

Section Seven — Probability and Statistics

Histograms and Frequency Density

Q4 The weight of honey collected from several beehives is shown in the table below.
  a) Complete the frequency table by calculating the frequency densities.
  b) Draw a histogram to represent this data.
  c) Use your histogram to estimate the number of beehives that produced more than 6 kg of honey.

Weight (w, in kg)	$0 \leq w < 2$	$2 \leq w < 4$	$4 \leq w < 7$	$7 \leq w < 9$	$9 \leq w < 15$
Frequency	3	2	6	9	12
Frequency density					

Q5 A group of students took part in a survey to see how much time they spent watching TV each week.

No. of hours (h)	Frequency	Frequency density
$0 \leq h < 1$	6	
$1 \leq h < 3$	13	
$3 \leq h < 5$	15	
$5 \leq h < 8$	9	
$8 \leq h < 10$	23	
$10 \leq h < 15$	25	
$15 \leq h < 20$	12	

  a) Complete the table by filling in the frequency density column.
  b) How many students took part in the survey?
  c) Write down the modal class.
  d) Represent the data as a histogram.
  e) Estimate the number of students that watch more than 7 but less than 13 hours each week.

Q6 A farmer keeps track of the amount of milk (C litres) produced by his cows each day.

Amount of Milk (C, in litres)	Frequency	Frequency Density	Mid-Interval	Frequency × Mid-Interval
$0 \leq C < 1$	6			
$1 \leq C < 5$	6			
$5 \leq C < 8$	6			
$8 \leq C < 10$	6			
$10 \leq C < 15$	6			
$15 \leq C < 20$	6			

  a) Complete the frequency table.
  b) Estimate the range of the amounts of milk produced each day.
  c) Use the mid-interval technique to estimate the mean.
  d) Draw a histogram to show the data.
  e) On how many days is less than 7 litres produced?

Section Seven — Probability and Statistics

Histograms and Frequency Density

Q7 A local newspaper employee has collected data on the salaries of 100 people living in the area. His data is shown in the table below.

Salary, S (£1000s)	$0 \leq S < 10$	$10 \leq S < 20$	$20 \leq S < 30$	$30 \leq S < 40$	$40 \leq S < 50$
Frequency	10	25	42	20	3
Frequency Density					

a) Complete the table and draw a histogram to show the data.

b) The newspaper prints this histogram alongside the one shown on the right. It represents data from an identical survey done 10 years earlier. Write a comment comparing current salaries with those from 10 years ago.

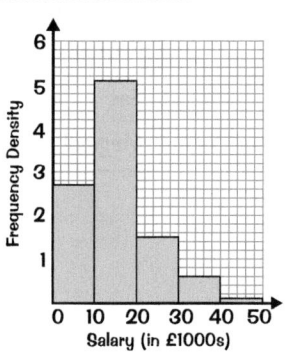

Q8 Mark collected the birth weights (w kg) of each student in his class. His data is shown in the table below.

Weight at birth (w, in kg)	Number of students
$0 \leq w < 3$	3
$3 \leq w < 3.5$	9
$3.5 \leq w < 4$	11
$4 \leq w < 5$	2

a) Mark drew the histogram on the right to illustrate his data. Explain what is wrong with Mark's histogram.

b) Draw an accurate histogram to represent Mark's data.

Q9 The histogram on the right shows the test scores of a year group of 1000 students.

Use the histogram to estimate the mean test score of the year group.

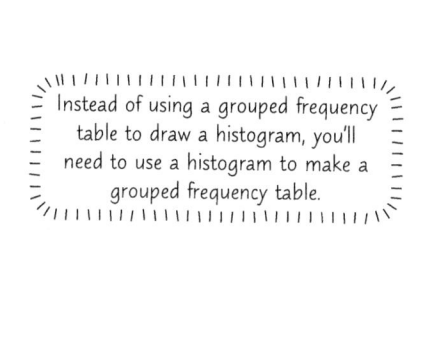

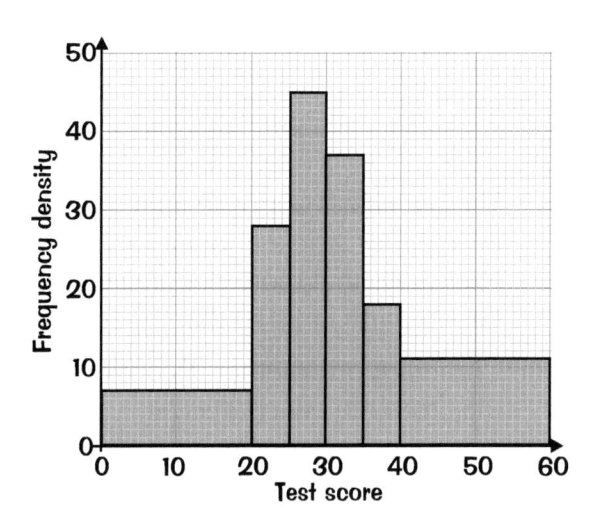

Instead of using a grouped frequency table to draw a histogram, you'll need to use a histogram to make a grouped frequency table.

Section Seven — Probability and Statistics

Other Graphs and Charts

Q1 A company that makes pies wants to add a nutritional information diagram to their packaging. Construct a pie chart to show the following nutritional data for one pie:

Contents of Pie	Amount per 100 g
Carbohydrate	35 g
Protein	15 g
Fat	10 g
Magical fairy dust	40 g

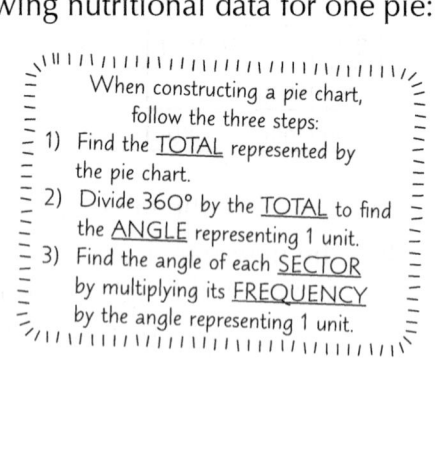

When constructing a pie chart, follow the three steps:
1) Find the TOTAL represented by the pie chart.
2) Divide 360° by the TOTAL to find the ANGLE representing 1 unit.
3) Find the angle of each SECTOR by multiplying its FREQUENCY by the angle representing 1 unit.

Q2 According to the tourist board for the Hindle Isles, 380 000 people visited the biggest island in the group, Sherrington, in 2014. The distribution of tourists for the whole group of islands is shown in the pie chart. Use a protractor on the diagram to find the number of tourists visiting the other islands in 2014 (rounded to the nearest 10 000).

Use the info you're given to find the number of tourists represented by 1°.

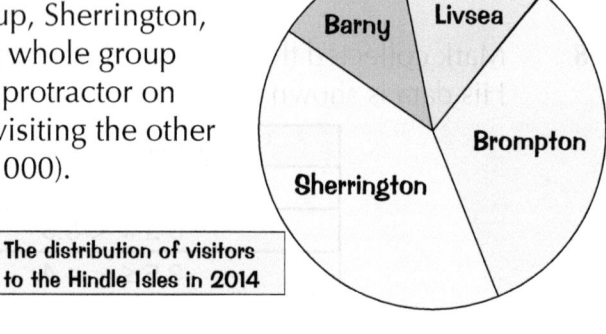

The distribution of visitors to the Hindle Isles in 2014

Q3 Megan records whether customers choose pizza or pasta in her Italian restaurant. The dual bar chart below shows the results over one week.

a) On which days was pizza more popular with Megan's customers?
b) On which day did she have the most customers?
c) Calculate the mean number of customers per day that ordered pizza.

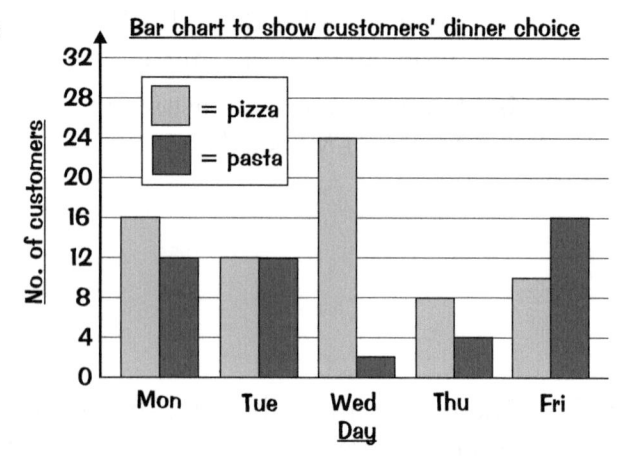

Q4 The pie charts opposite appear in a newspaper article about a local election. Nicki says that more people voted for the Green party in 2010 than in 2005.

Comment on whether it's possible to tell this from the pie charts.

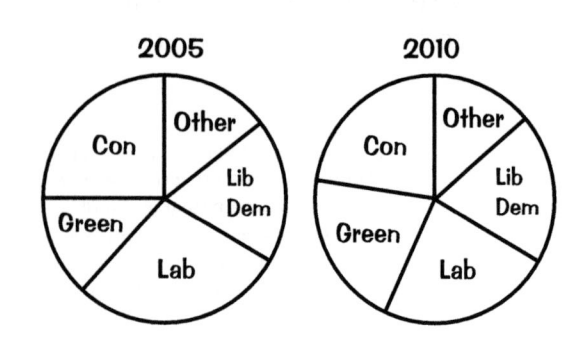

Section Seven — Probability and Statistics

Other Graphs and Charts

Q5 The graphs below show some statistics on marital status for people over 65 years old.

Marital status of people aged 65 and over: by sex and age, 2001

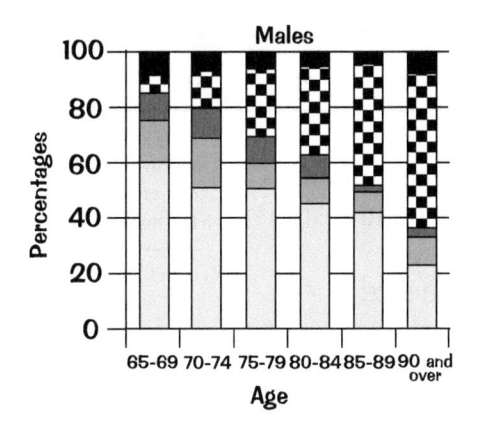

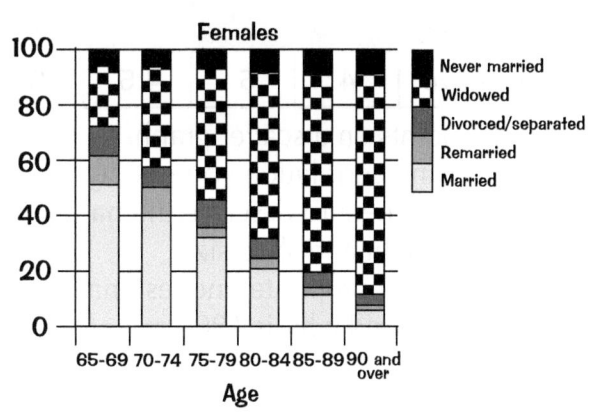

(Stacked bar charts showing percentages for Males and Females by age group 65-69, 70-74, 75-79, 80-84, 85-89, 90 and over. Categories: Never married, Widowed, Divorced/separated, Remarried, Married.)

a) What percentage of males aged 65-69 are married?

b) What percentage of females aged 70-74 have remarried?

These are a bit like bar charts where the bars have been broken down into chunks. Use the vertical axis to find the size of each chunk.

Q6 The table below shows the amount spent on sun cream each season by a British actor living in Hollywood over four years.

Season	Spring 2011	Summer 2011	Autumn 2011	Winter 2011	Spring 2012	Summer 2012	Autumn 2012	Winter 2012
Amount spent ($)	20	27	24	12	22	29	26	21
Season	Spring 2013	Summer 2013	Autumn 2013	Winter 2013	Spring 2014	Summer 2014	Autumn 2014	Winter 2014
Amount spent ($)	25	30	28	20	25	33	31	14

a) Plot the data from the table above in a time-series plot.
b) State the period of the data.
c) Plot a suitable set of moving averages on the graph, and describe the trend in the data.

Q7 Having seen the time-series graph shown here, a Quality Control Manager said:

"Admittedly we do have some complaints about our products, but from July the number of complaints has stopped rising, meaning our products must be of a better quality."

From the graph, do you think this statement is correct? Why/Why not?

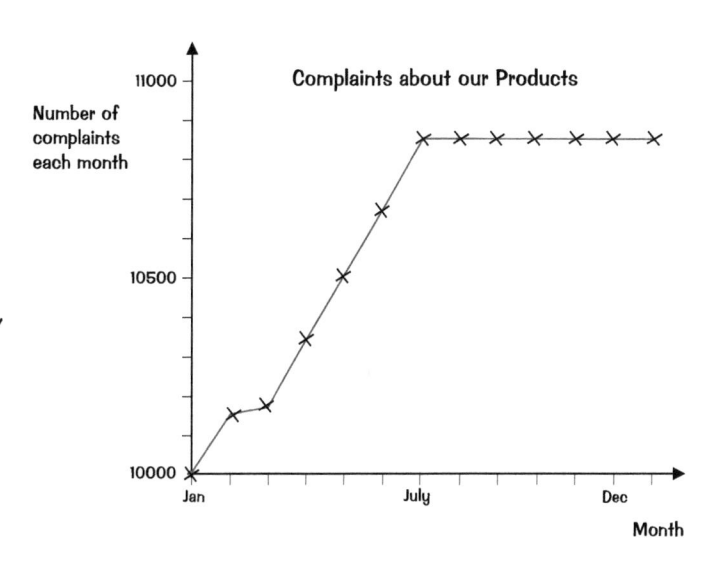

(Time-series graph titled "Complaints about our Products" showing Number of complaints each month from Jan to Dec, rising from about 10000 in January to about 10750 in July, then remaining flat until December.)

Section Seven — Probability and Statistics

Scatter Graphs

Q1 8 friends are comparing heights and shoe sizes to see if they are correlated. The data is shown below:

Height	135 cm	140 cm	150 cm	155 cm	165 cm	180 cm	200 cm	215 cm
Shoe size	4	5	4.5	5	6	8	9	12

a) Plot the points on a scatter graph.
b) Describe any correlation you notice between the variables.
c) Write a statement to describe the nature of the relationship between height and shoe size.
d) By fitting an appropriate line, estimate the shoe size of another friend who is 190 cm.

To draw a scatter graph, just plot one of the variables on the horizontal axis and the other on the vertical axis.

Q2 10 people took 2 exams in Welding for Beginners. The table shows the marks obtained.

Candidate	1	2	3	4	5	6	7	8	9	10
Exam 1 (%)	85	30	55	10	40	20	0	95	65	40
Exam 2 (%)	70	25	50	15	70	25	5	80	60	35

a) Draw a scatter graph representing this information.
b) Draw a line of best fit.
c) Identify the candidate whose scores lead to an outlier on your scatter graph.
d) Clive only sat the first exam, obtaining a mark of 50%. Use your scatter graph to estimate the mark that he might have achieved on the second exam.

Q3 Janine is convinced that cookery books that are more expensive contain more pages. To test out her theory, she has compiled this table:

Price	£4.25	£5.00	£4.75	£6.25	£7.50	£8.25	£4.75	£5.00	£6.75	£3.25	£3.75
No. of pages	204	220	118	184	196	328	158	96	144	84	48

a) Draw a scatter graph to represent this information.
b) Draw in a line of best fit on your scatter graph.
c) Describe the correlation between the price of a cookery book and the number of pages it contains.
d) Use your line to estimate the price of a book containing 250 pages.
e) Explain why using your line to estimate the price of a book containing 450 pages may lead to an unreliable result.

Q4 A local electrical store has kept a log of the number of CD players sold at each price:

Price (£)	£80	£150	£230	£310	£380	£460
No. Sold	27	24	22	19	17	15

a) Draw this information as a scatter graph, using suitable axes.
b) Draw a line of best fit and use it to estimate:
  i) the number of CD players the shopkeeper could expect to sell for £280
  ii) how much the shopkeeper should charge if he wanted to sell exactly 25 CD players.
c) Describe the correlation between the price of a CD player and the number sold.

Section Seven — Probability and Statistics

Section Seven — Mixed Questions

Mixed Questions

You might struggle to believe this, but you've almost reached the end of Section Seven.
Why not treat yourself with these last few mixed questions — oh go on, you know you want to...

Q1 Jeanie is playing a game. She splits a pack of number cards into two piles, then picks one card at random from each pile and adds them together to get a total score.
  a) Complete the table of possible outcomes on the right.
  b) What is the probability of scoring:
     i) 12?   ii) 13?   iii) An odd number?

	Pile 1			
		4		11
Pile 2	2		10	
	4			14
	5		13	

Q2 Jess rolls three fair 20-sided dice, with faces numbered 1-20.
  a) How many different outcomes are possible from rolling the three dice?
  b) What is the probability of getting odd numbers on all three dice?

Q3 Sophie has run 20 races this year. Her results are shown in the frequency table.
  a) Based on her results, estimate the probability that she'll come third in her next race.
  b) Estimate how times Sophie will come second in her next 15 races.

Result	1st	2nd	3rd	Not Placed
Frequency	2	8	5	5

Q4 A bag contains 20 beads: 5 red, 5 green, 9 blue and 1 yellow.
Ahmann randomly selects a bead, then replaces it before selecting another bead.
What is the probability that Ahmann selects:
  a) a yellow bead twice in a row?   b) a red bead and a yellow bead, in either order?

Q5 Jack will eat either pasta or a jacket potato for lunch.
The probability that he eats pasta is 0.6. The probability that he will have cheese if he has pasta is 0.5. The probability that he will have cheese if he has a potato is 0.8.
  a) Draw a tree diagram showing all of the possible outcomes.
  b) What is the probability Jack will have cheese with his lunch?

Q6 A lucky dip contains 12 prizes in identically shaped boxes: 4 bouncy balls and 8 toy cars. Dana picks three prizes at random, without replacement.
Find the probability that at least one of Dana's prizes is a bouncy ball.

Q7 The Venn diagram on the right shows the numbers of students in Year 10 studying Spanish and French.
What is the probability that a randomly selected student:
  a) studies both languages?
  b) studies Spanish given they don't study French?

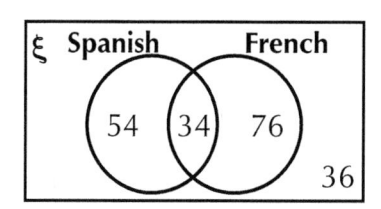

ξ Spanish   French
54 (34) 76
                36

Q8 Mya wants to know the average weight of babies born at her local hospital. She calculates the mean weight at 5.5 pounds using the birth weight of her newborn twin brothers.
Give one reason why this sample may not give her a true estimate.

Q9 The ages of a group of friends are 19, 22, 32, 45, 22, 26, 38 and 24. Find the:
  a) range   c) mode
  b) mean   d) median

More mixed practice on the next page...

Mixed Questions

Q10 Lionel and his friends grew sunflowers.
The table shows the heights of the plants after 8 weeks.
a) Which is the modal class?
b) Which group contains the median?
c) Estimate the mean height to 1 d.p.
d) What percentage of sunflowers were 30 cm or less?

Height (cm)	Frequency
0 < h ≤ 15	5
15 < h ≤ 30	7
30 < h ≤ 45	10
45 < h ≤ 60	14
60 < h ≤ 75	4

Q11 The numbers of birds that turn up at a bird table are recorded each day. The box plots represent the data recorded for three different species over the past nine days.

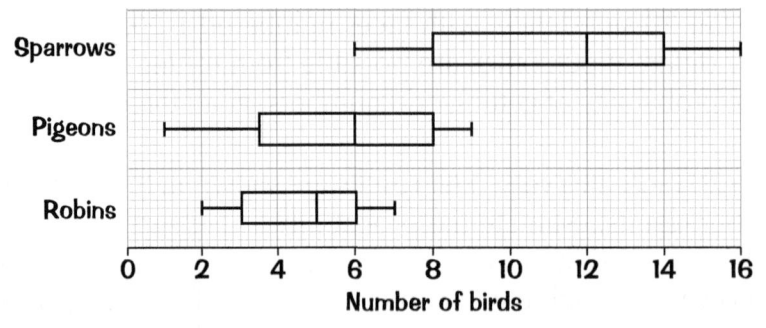

a) Which species had the most variation in how many birds turned up each day?
b) Which species turned up least frequently on average?
c) Jake says that according to the box plots, there were no days where more robins turned up than sparrows. Is he correct? Explain your answer.
d) For each species calculate: i) the range.   ii) the interquartile range.

Q12 Dog owners replied to a survey asking about the masses of their pets. The results are shown on the cumulative frequency graph on the right.
a) Estimate the median mass.
b) Estimate the lower and upper quartile values.
c) Estimate the interquartile range.

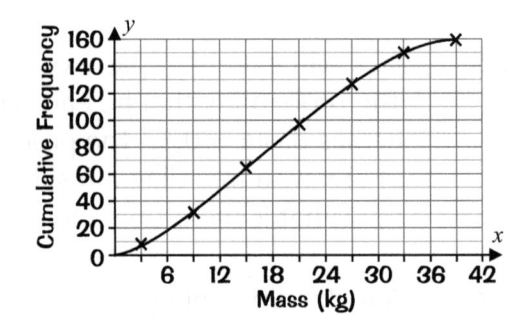

Q13 Farmer Frankie grows pumpkins. Their masses are shown in the table below.

Mass (M, in kg)	0 ≤ M < 2	2 ≤ M < 5	5 ≤ M < 7	7 ≤ M < 8	8 ≤ M < 12	12 ≤ M < 16
Frequency	2	6	10	6	6	1
Frequency Density						

a) Complete the frequency table by calculating the frequency densities.
b) Draw a histogram to represent this data.
c) Use your histogram to estimate the number of pumpkins that were less than 6 kg.

Q14 10 people volunteered to plant trees. The table shows how long they volunteered for and the number of trees they planted:

Hours Volunteered	2.5	3.5	1	2.5	3	2	3	1.5	2.75	3.5
Trees Planted	40	55	20	42	48	34	52	28	47	57

a) Draw a scatter graph representing this information including a line of best fit.
b) Use your line to estimate how many trees someone could plant in 1 hour 45 minutes.